Chi's Sweet Home

チーズ スイートホーム

2

Konami Kanata

contents
homemade 21~38+

homemade 21: a cat is moved

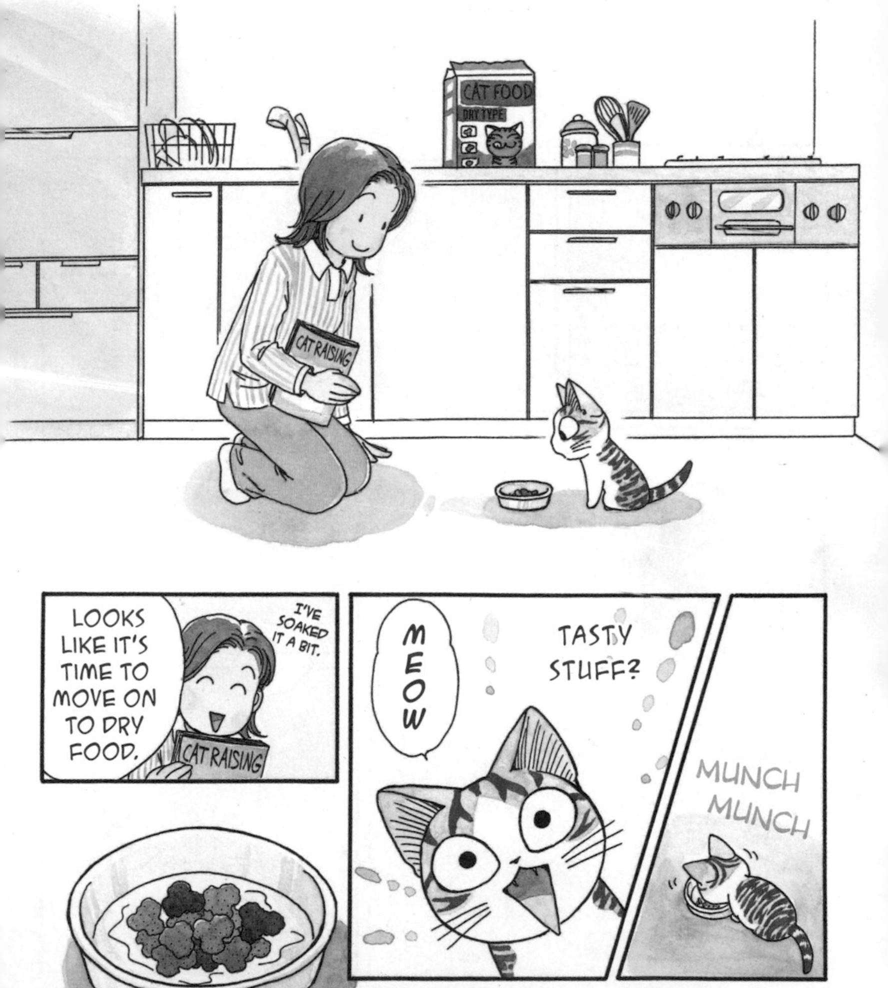
CAT FOOD
DRY TYPE
CAT RAISING
LOOKS LIKE IT'S TIME TO MOVE ON TO DRY FOOD.
I'VE SOAKED IT A BIT.
CAT RAISING
MEOW
TASTY STUFF?
MUNCH MUNCH

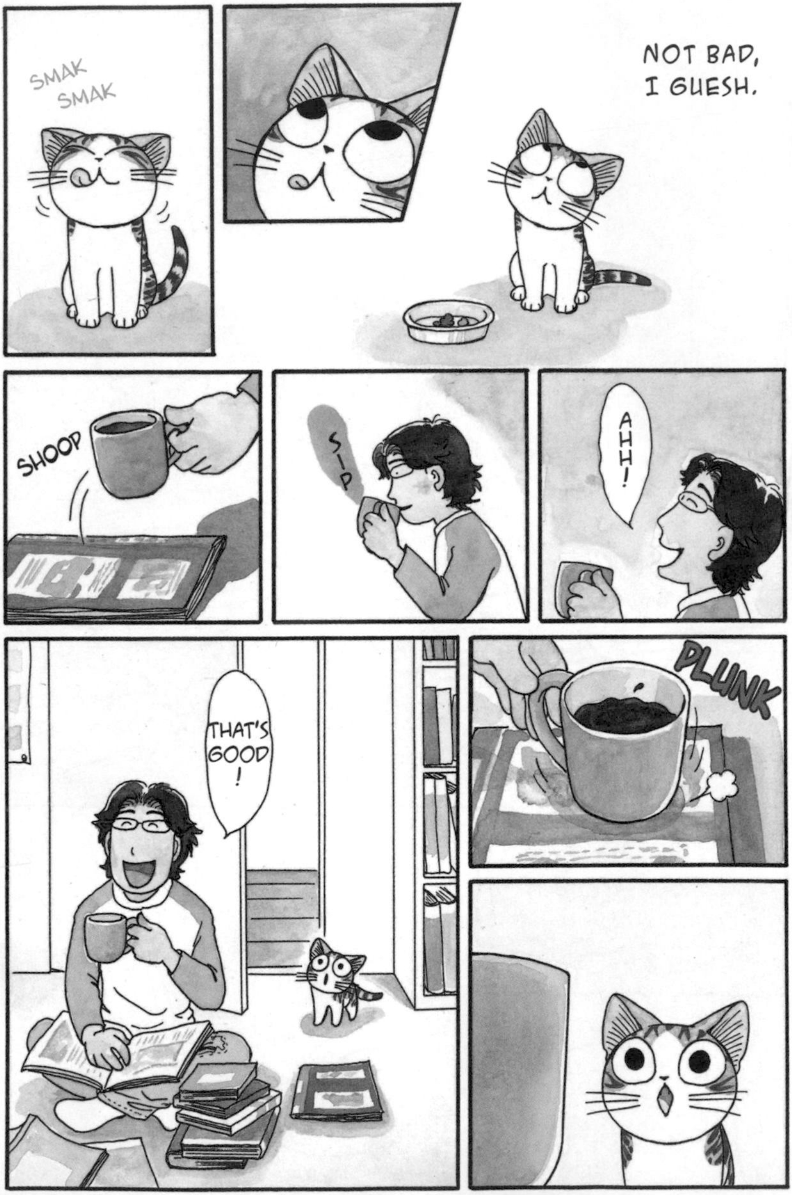
SMAK SMAK
NOT BAD, I GUESH.
SHOOP
SIP
AHH!
THAT'S GOOD!
PLUNK

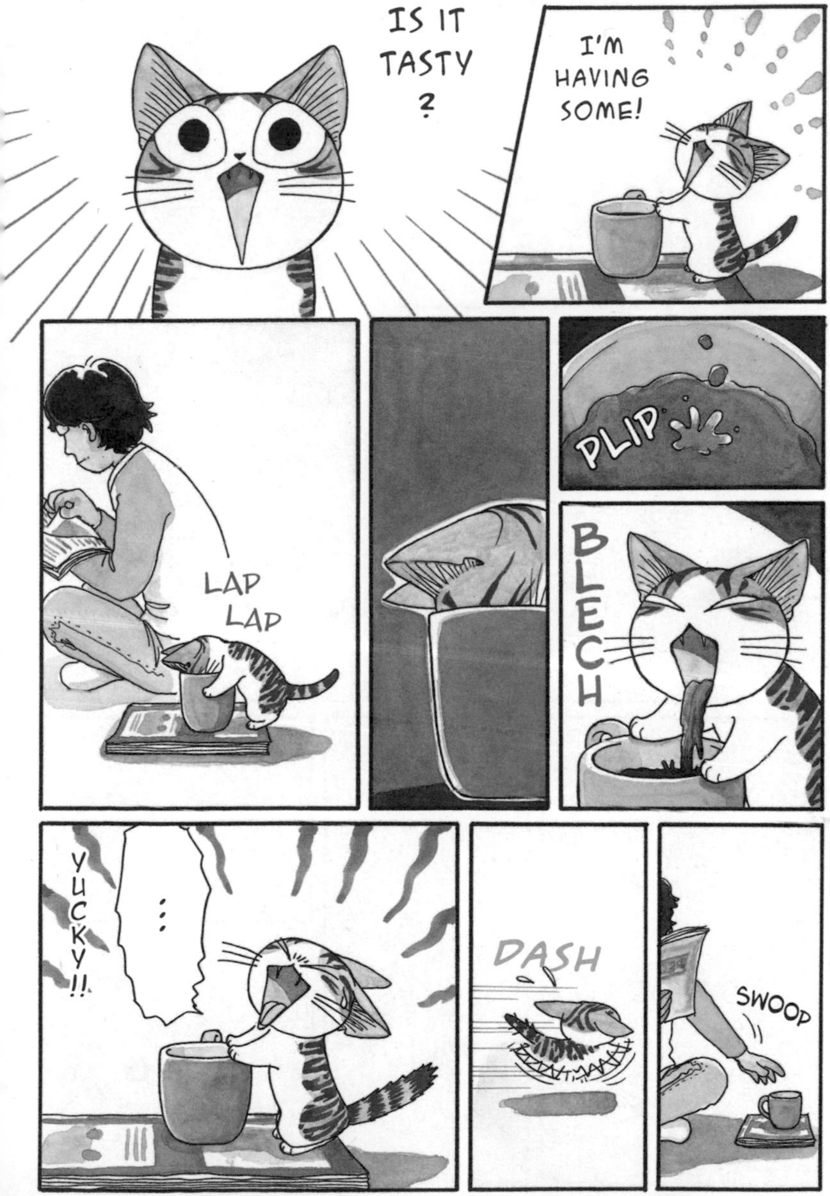
IS IT TASTY ?
I'M HAVING SOME!
LAP LAP
PLIP
BLECH
YUCKY!!
...
DASH
SWOOP

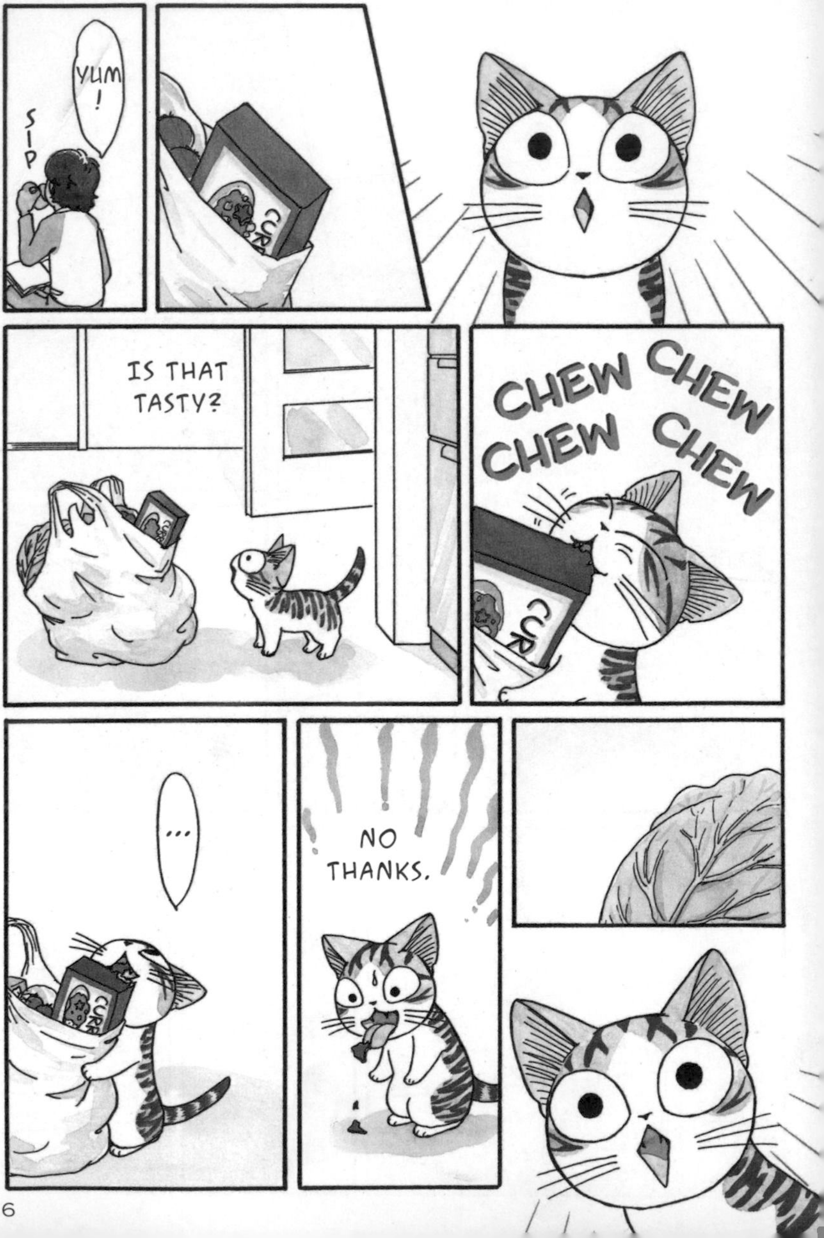
YUM!
SIP
CURR
IS THAT TASTY?
CHEW CHEW CHEW CHEW
CUR
...
CURR
NO THANKS.

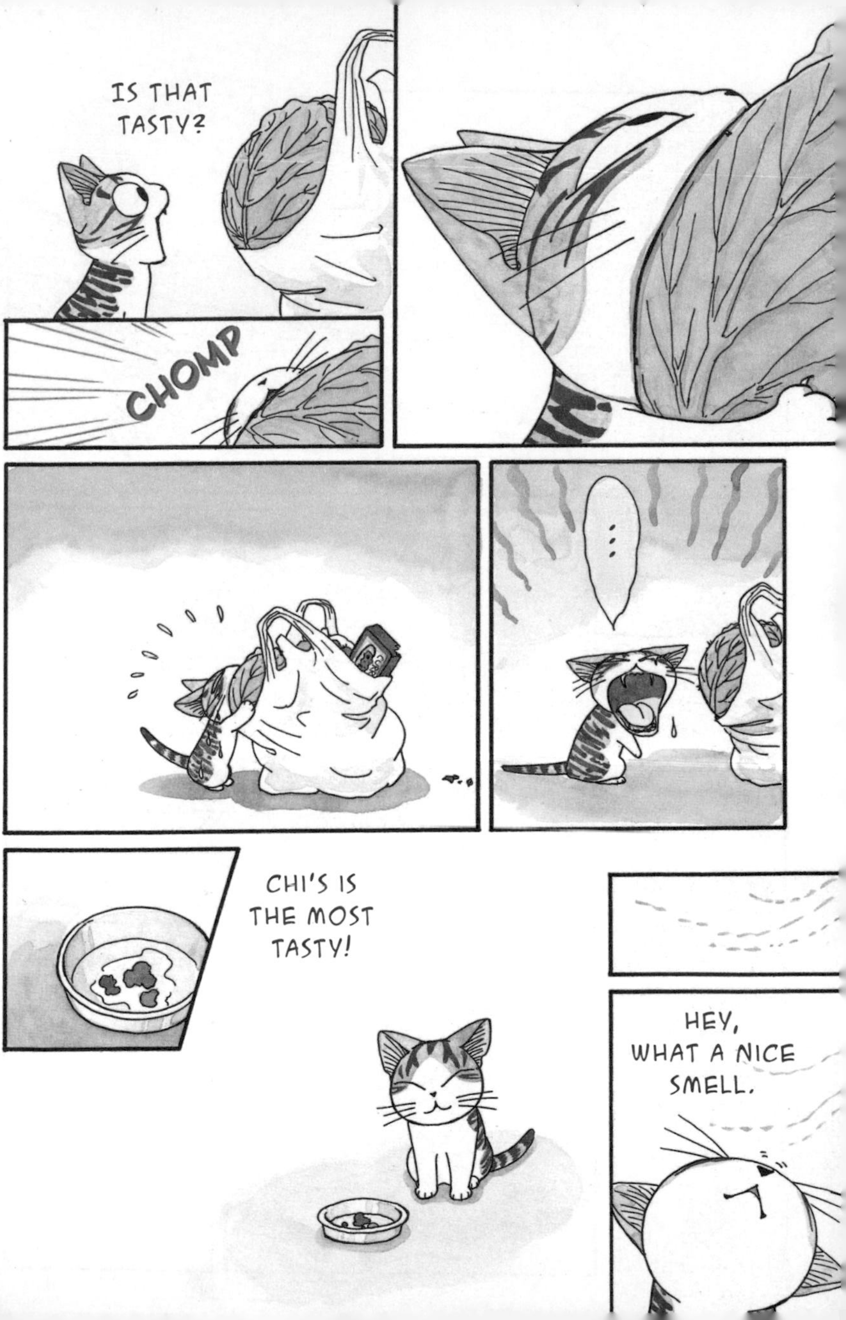
IS THAT TASTY?
CHOMP
...
CHI'S IS THE MOST TASTY!
HEY, WHAT A NICE SMELL.

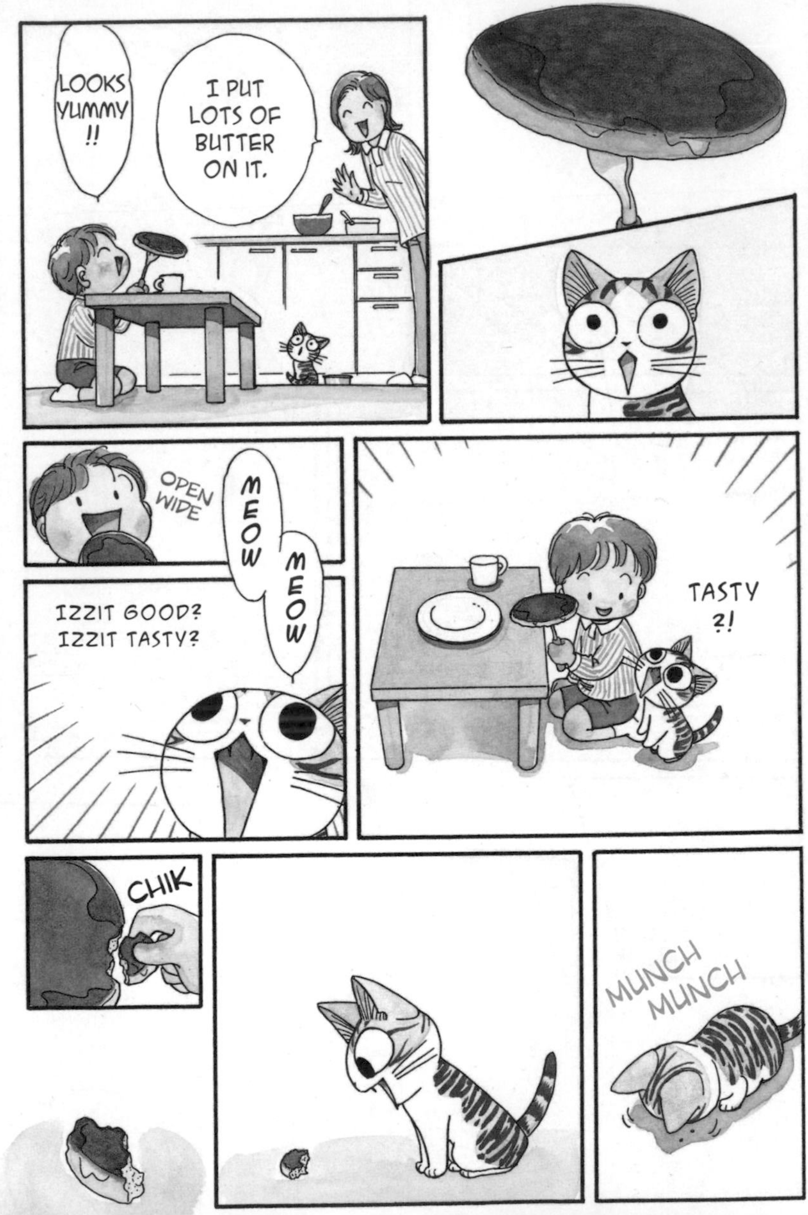
LOOKS YUMMY !!
I PUT LOTS OF BUTTER ON IT.
OPEN WIDE
MEOW
MEOW
IZZIT GOOD? IZZIT TASTY?
TASTY ?!
CHIK
MUNCH MUNCH

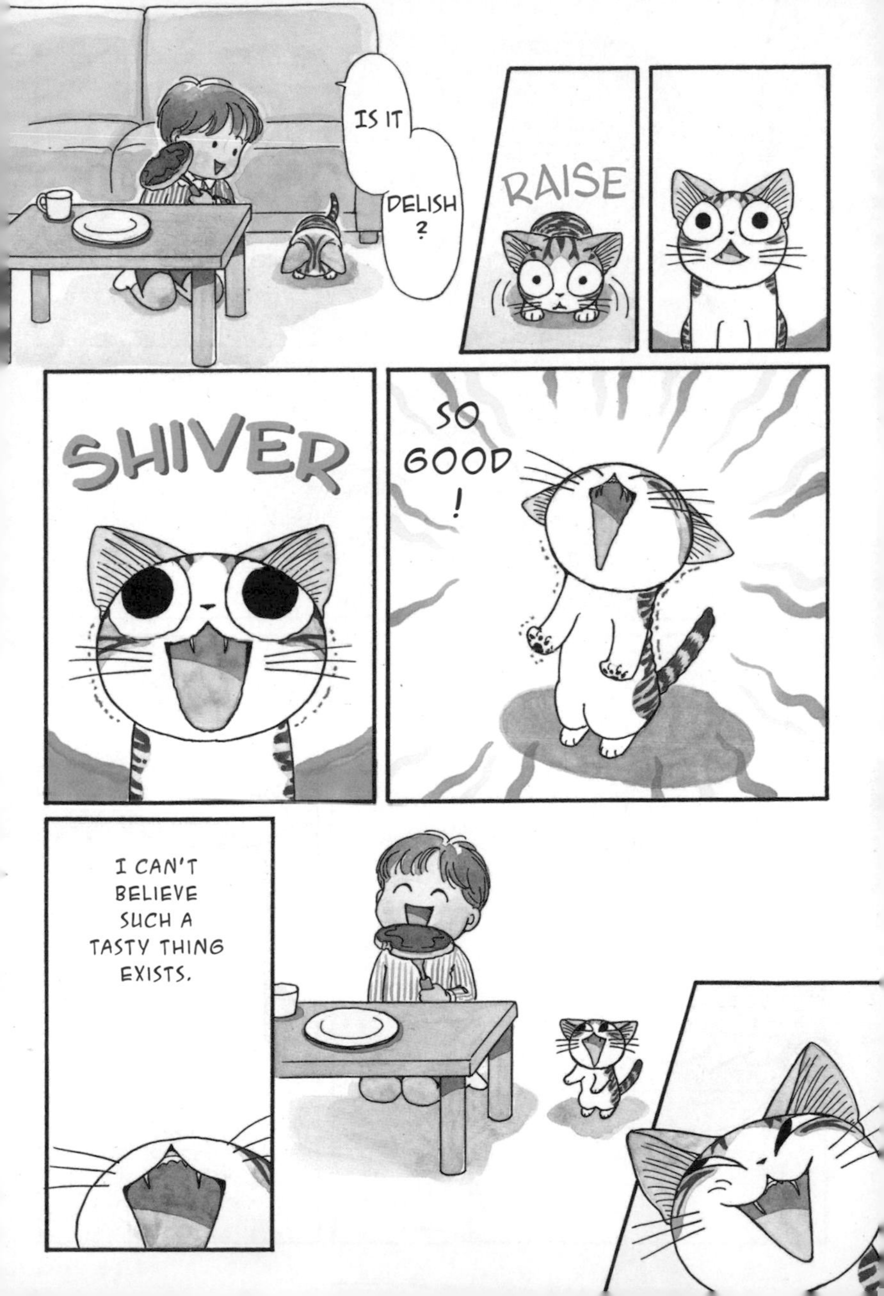
IS IT
DELISH ?
RAISE
SHIVER
SO GOOD !
I CAN'T BELIEVE SUCH A TASTY THING EXISTS.

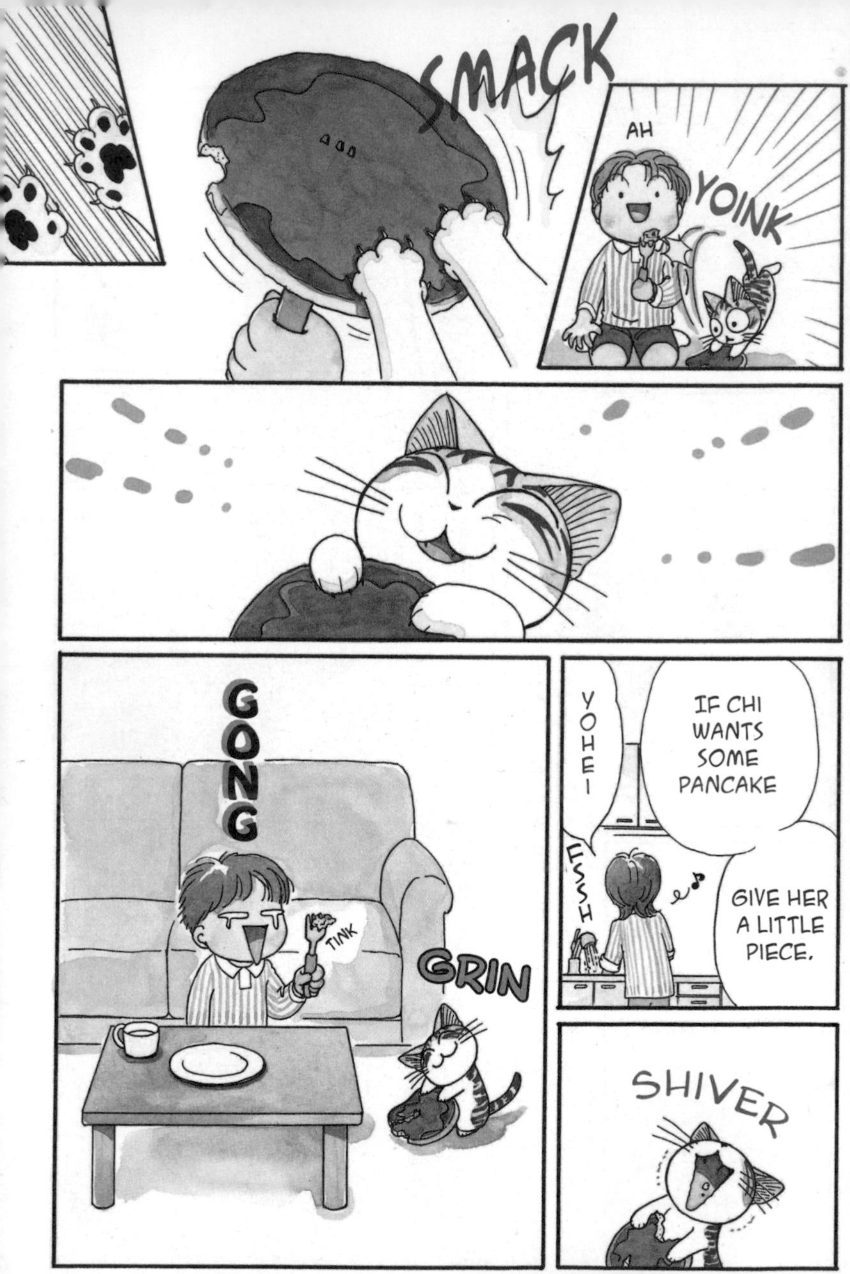
SMACK
AH
YOINK
GONG
TINK
GRIN
YOHEI
IF CHI WANTS SOME PANCAKE
FSSH
GIVE HER A LITTLE PIECE.
SHIVER

the end

homemade 22: a cat takes a bath

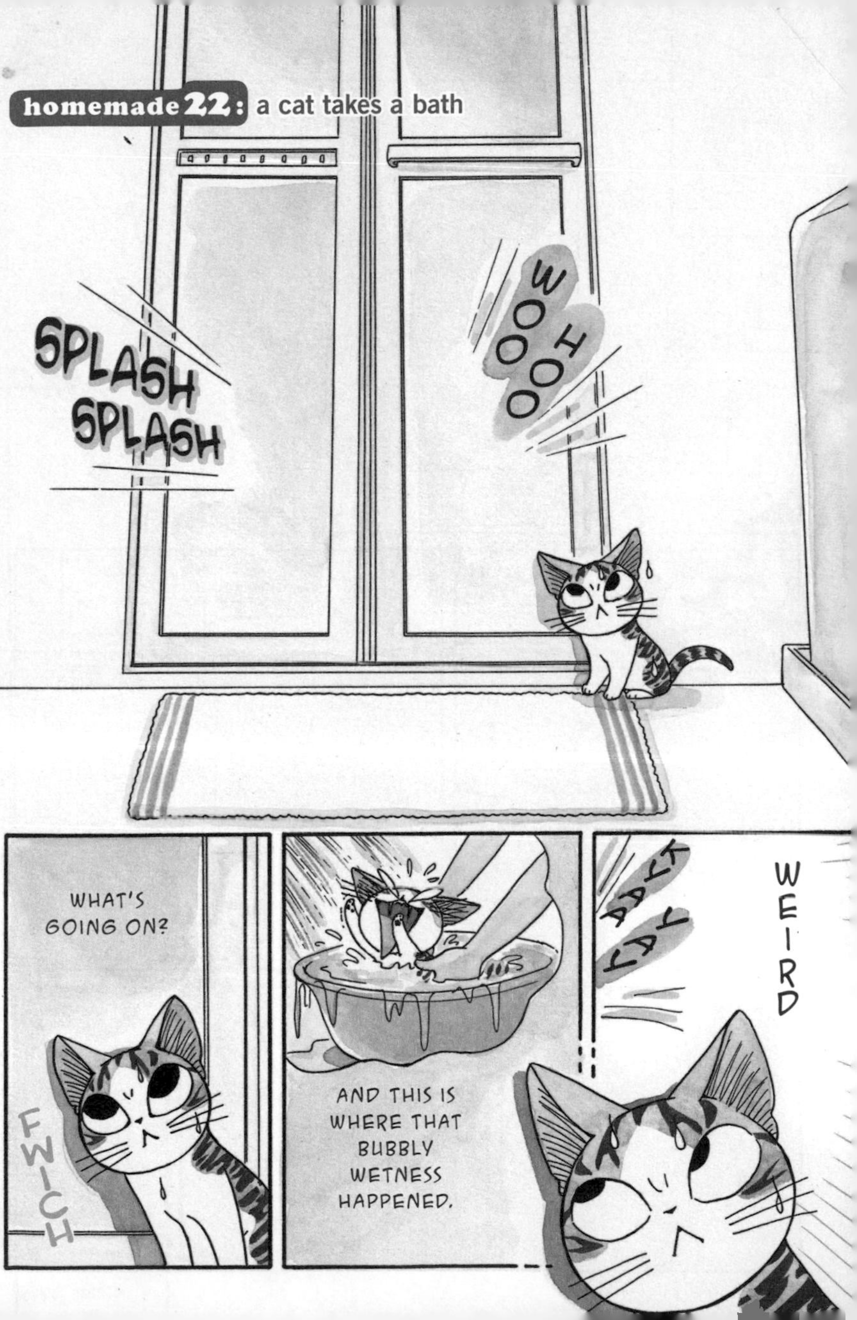
SPLASH
SPLASH
WOOOHOO
WHAT'S GOING ON?
FWICH
AND THIS IS WHERE THAT BUBBLY WETNESS HAPPENED.
AAYK
YAY
WEIRD

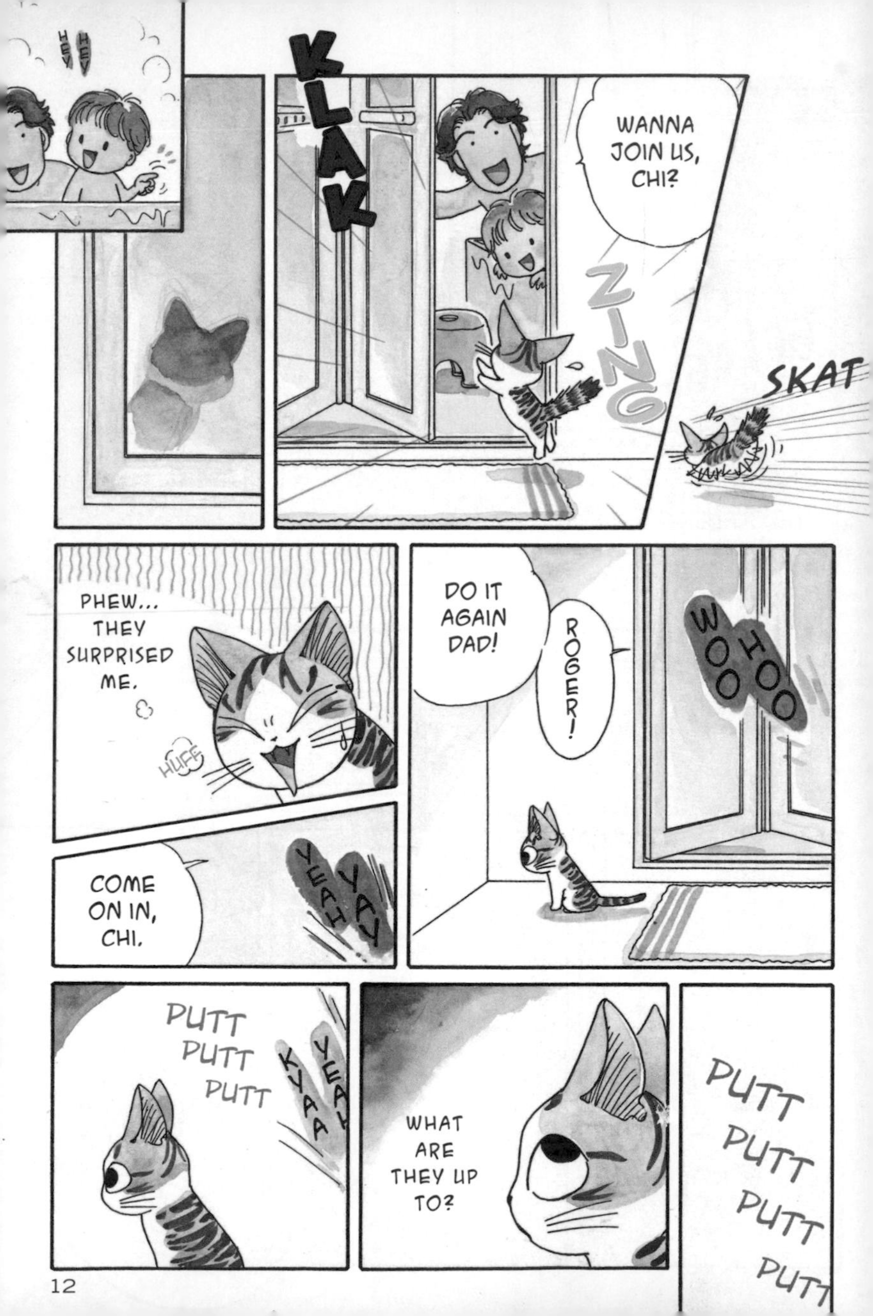
HEY HEY
KLAK
WANNA JOIN US, CHI?
ZING
SKAT
PHEW... THEY SURPRISED ME.
HUFF
COME ON IN, CHI.
YEAH YAY
DO IT AGAIN DAD!
ROGER!
WOO HOO
PUTT PUTT PUTT
KYAAA YEAH
WHAT ARE THEY UP TO?
PUTT PUTT PUTT PUTT

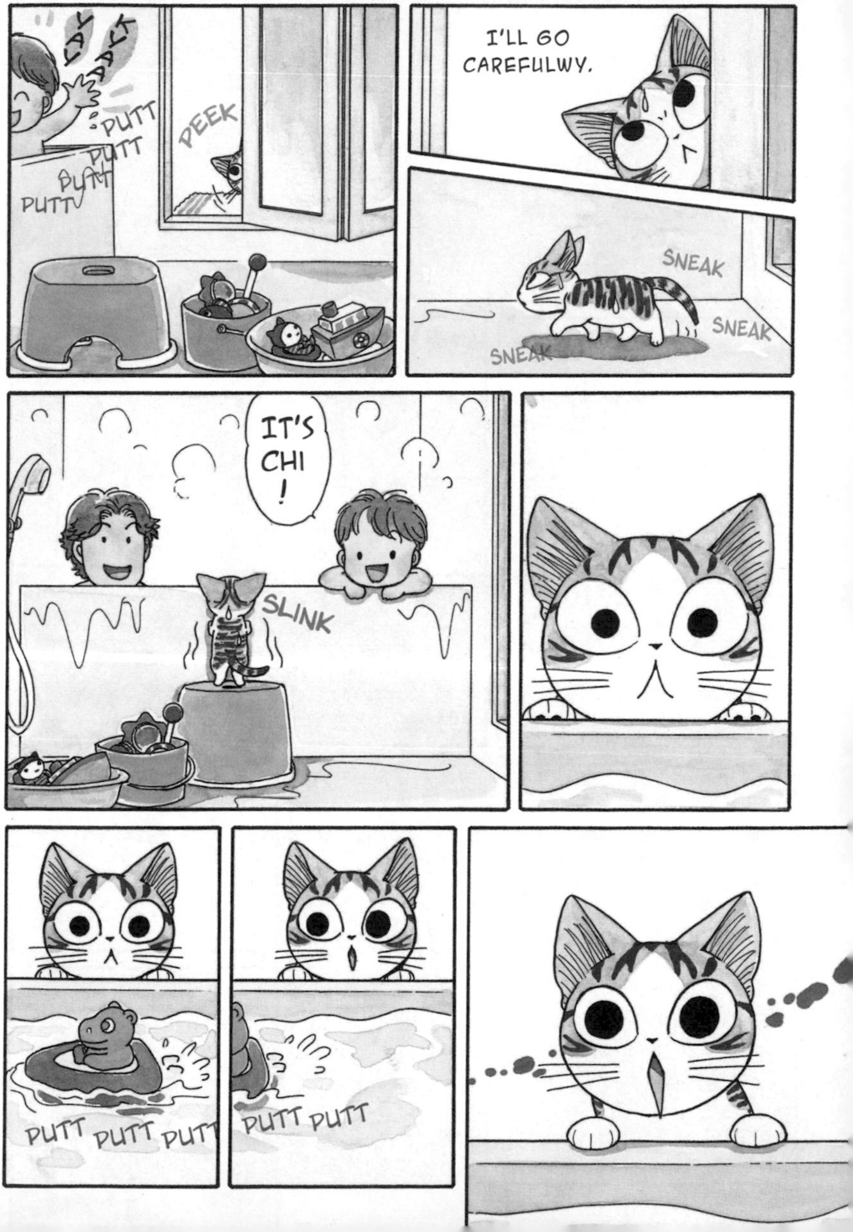
KYAA
YAY
PUTT
PUTT
PUTT
PUTT
PEEK
I'LL GO CAREFULWY.
SNEAK
SNEAK
SNEAK
IT'S CHI!
SLINK
PUTT PUTT PUTT
PUTT PUTT

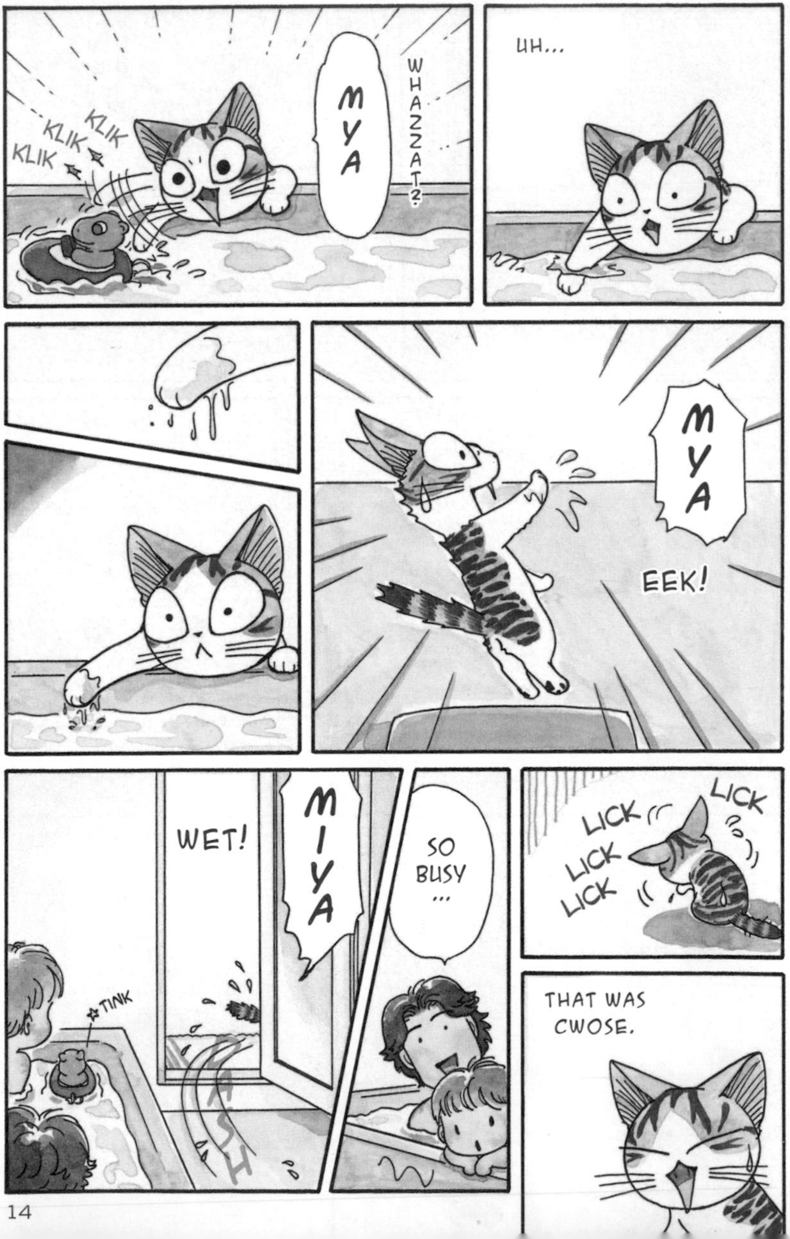
KLIK
KLIK
KLIK
MYA
WHAZZAT?
UH...
MYA
EEK!
WET!
TINK
MIYA
SO BUSY ...
LICK
LICK
LICK
LICK
THAT WAS CWOSE.

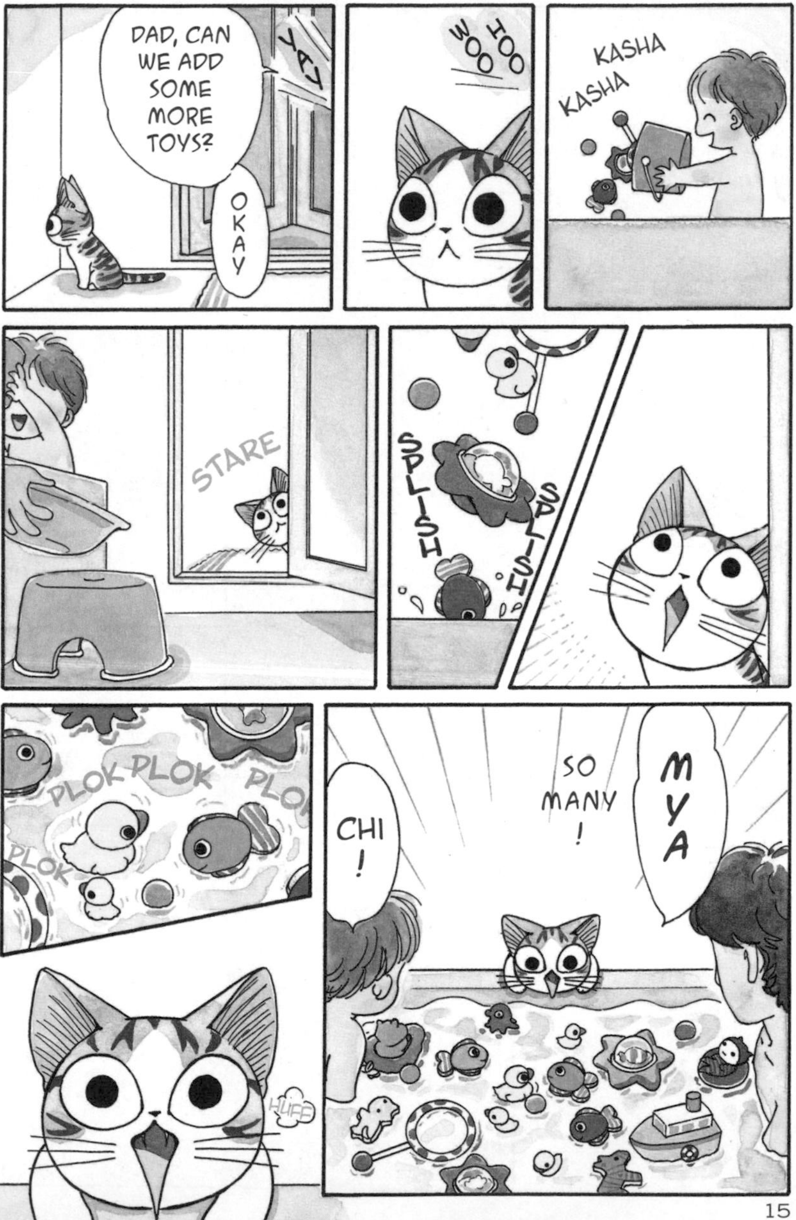
DAD, CAN WE ADD SOME MORE TOYS?
YAY
OKAY
WOOO HOOO
KASHA KASHA
STARE
SPLISH SPLISH
PLOK PLOK PLOK PLOK
HUFF
CHI!
SO MANY!
MYA

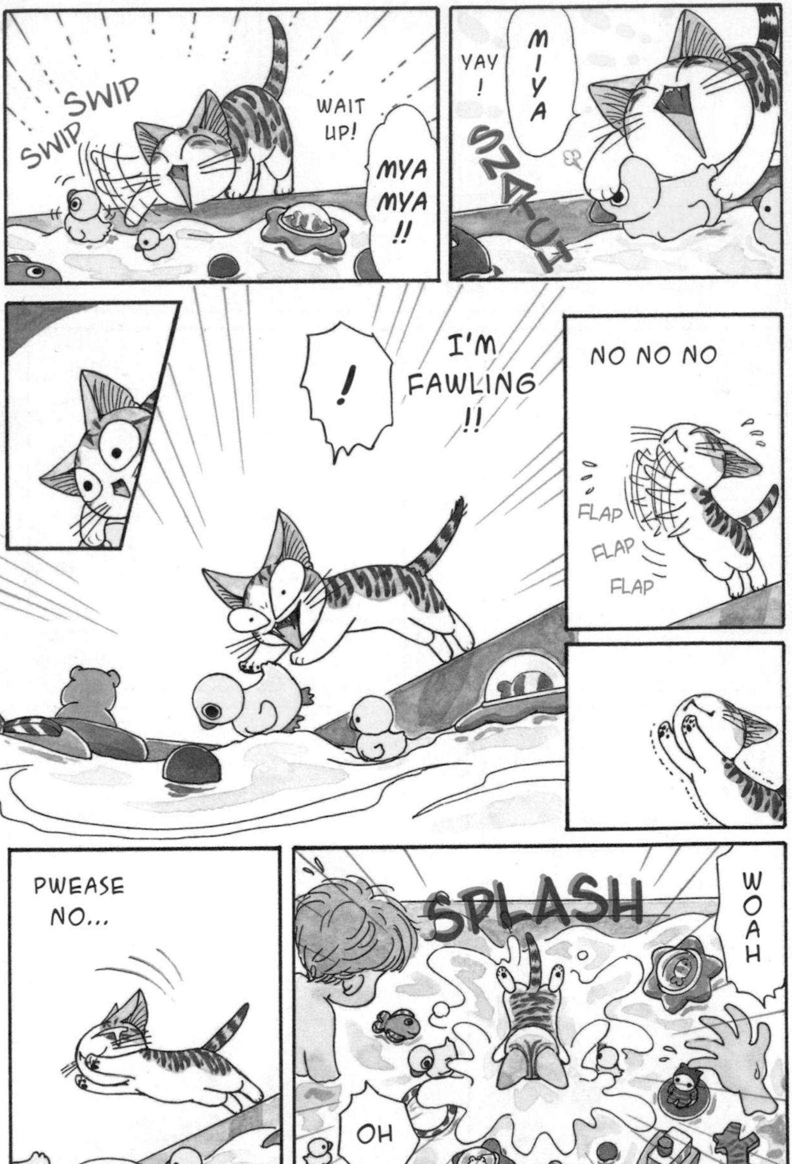

SWIP
SWIP
WAIT UP!
MYA MYA !!
YAY!
MIYA
SNATCH
!
I'M FAWLING !!
NO NO NO
FLAP
FLAP
FLAP
PWEASE NO...
SPLASH
WOAH
OH

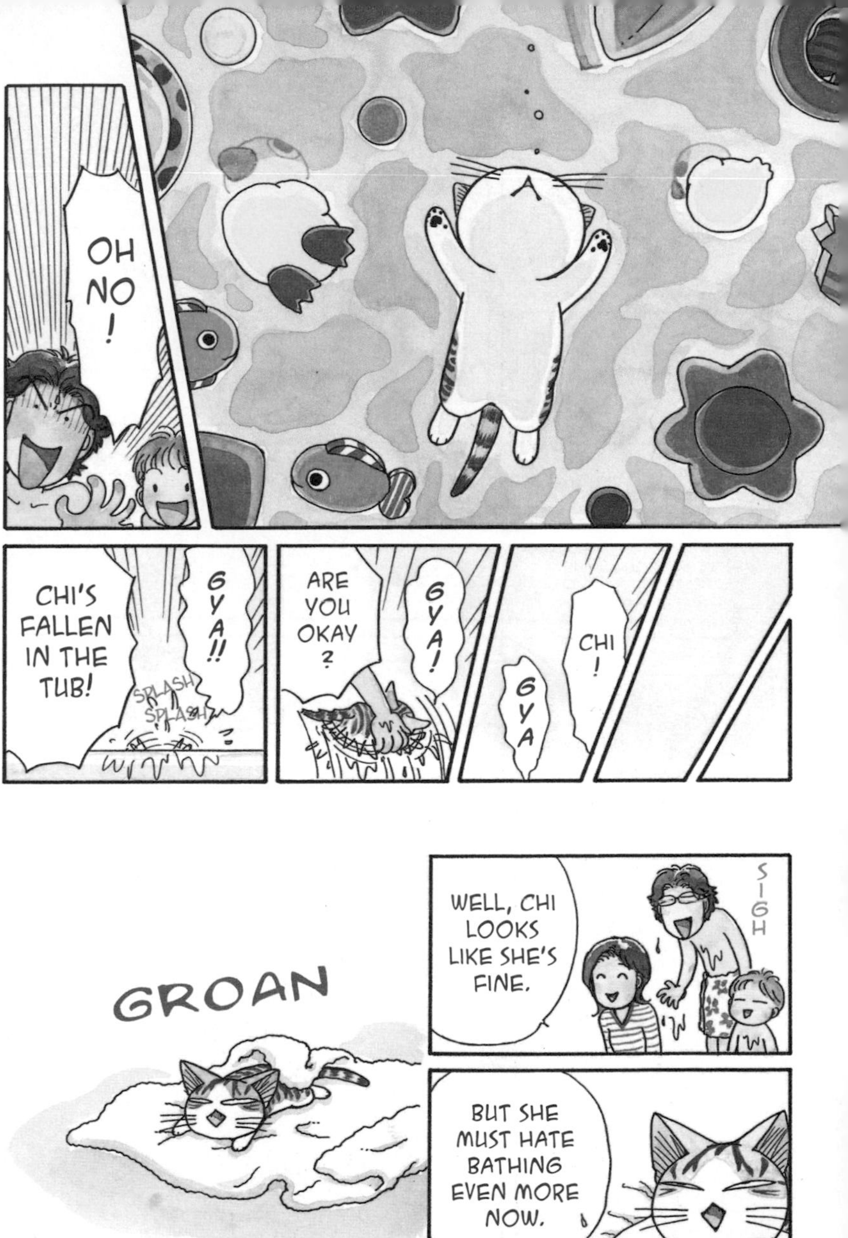
OH NO!
CHI'S FALLEN IN THE TUB!
GYA!!
SPLASH
SPLASH
ARE YOU OKAY?
GYA!
CHI!
GYA
GROAN
WELL, CHI LOOKS LIKE SHE'S FINE.
SIGH
BUT SHE MUST HATE BATHING EVEN MORE NOW.

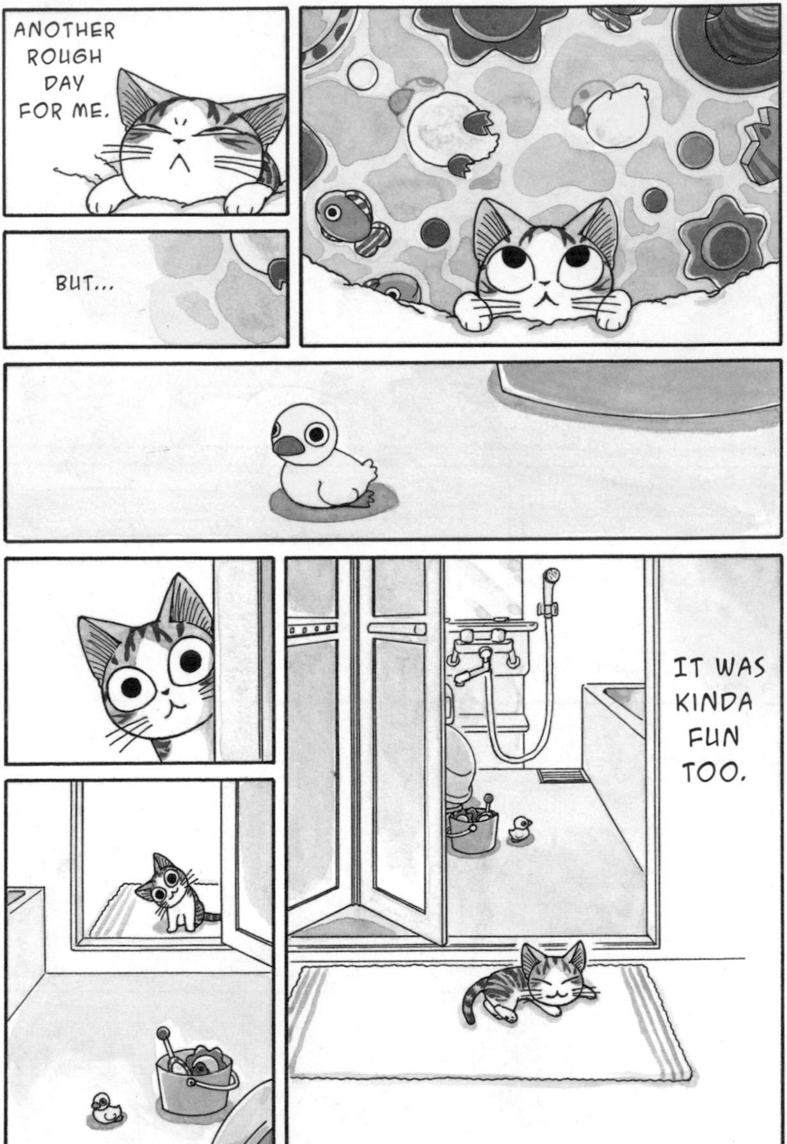
ANOTHER ROUGH DAY FOR ME.
BUT...
IT WAS KINDA FUN TOO.

the end

homemade 23: a cat throws down

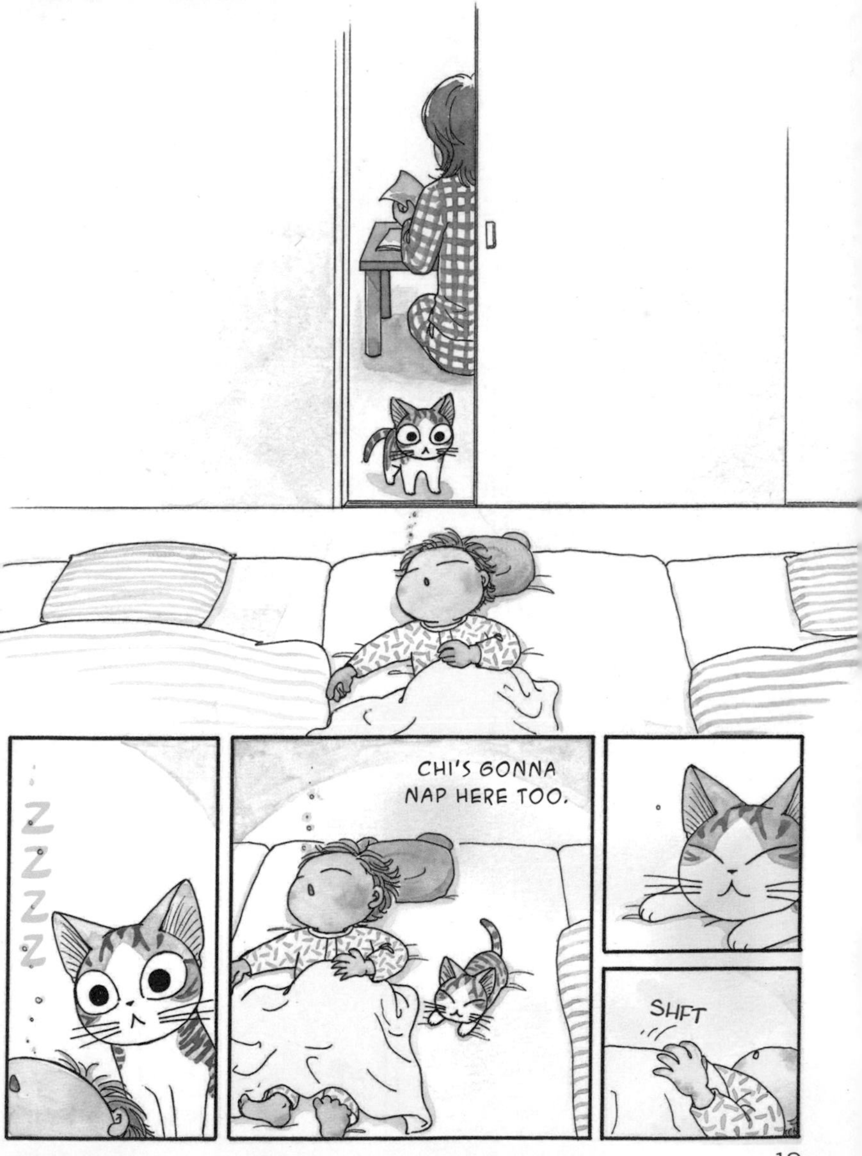
Z Z Z Z
CHI'S GONNA NAP HERE TOO.
SHFT

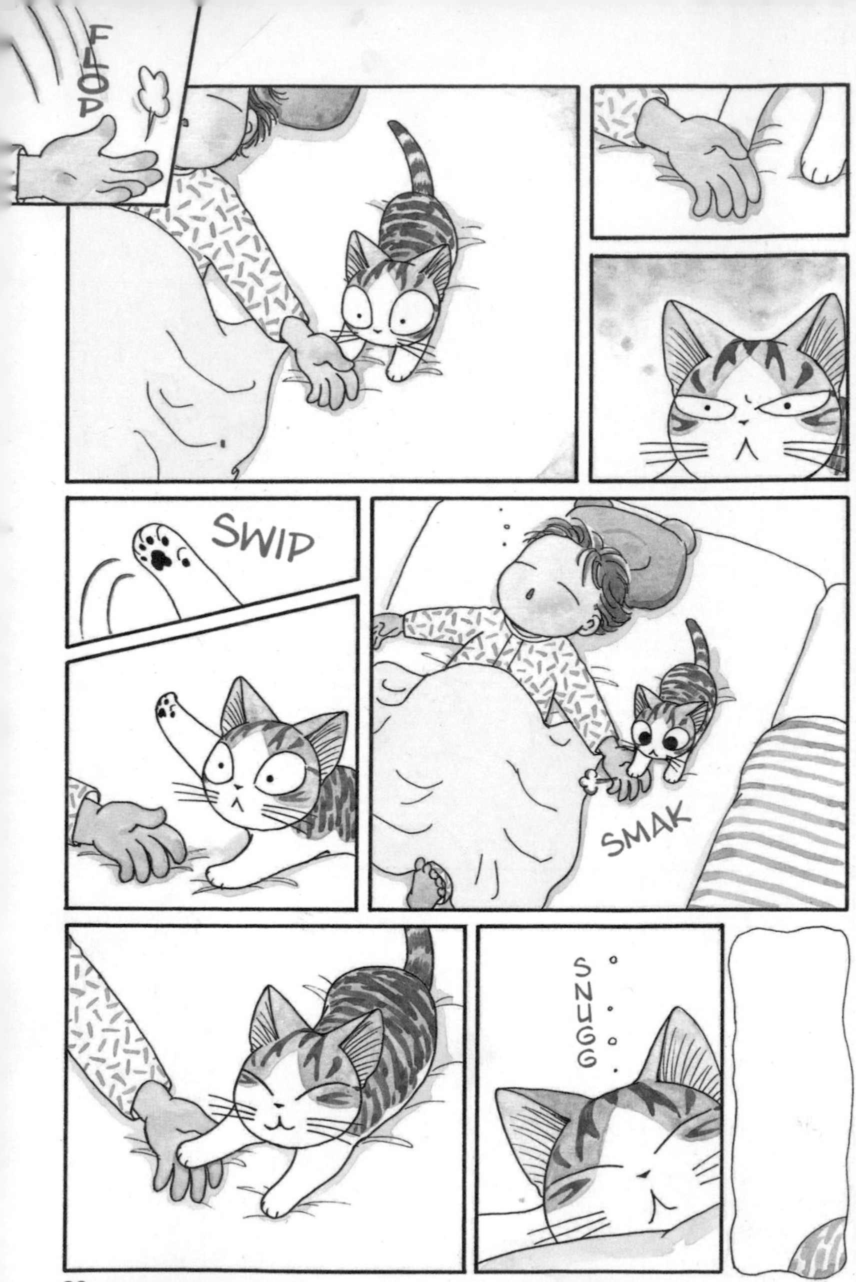
FLOP
SWIP
SMAK
SNUGG

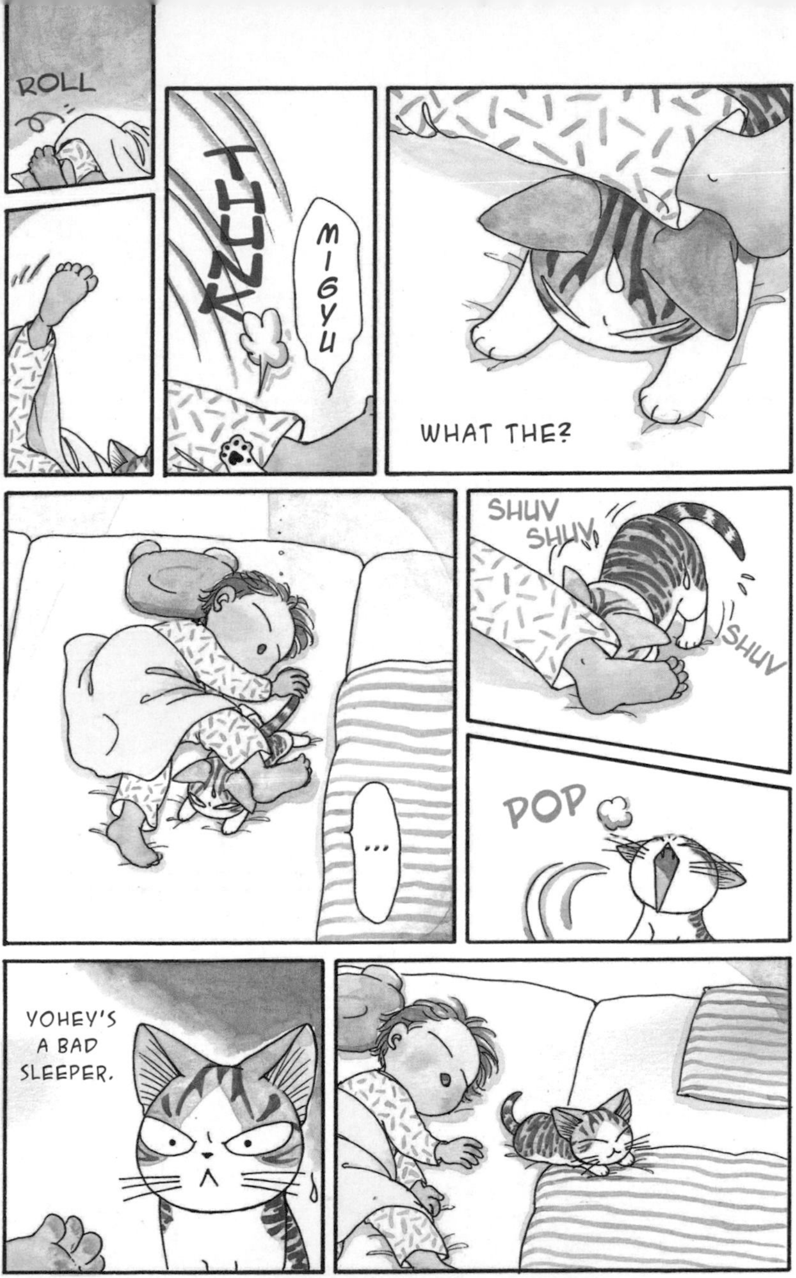
ROLL
THUNK
MIGYU
WHAT THE?
...
SHUV
SHUV
SHUV
POP
YOHEY'S A BAD SLEEPER.

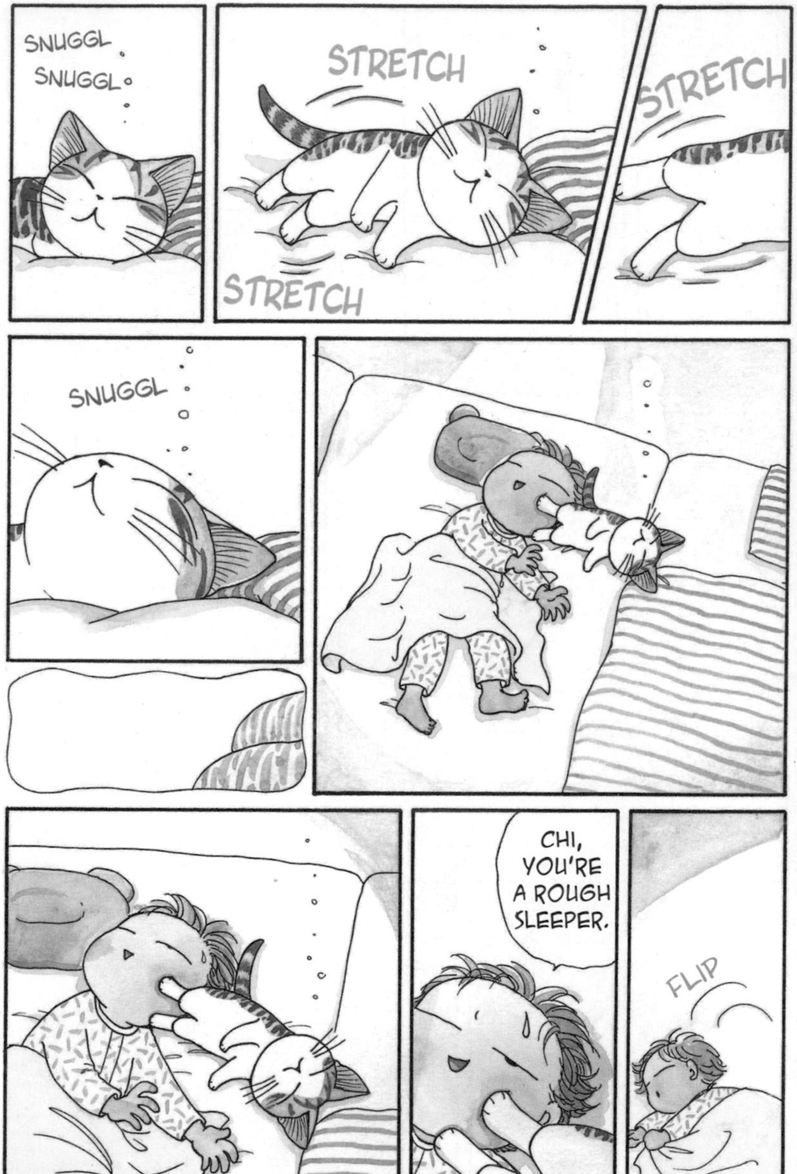
SNUGGL
SNUGGL
STRETCH
STRETCH
STRETCH
SNUGGL
CHI, YOU'RE A ROUGH SLEEPER.
FLIP

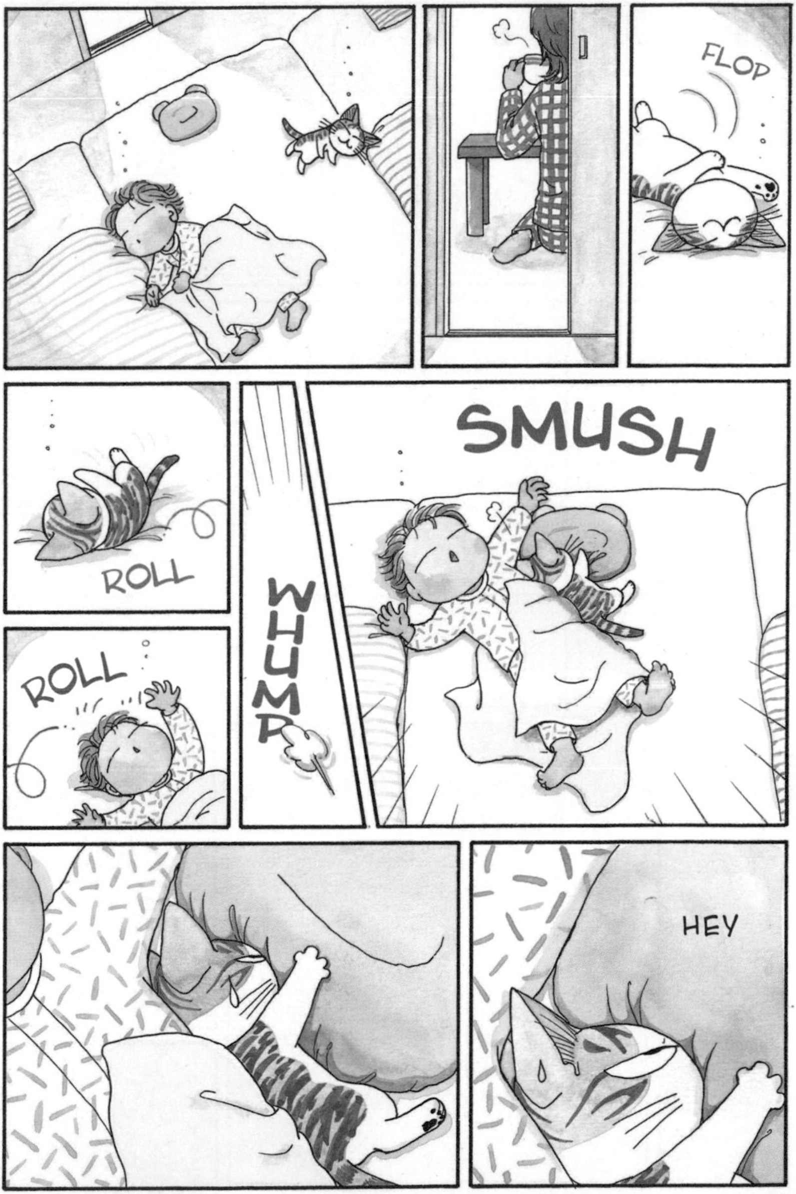
FLOP
ROLL
ROLL
WHUMP
SMUSH
HEY

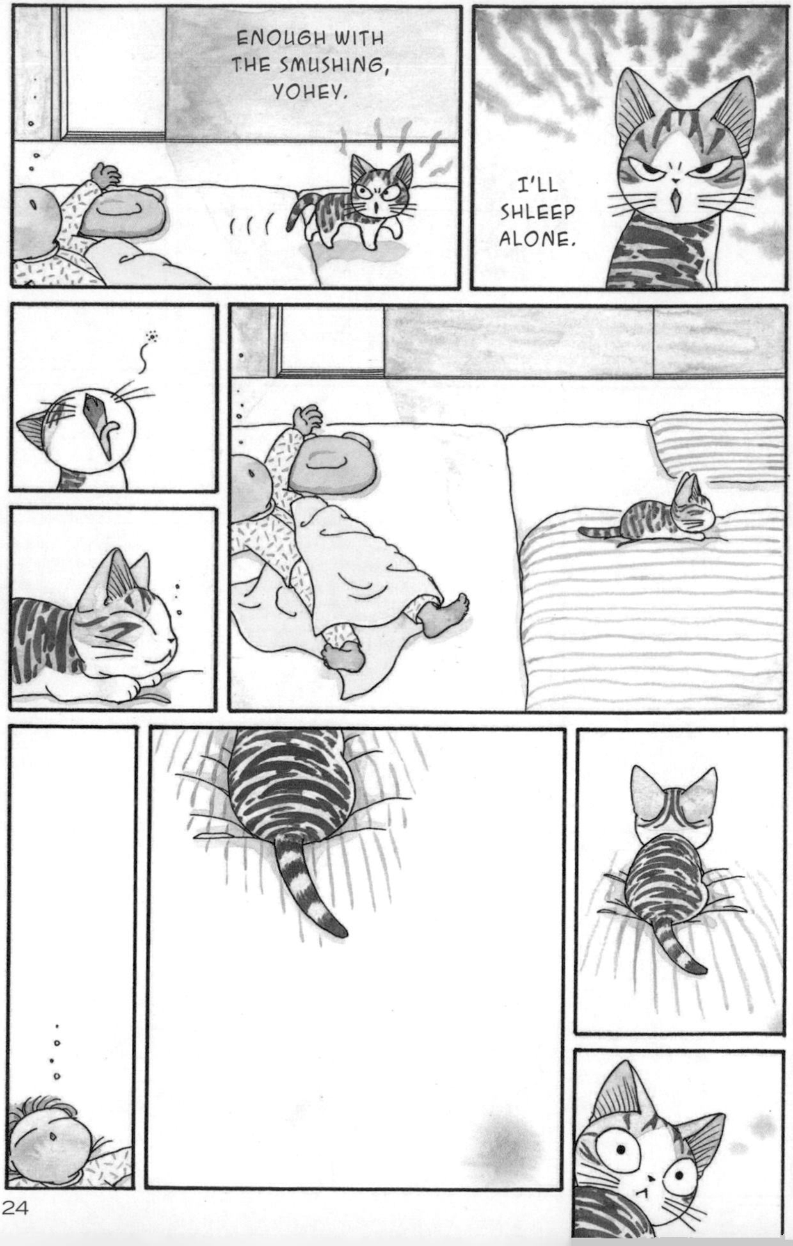
ENOUGH WITH THE SMUSHING, YOHEY.
I'LL SHLEEP ALONE.

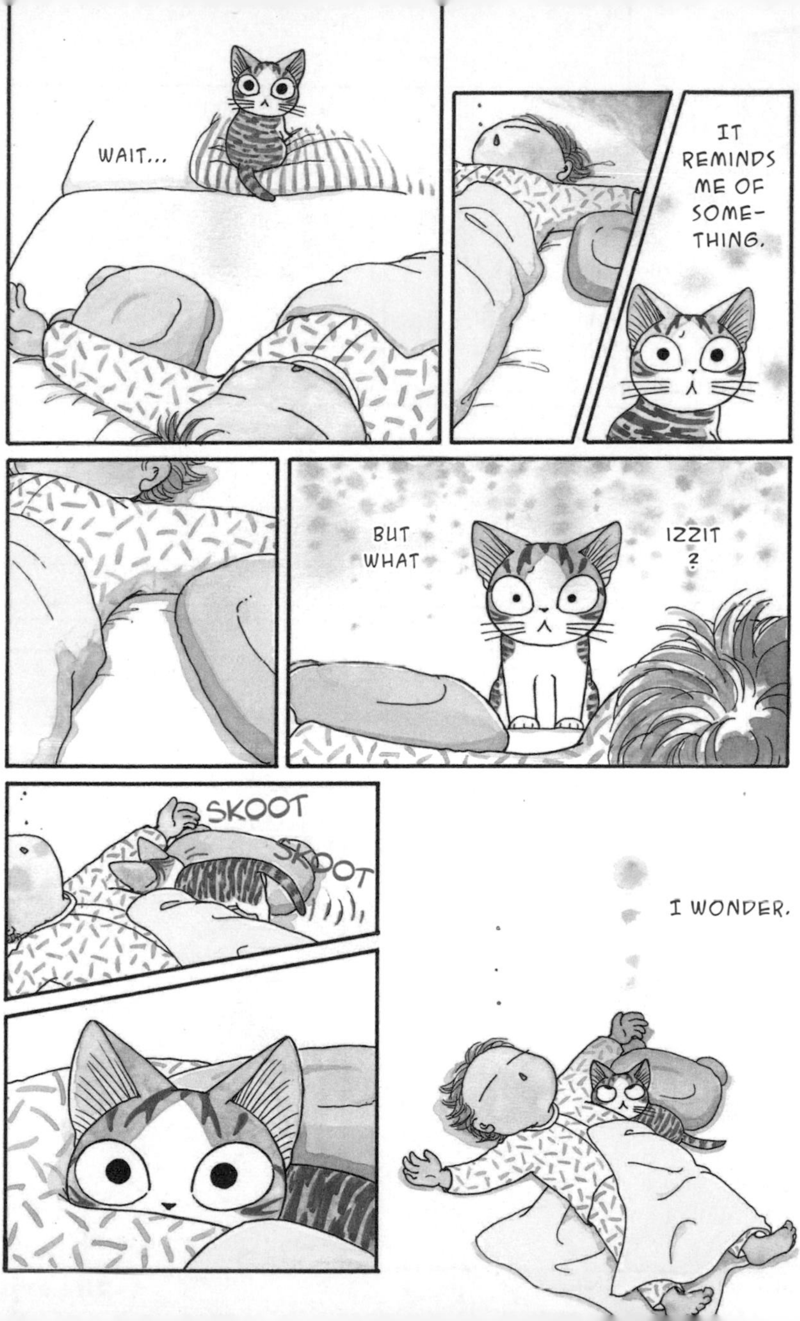
WAIT...
IT REMINDS ME OF SOME-THING.
BUT WHAT
IZZIT?
SKOOT
SKOOT
I WONDER.

WEL-COME HOME.

IS YOHEI ASLEEP?

YUP.

AW

AND WITH CHI.

Z Z Z

SNUG

THEY LOOK JUST LIKE

THE DEAREST OF HUMAN SIBLINGS.

HEE HEE

SHOOP

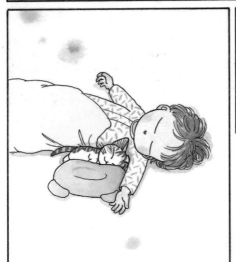

the end

homemade 24: a cat asserts itself

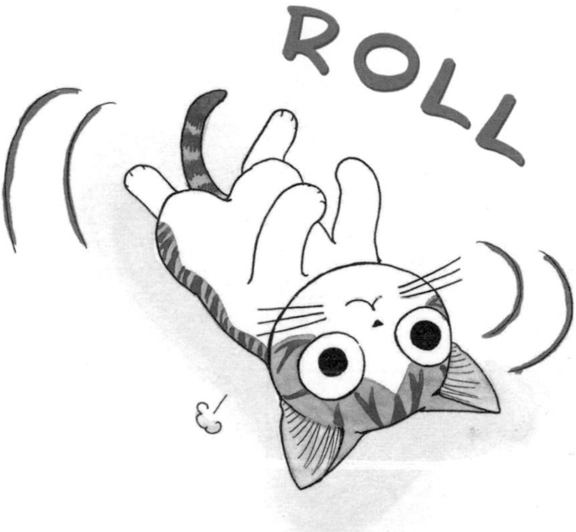
ROLL

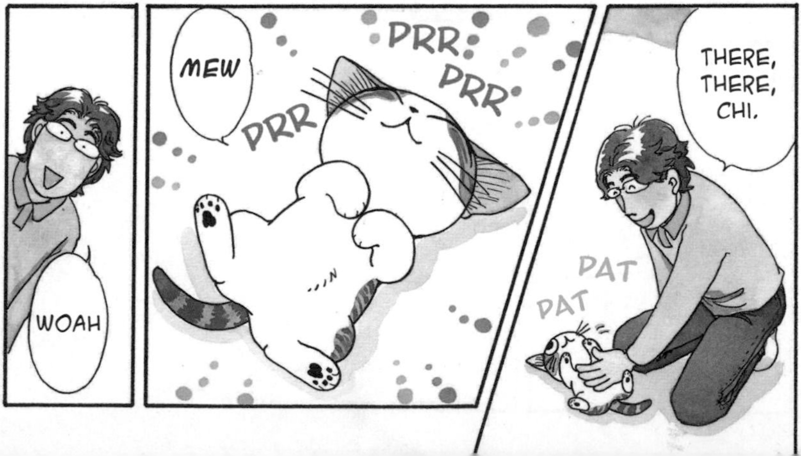
WOAH
MEW
PRR
PRR
PRR
THERE, THERE, CHI.
PAT
PAT

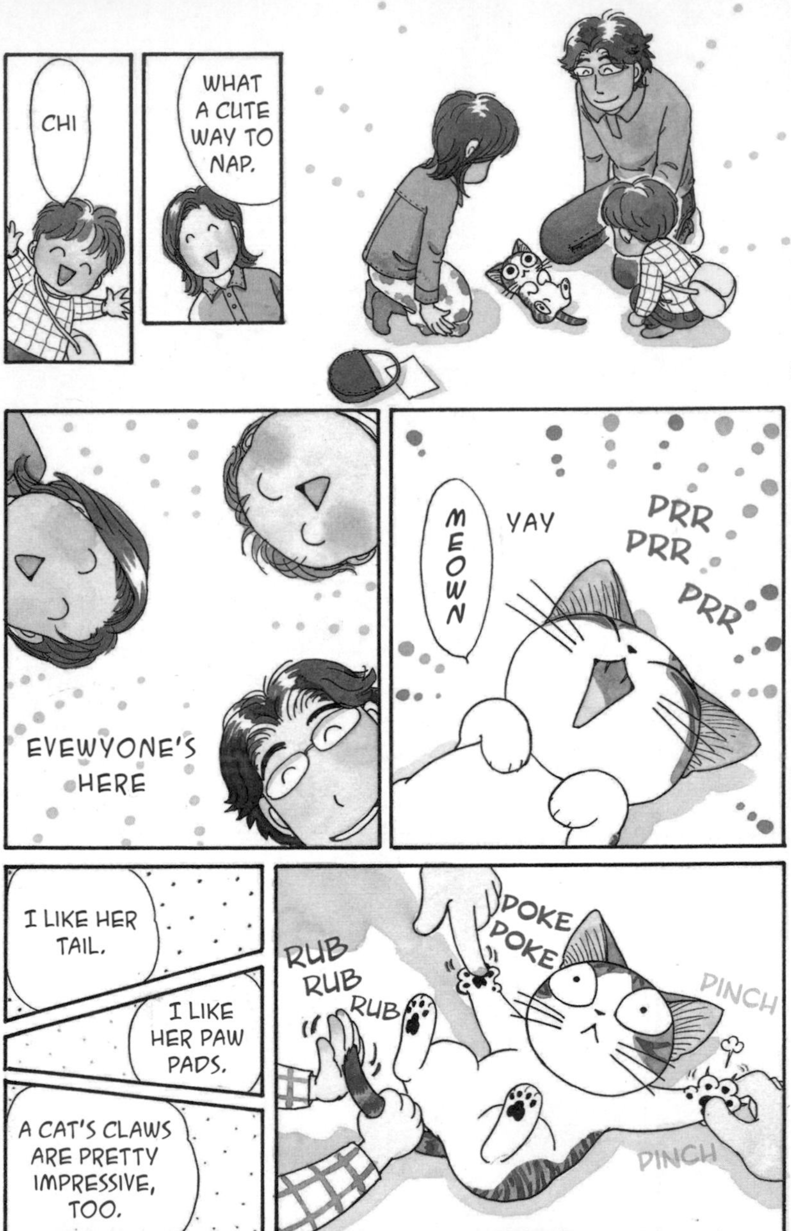
CHI
WHAT A CUTE WAY TO NAP.
EVEWYONE'S HERE
MEOWN
YAY
PRR PRR PRR
I LIKE HER TAIL.
I LIKE HER PAW PADS.
A CAT'S CLAWS ARE PRETTY IMPRESSIVE, TOO.
RUB RUB RUB
POKE POKE
PINCH
PINCH

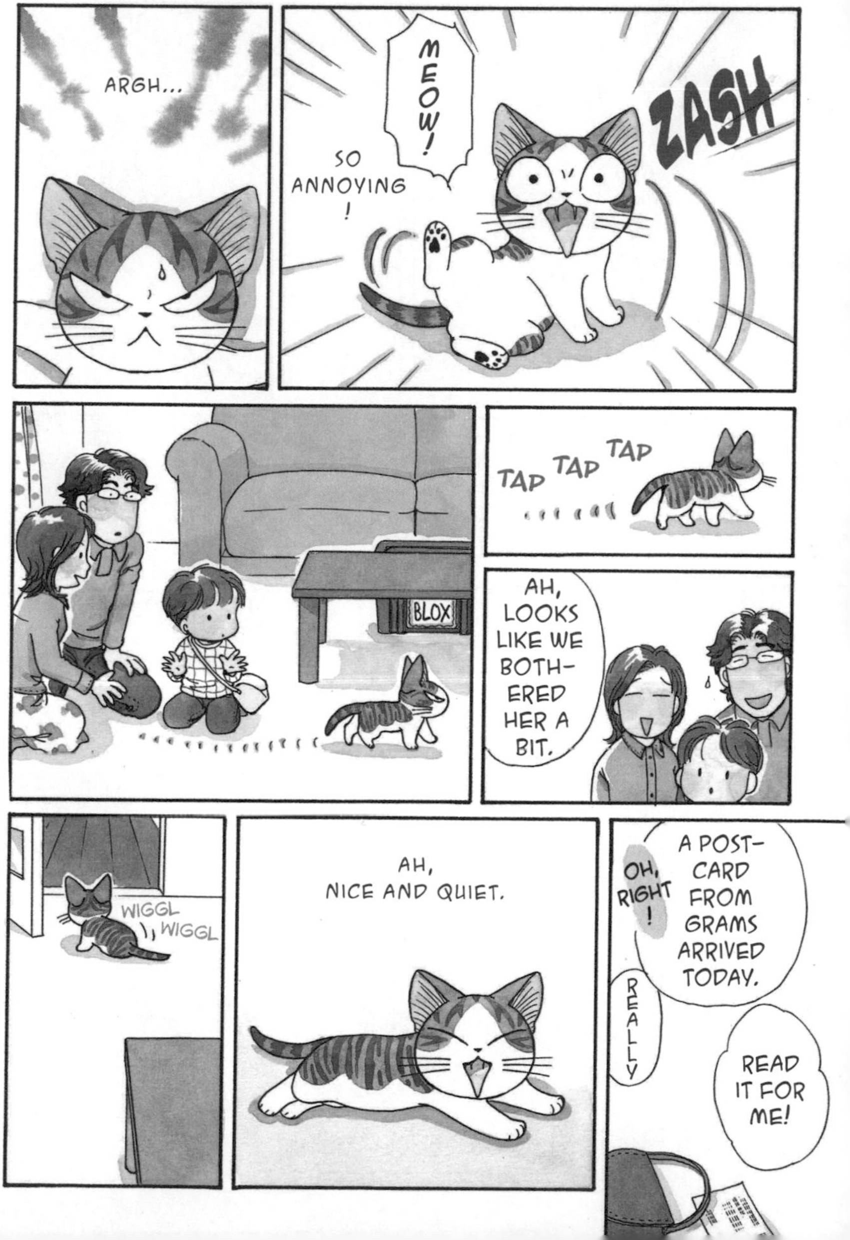
ARGH...
SO ANNOYING!
MEOW!
ZASH
TAP TAP TAP
BLOX
AH, LOOKS LIKE WE BOTHERED HER A BIT.
WIGGL WIGGL
AH, NICE AND QUIET.
OH, RIGHT!
A POSTCARD FROM GRAMS ARRIVED TODAY.
REALLY
READ IT FOR ME!

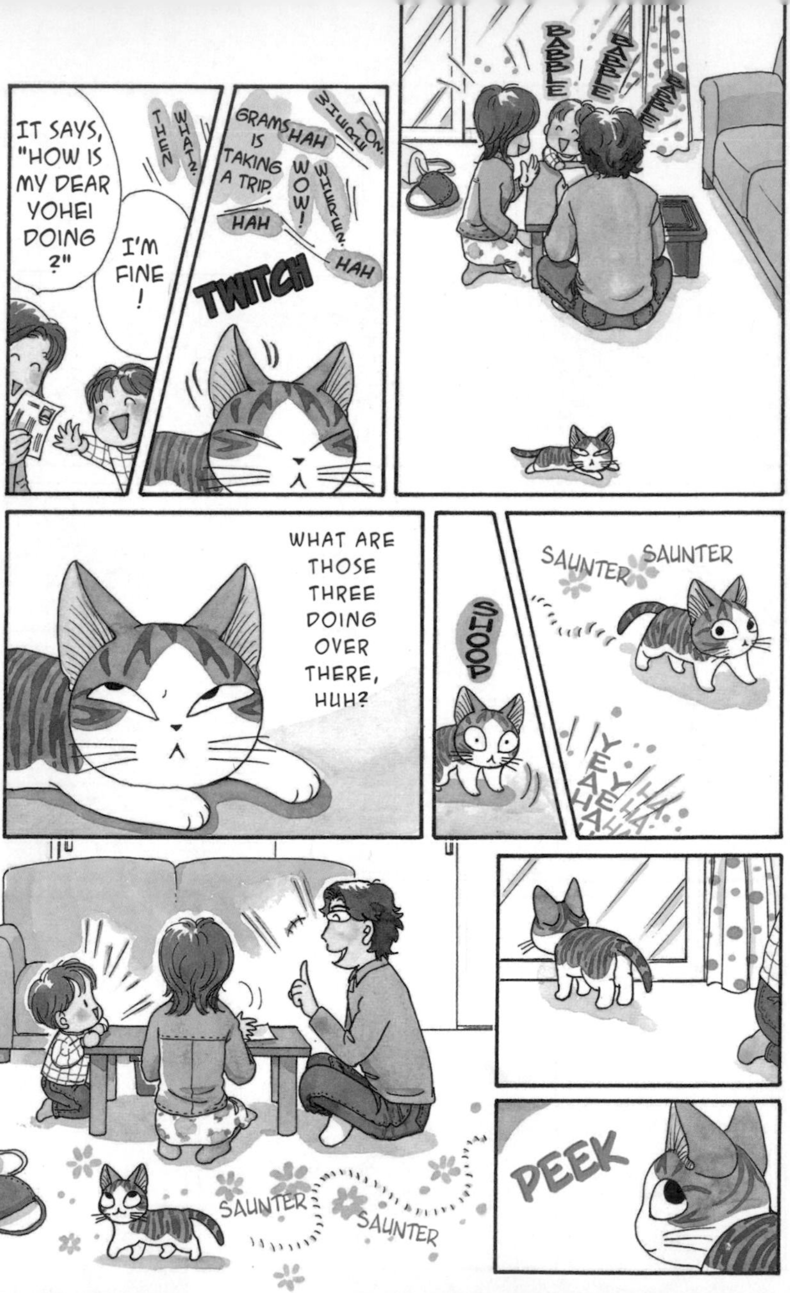
IT SAYS, "HOW IS MY DEAR YOHEI DOING?"
THEN WHAT?
I'M FINE!
HOW NICE!
GRAMS IS TAKING A TRIP.
HAH
WOW!
WHERE?
HAH
HAH
TWITCH
BABBLE
BABBLE
BABBLE
WHAT ARE THOSE THREE DOING OVER THERE, HUH?
SHOOP
SAUNTER
SAUNTER
YEAH
HA HA HA
SAUNTER
SAUNTER
PEEK

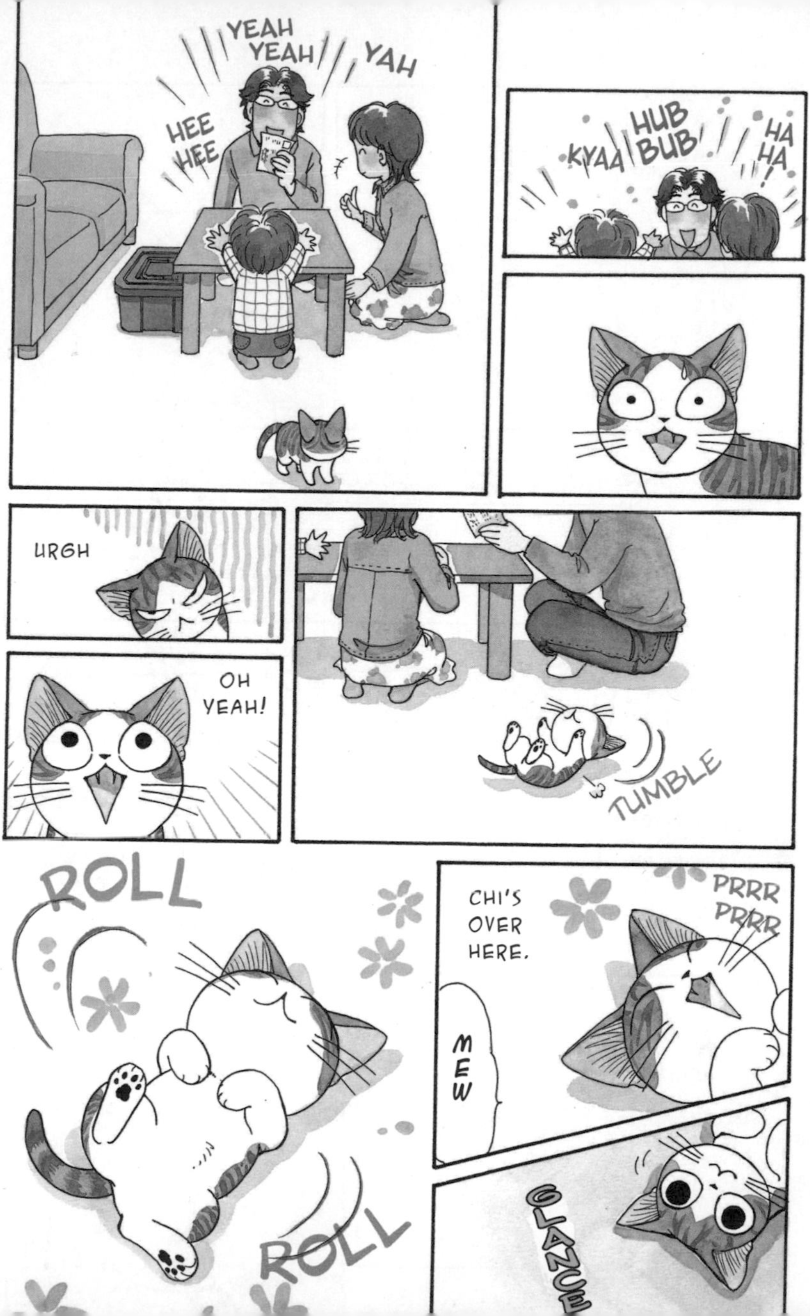
YEAH YEAH
YAH
HEE HEE
KYAA
HUB BUB
HA HA!
URGH
OH YEAH!
TUMBLE
ROLL
ROLL
CHI'S OVER HERE.
PRRR PRRR
MEW
GLANCE

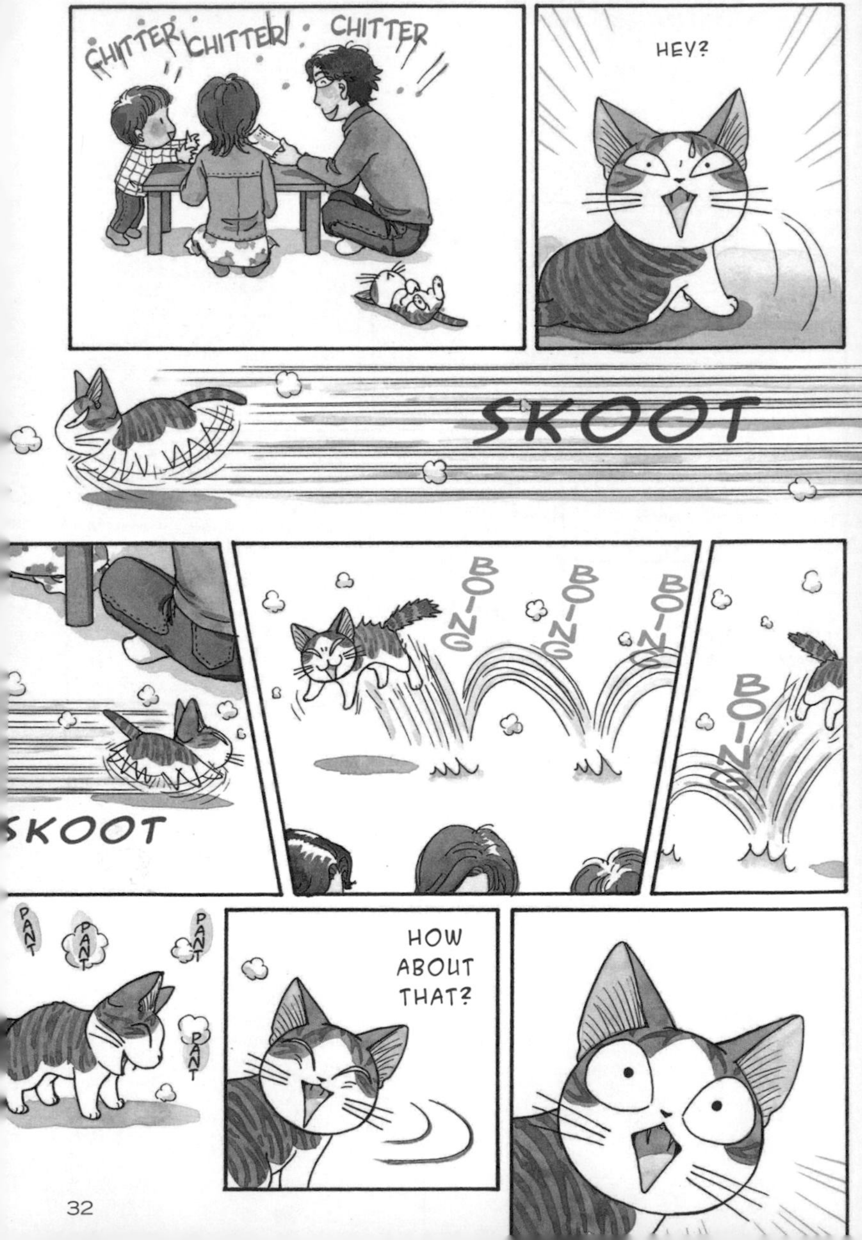

CHITTER CHITTER CHITTER
HEY?
SKOOT
SKOOT
BOING BOING BOING
BOING
PANT PANT PANT PANT
HOW ABOUT THAT?

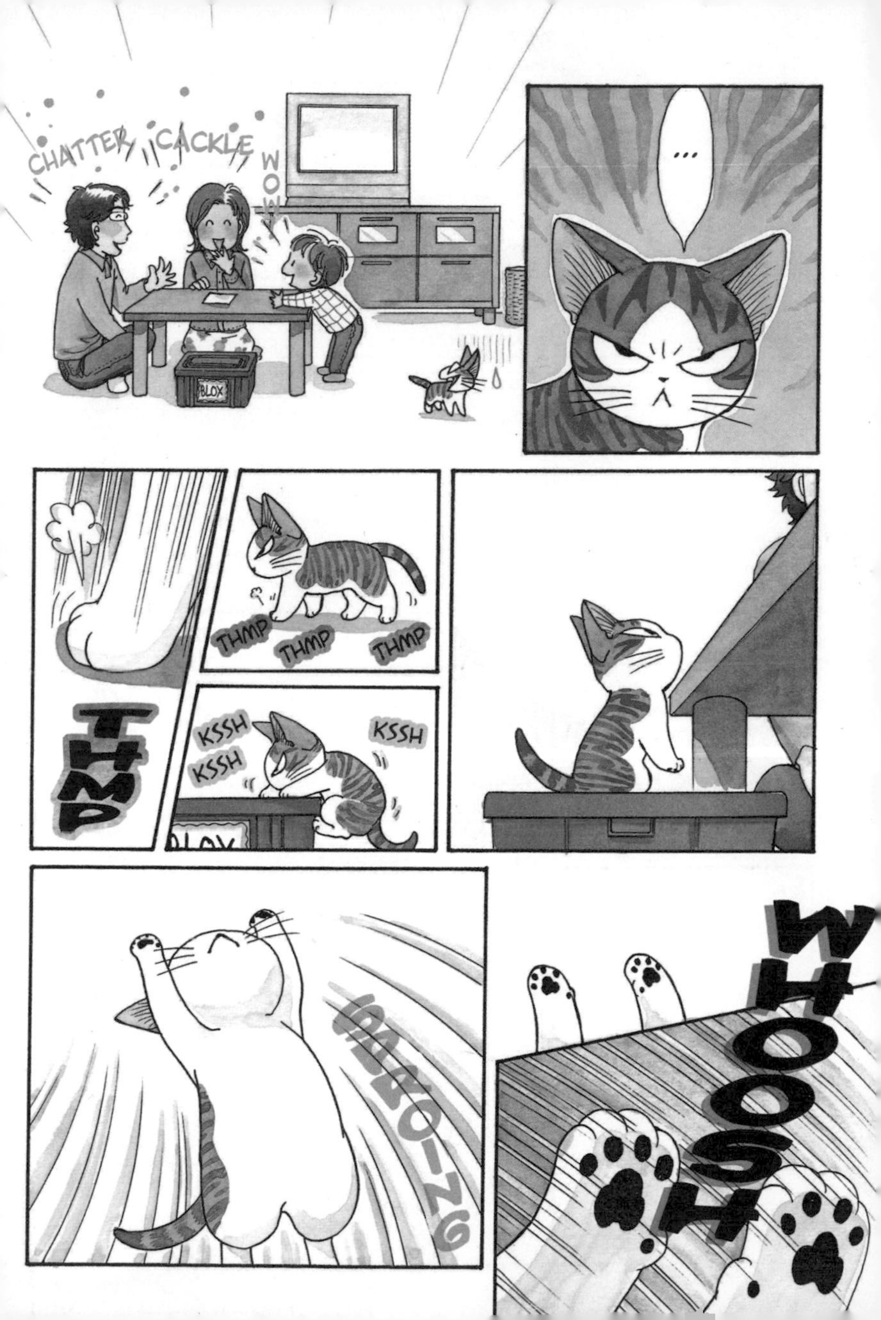
CHATTER
CACKLE
WOW
...
THMP
THMP
THMP
THMP
KSSH
KSSH
KSSH
BLOX
BOIOING
WHOOSH

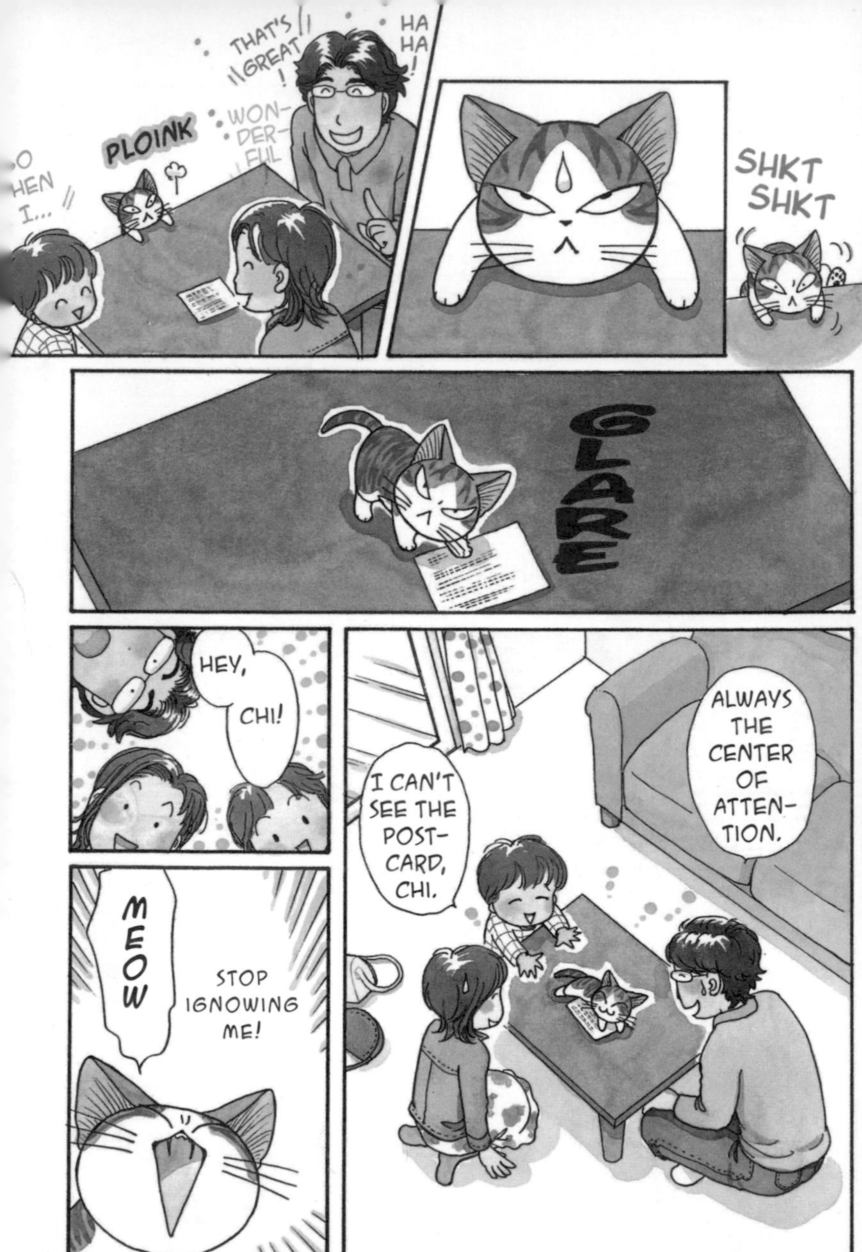
O
HEN
I...
PLOINK
WON-DER-FUL
THAT'S GREAT!
HA HA!
SHKT SHKT
GLARE
HEY,
CHI!
MEOW
STOP IGNOWING ME!
I CAN'T SEE THE POST-CARD, CHI.
ALWAYS THE CENTER OF ATTEN-TION.

the end

homemade 25: a cat stands firm

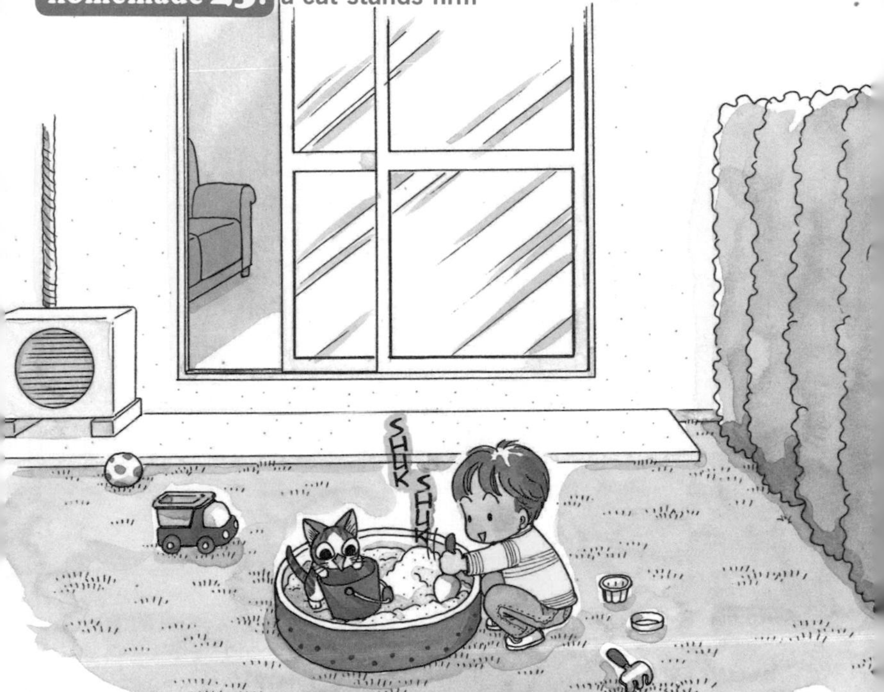
SHUK
SHUK

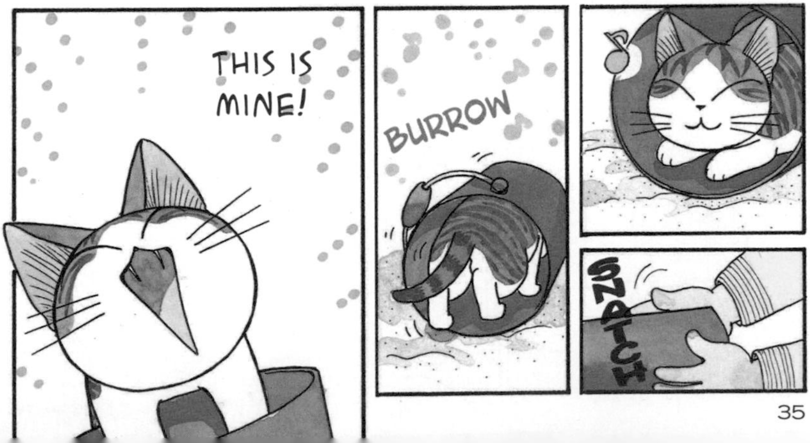
THIS IS MINE!
BURROW
SNATCH

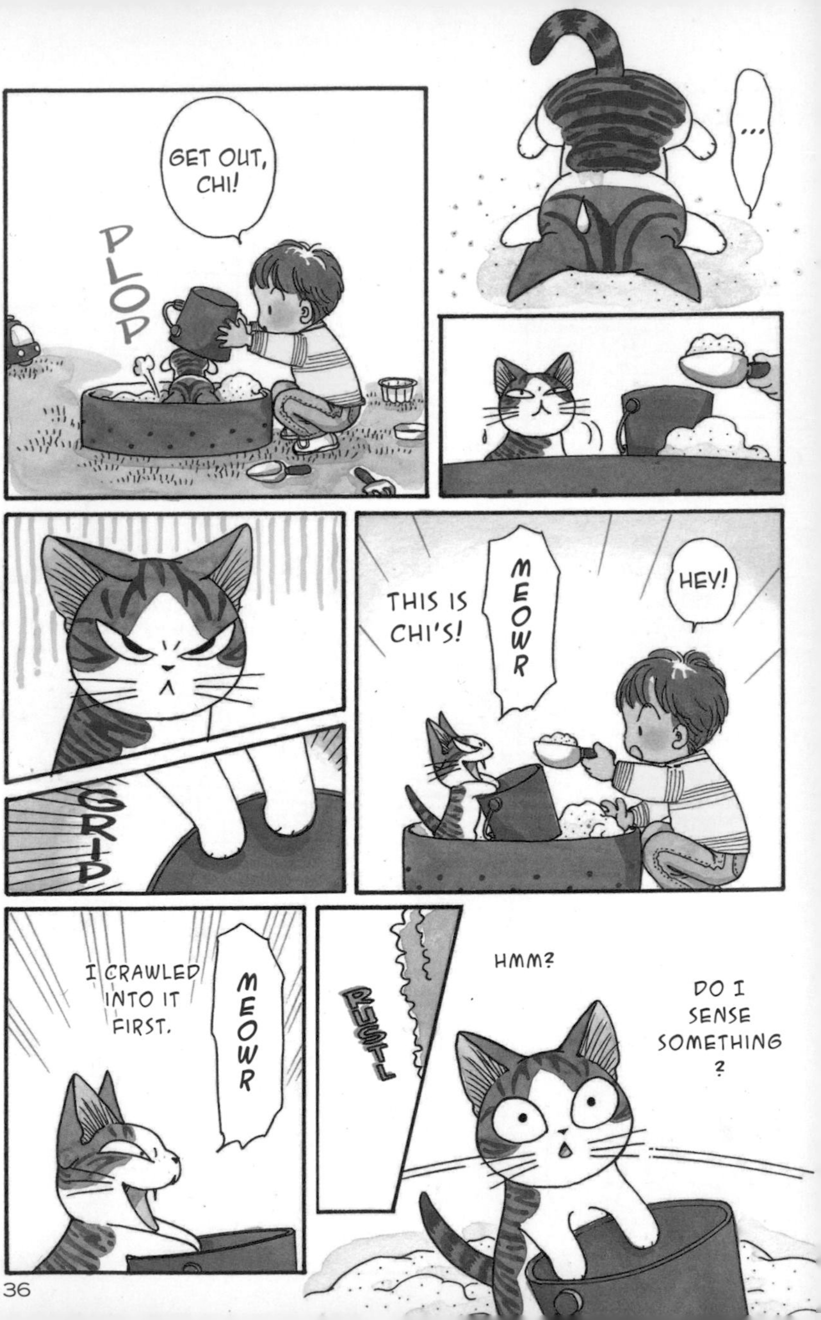

GET OUT, CHI!
PLOP
...
GRIP
THIS IS CHI'S!
MEOWR
HEY!
I CRAWLED INTO IT FIRST.
MEOWR
RUSTL
HMM?
DO I SENSE SOMETHING?

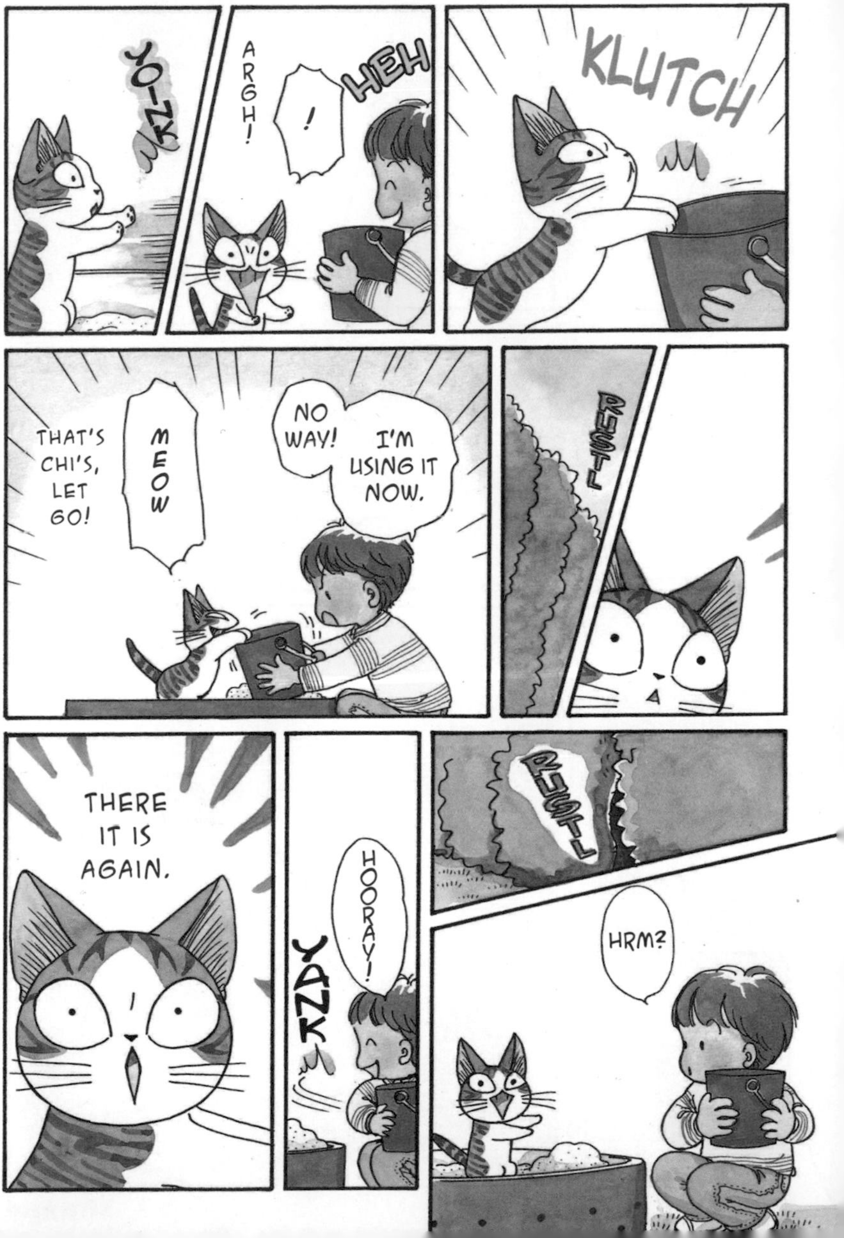

YOINK
ARGH!
!
HEH
KLUTCH
THAT'S CHI'S, LET GO!
MEOW
NO WAY!
I'M USING IT NOW.
RUSTL
THERE IT IS AGAIN.
HOORAY!
YANK
RUSTL
HRM?

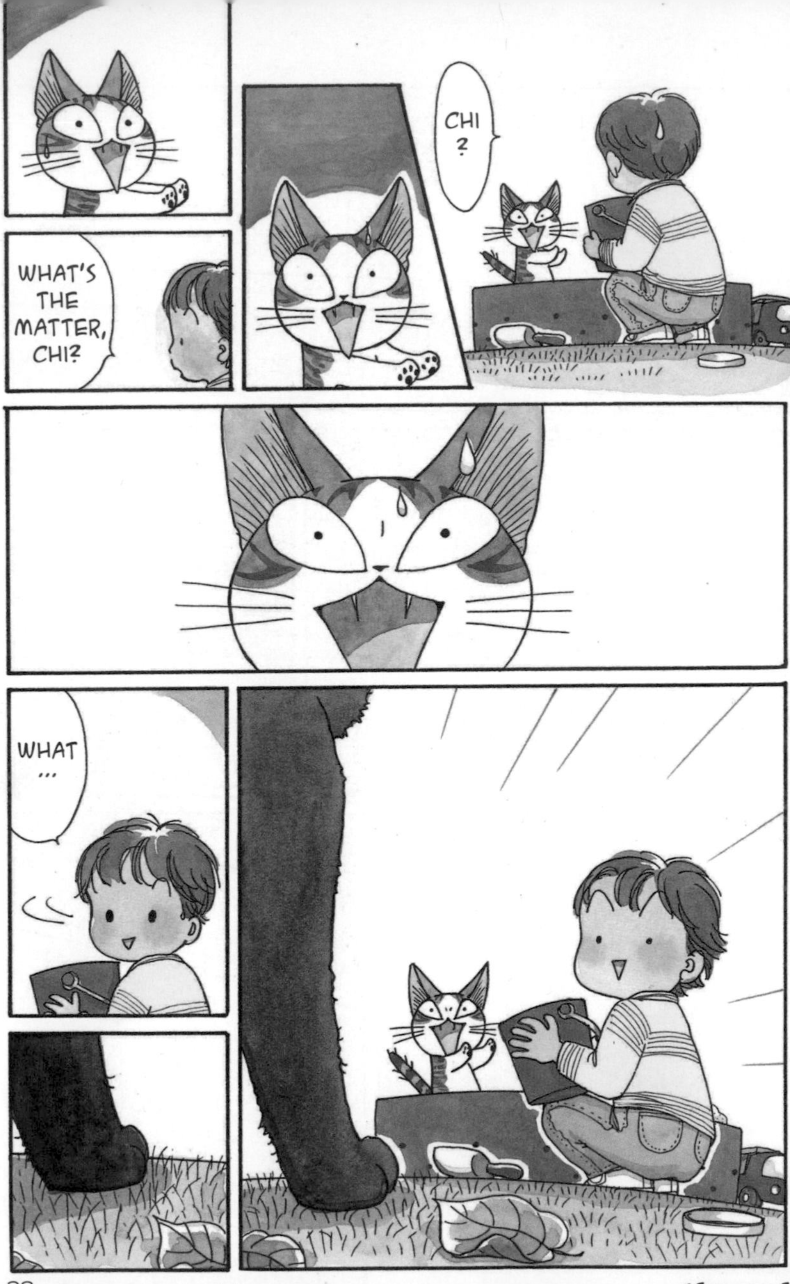
CHI
?
WHAT'S THE MATTER, CHI?
WHAT
...

the end

homemade 26: a cat encounters

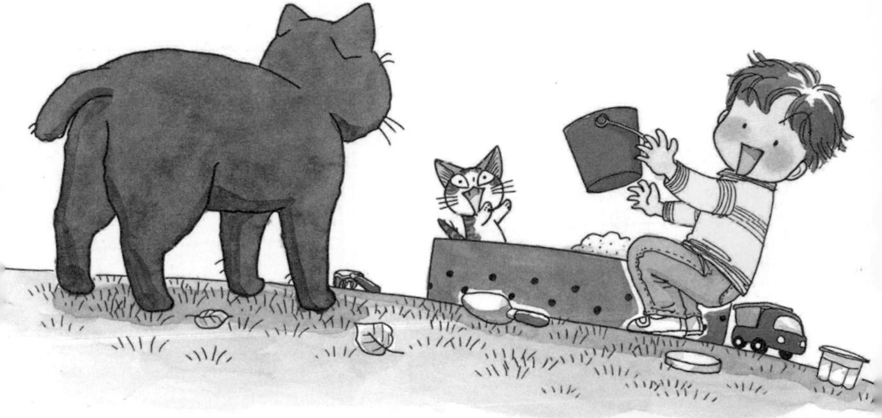

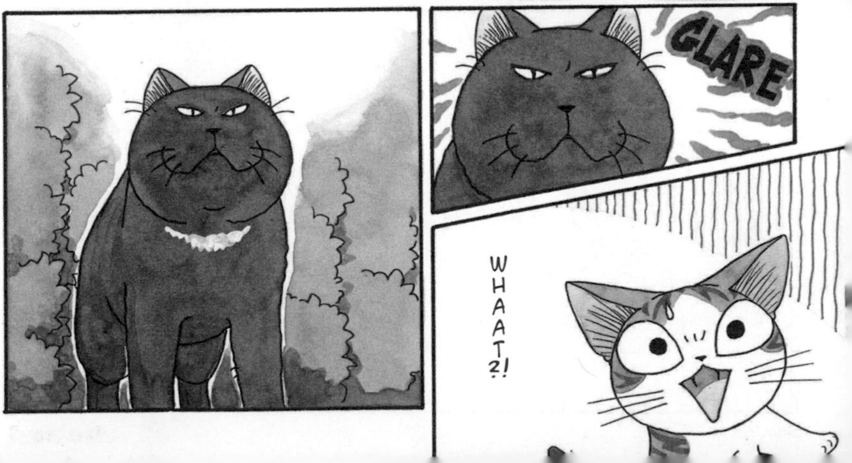
GLARE
WHAAAT?!

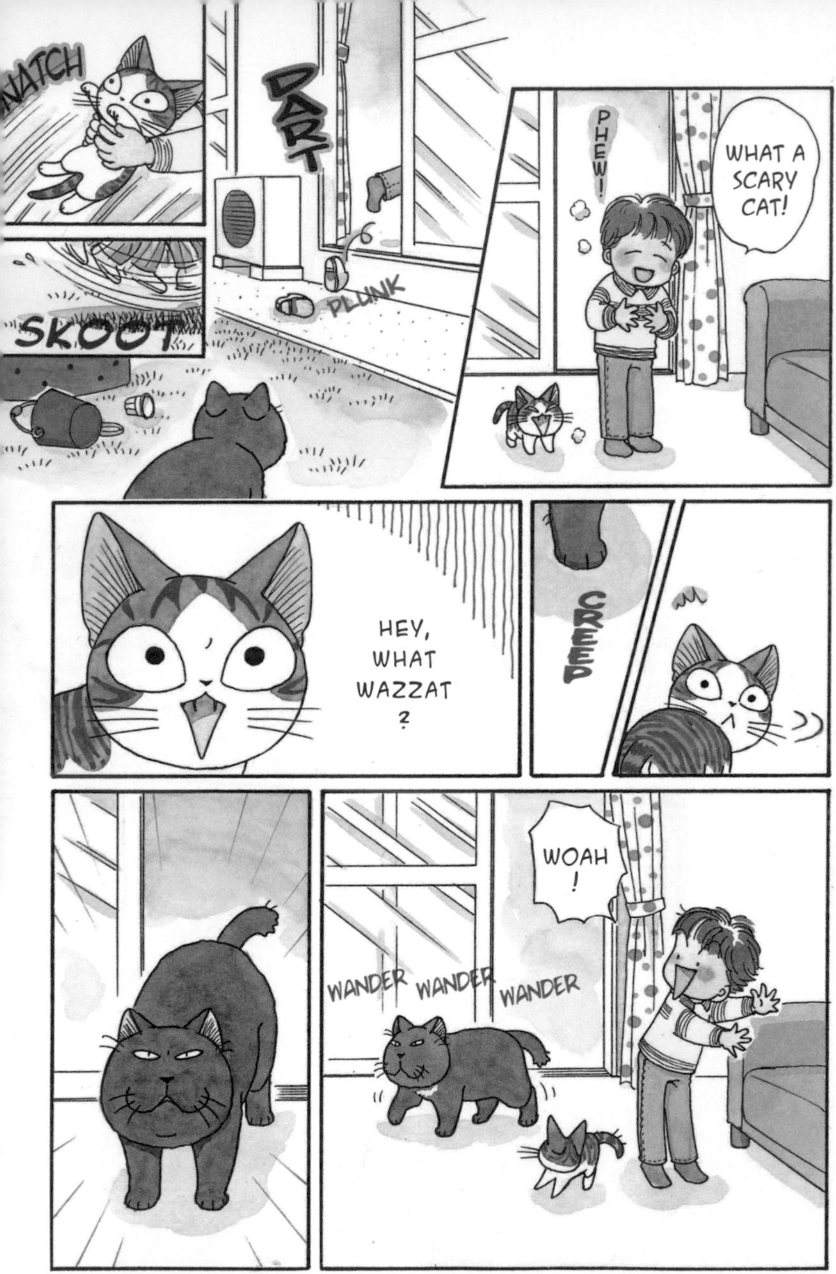
NATCH
SKOOT
DART
PLUNK
PHEW!
WHAT A SCARY CAT!
HEY, WHAT WAZZAT?
CREEP
WANDER
WANDER
WANDER
WOAH!

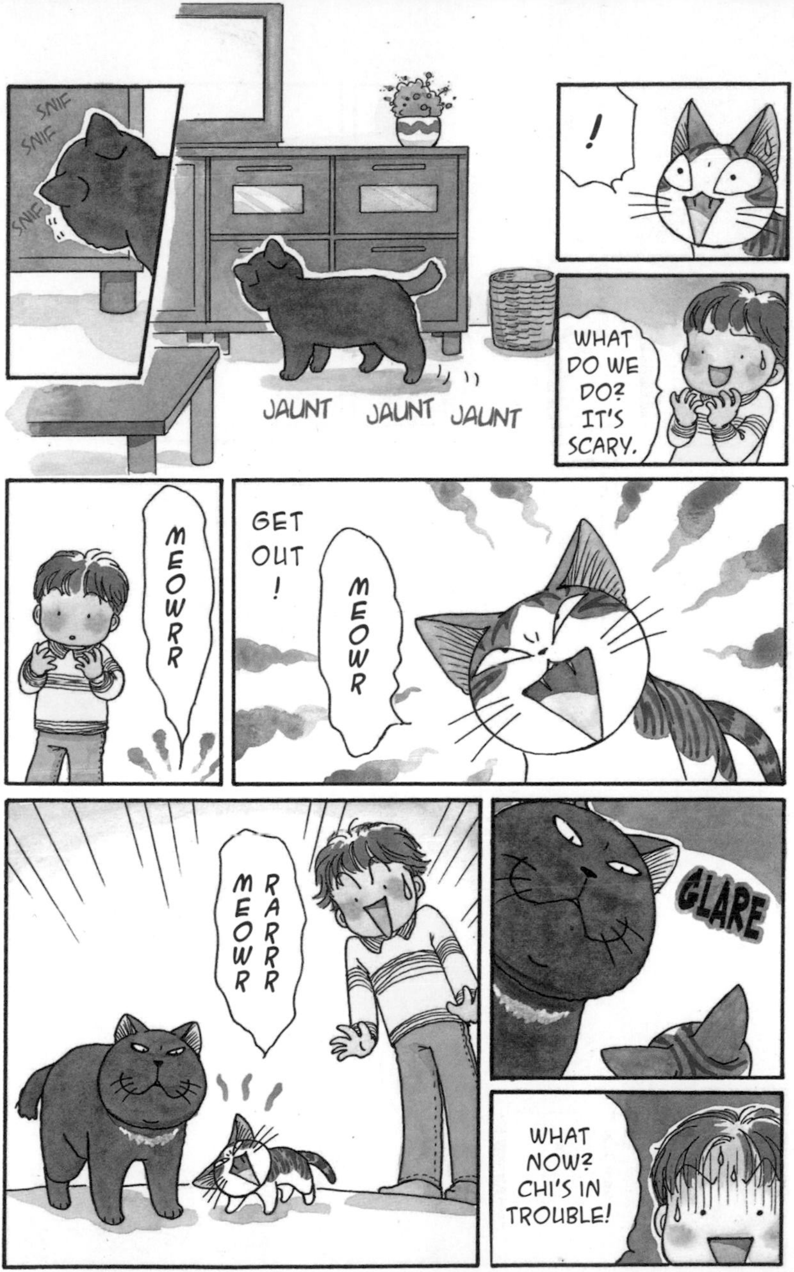
SNIF
SNIF
SNIF
JAUNT JAUNT JAUNT
!
WHAT DO WE DO? IT'S SCARY.
MEOWRR
GET OUT!
MEOWR
RARRR MEOWR
GLARE
WHAT NOW? CHI'S IN TROUBLE!

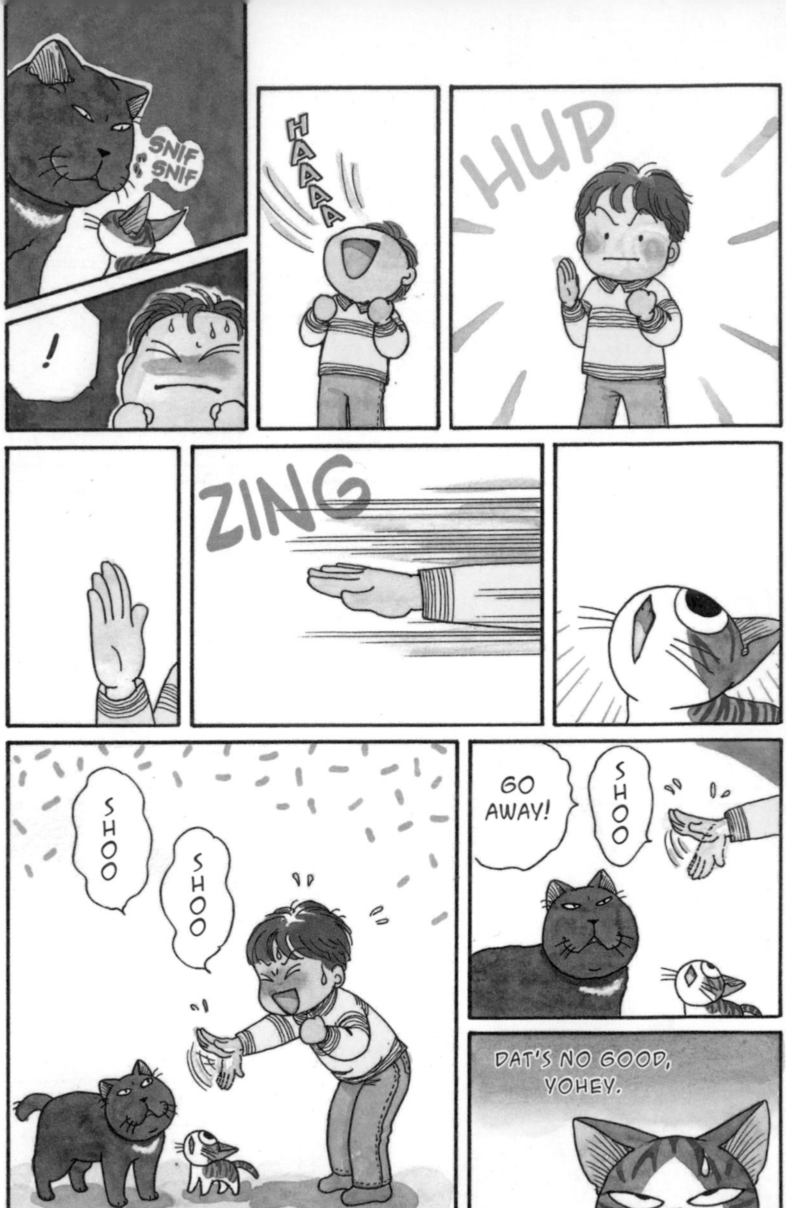
SNIF SNIF
!
HAAAAA
HUP
ZING
SHOO
SHOO
GO AWAY!
SHOO
DAT'S NO GOOD, YOHEY.

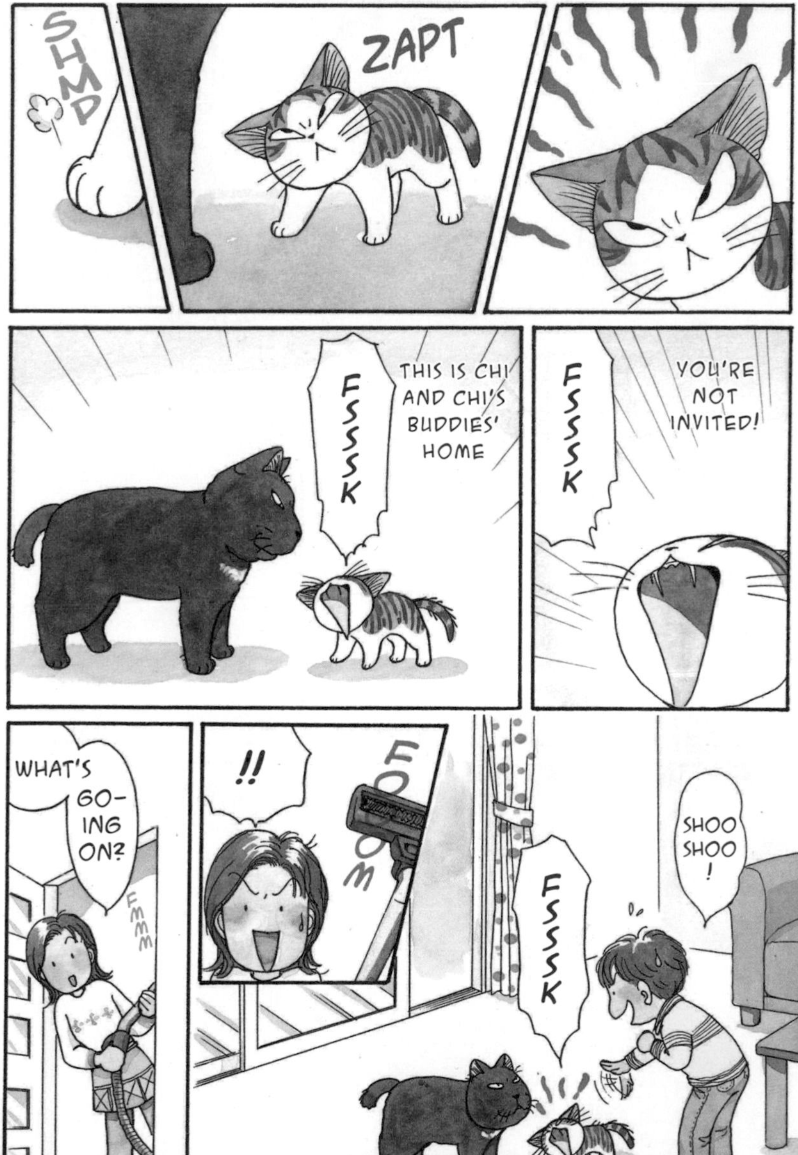
SHMP
ZAPT
FSSSK
THIS IS CHI AND CHI'S BUDDIES' HOME
FSSSK
YOU'RE NOT INVITED!
WHAT'S GO-ING ON?
FMMM
!!
FOOOOM
FSSSK
SHOO SHOO!

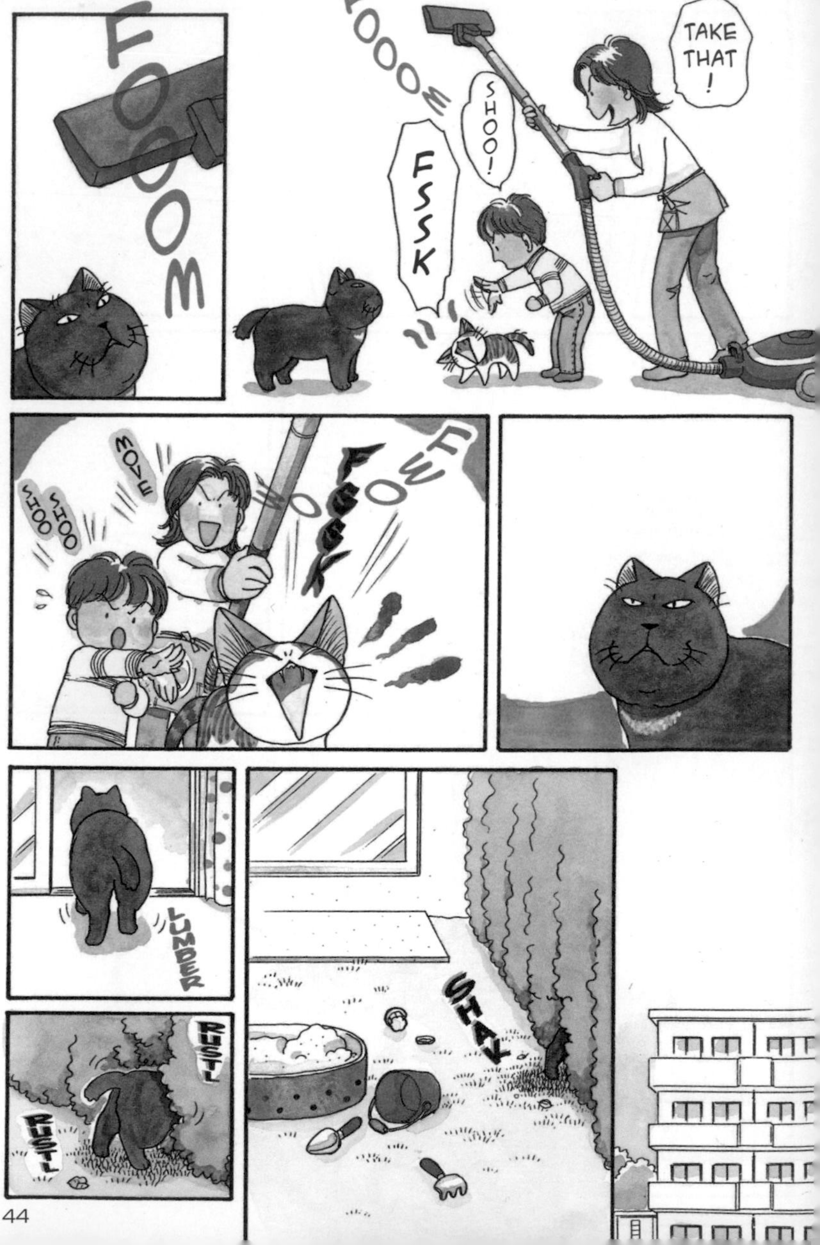
FOOOM
FOOOE
SHOO!
FSSK
TAKE THAT!
MOVE
SHOO SHOO
FSSK
FWOOW
LUMBER
RUSTL
RUSTL
SHAK

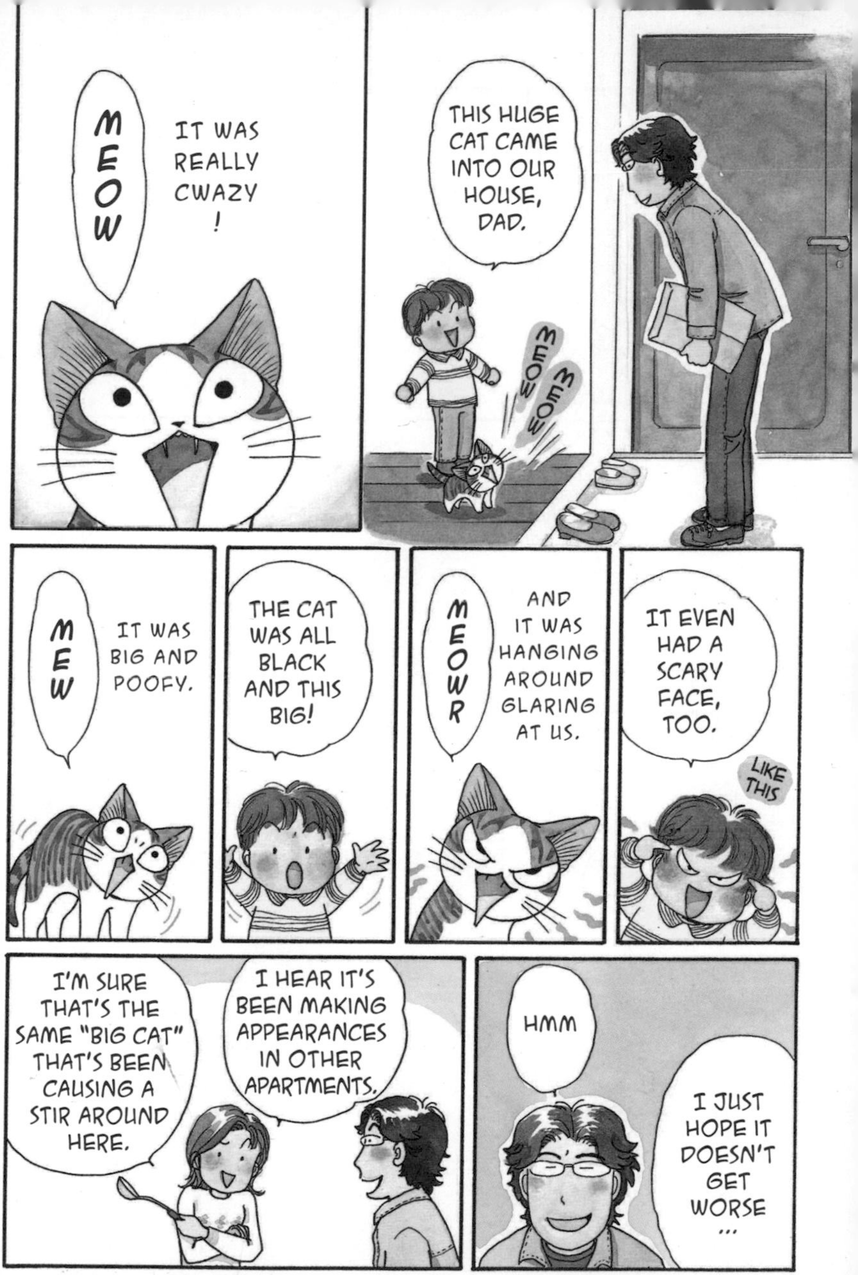
MEOW
IT WAS REALLY CWAZY !
THIS HUGE CAT CAME INTO OUR HOUSE, DAD.
MEOW
MEOW
MEW
IT WAS BIG AND POOFY.
THE CAT WAS ALL BLACK AND THIS BIG!
MEOWR
AND IT WAS HANGING AROUND GLARING AT US.
IT EVEN HAD A SCARY FACE, TOO.
LIKE THIS
I'M SURE THAT'S THE SAME "BIG CAT" THAT'S BEEN CAUSING A STIR AROUND HERE.
I HEAR IT'S BEEN MAKING APPEARANCES IN OTHER APARTMENTS.
HMM
I JUST HOPE IT DOESN'T GET WORSE ...

IT'S NOT LIKE WE HAVEN'T GOT CHI HERE.

WHAT A MESS.

AH, CATS...

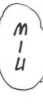
MIU

HEY, DADDY!

YOHEY WAS IN REALLY BIG TWOUBLE.

MEOW

CHI WAS IN DANGER, SO I STEPPED IN.

MEW

RIGHT, YOHEY?

BUT...

WHAT WAS THAT STWANGE CWEATURE, ANYWAY?

MYA?

46

the end

homemade 27: a cat intrudes

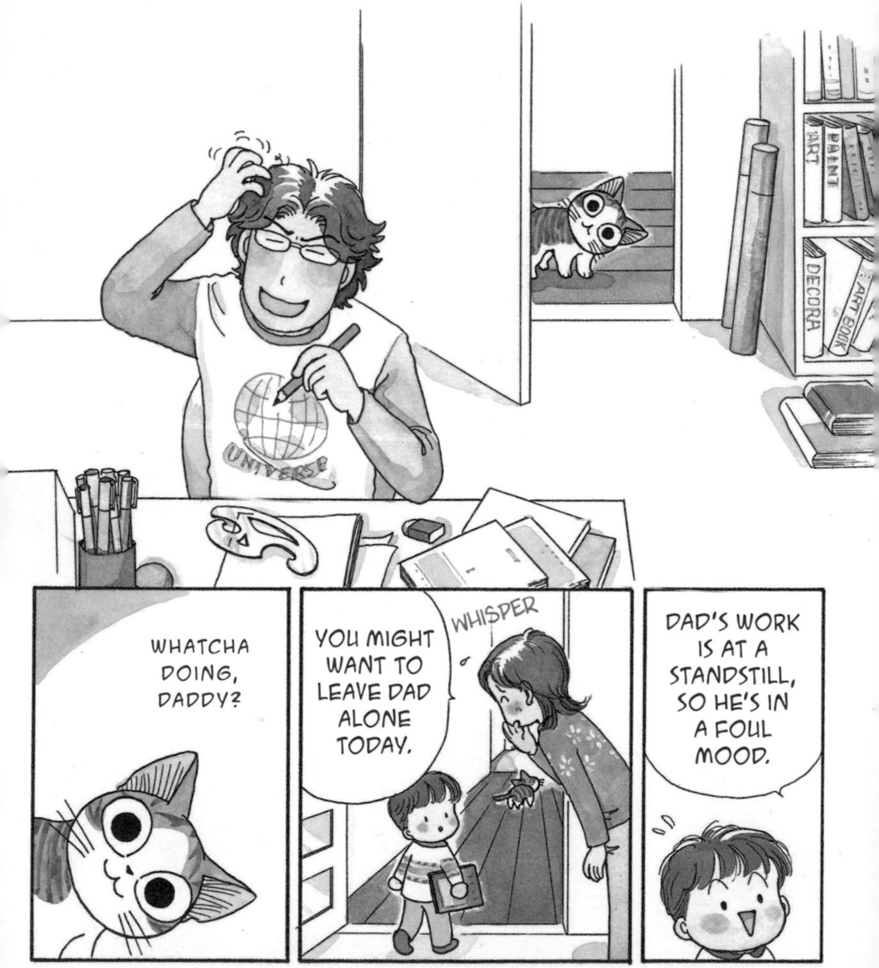
ART
PAINT
DECORA
ART BOOK
UNIVERSE
WHATCHA DOING, DADDY?
YOU MIGHT WANT TO LEAVE DAD ALONE TODAY.
WHISPER
DAD'S WORK IS AT A STANDSTILL, SO HE'S IN A FOUL MOOD.

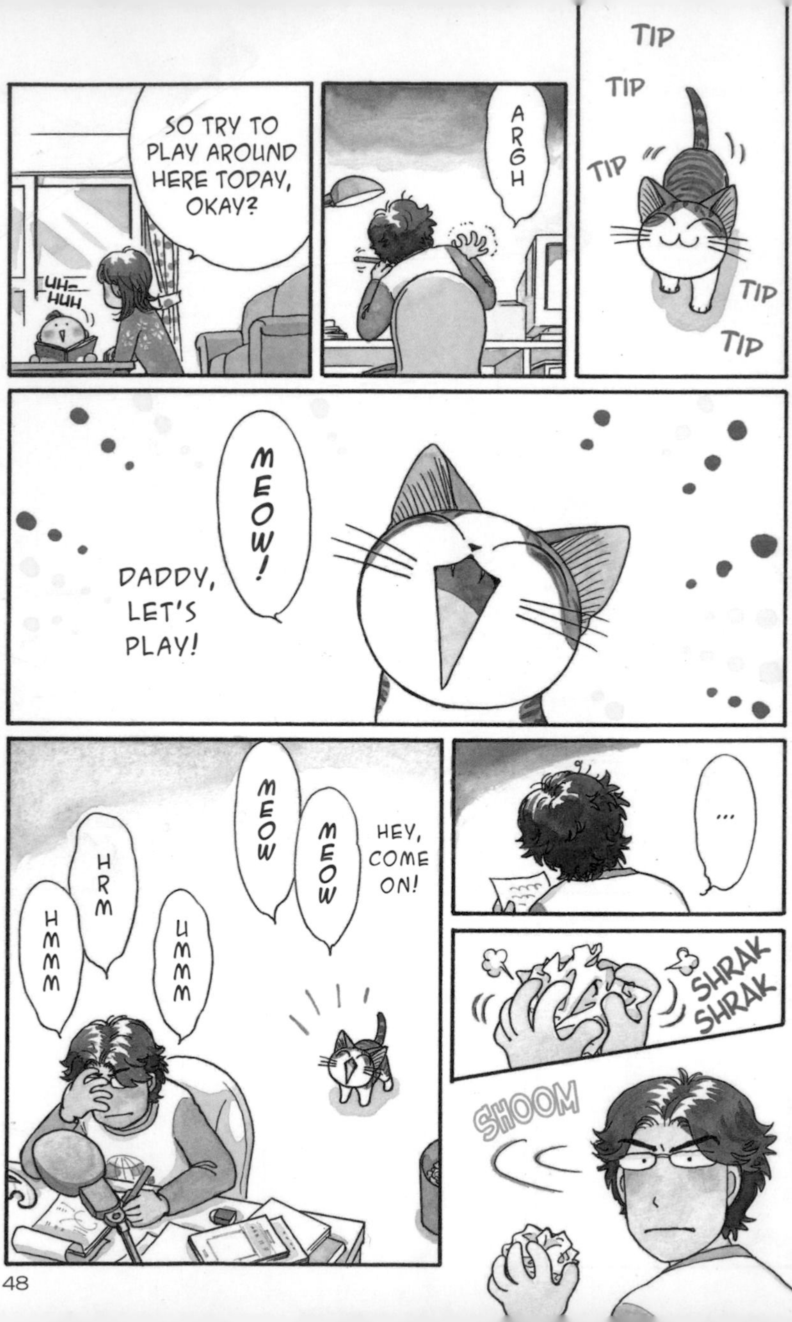
SO TRY TO PLAY AROUND HERE TODAY, OKAY?
UH-HUH
ARGH
TIP
TIP
TIP
TIP
TIP
MEOW!
DADDY, LET'S PLAY!
HMMM
HRM
UMMM
MEOW
MEOW
HEY, COME ON!
...
SHRAK SHRAK
SHOOM

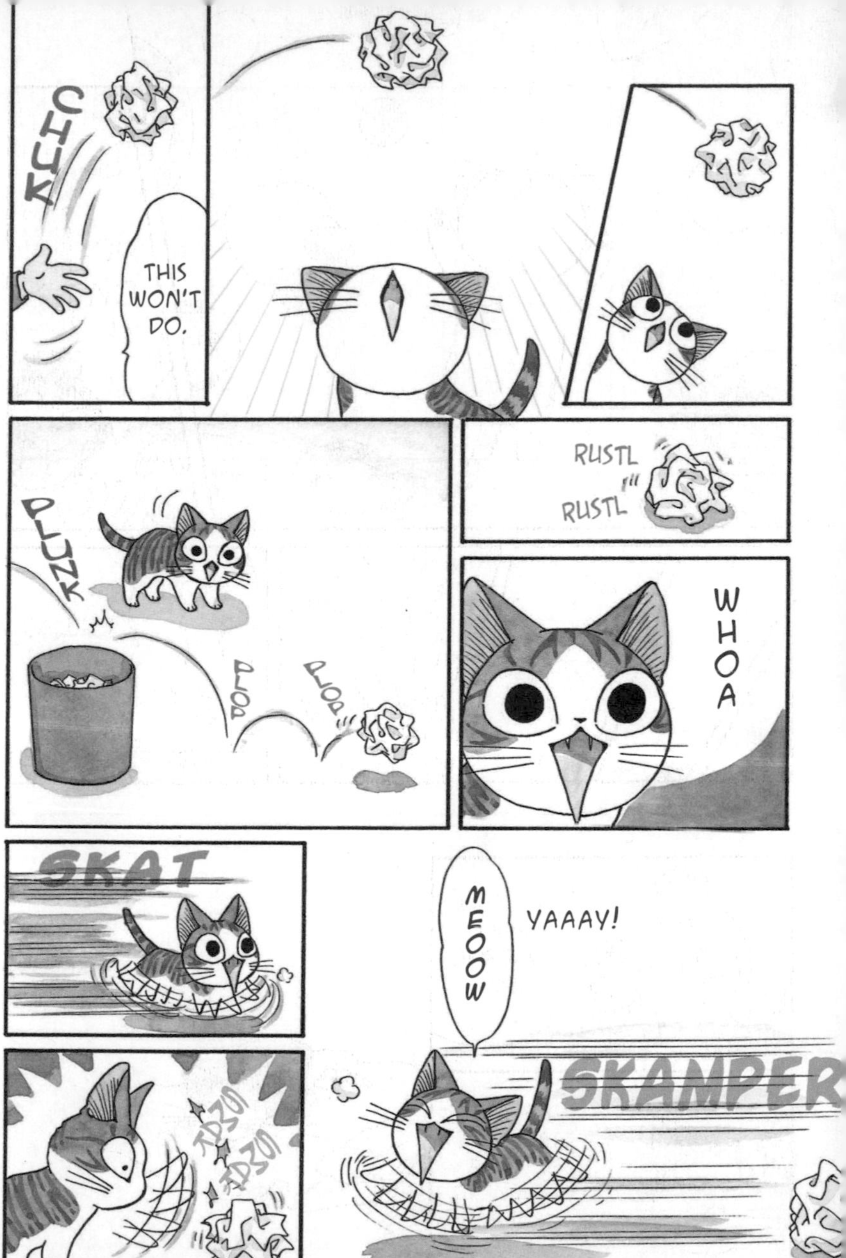
CHUK
THIS WON'T DO.
PLUNK
PLOP
PLOP
RUSTL
RUSTL
WHOA
SKAT
MEOOW
YAAAY!
SKAMPER

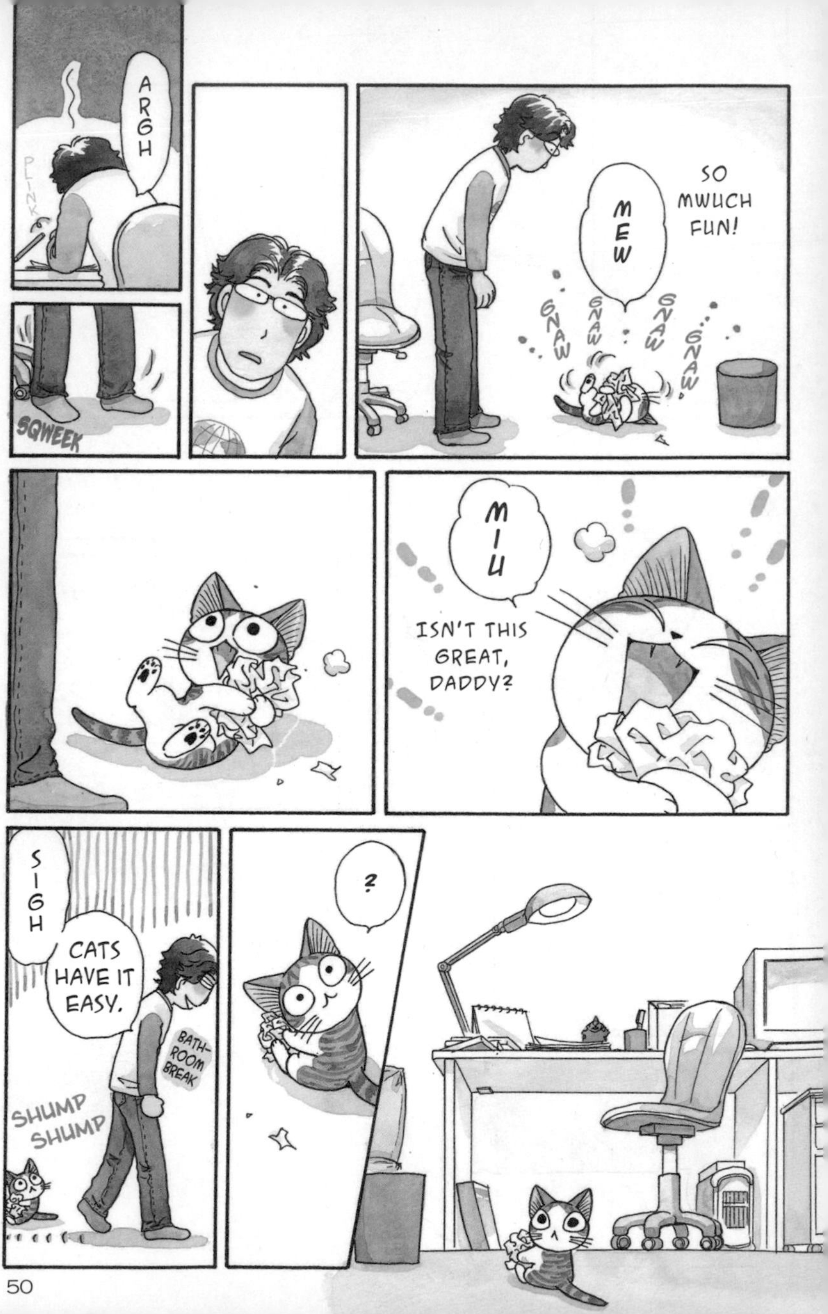

ARGH
PLINK
SQWEEK
SO MWUCH FUN!
MEW
GNAW
GNAW
GNAW
GNAW
MIU
ISN'T THIS GREAT, DADDY?
SIGH
CATS HAVE IT EASY.
BATH-ROOM BREAK
SHUMP SHUMP
?

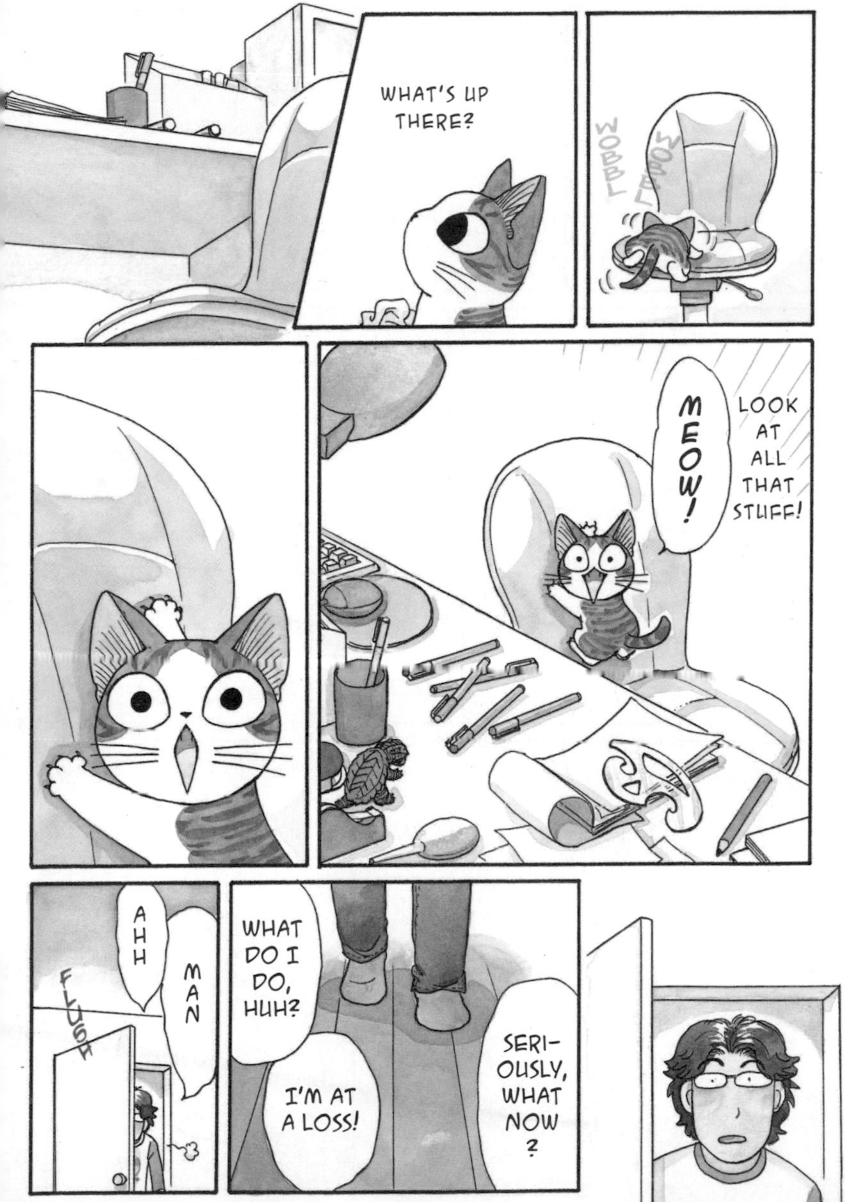
WHAT'S UP THERE?
WOBBL
WOBBL
MEOW!
LOOK AT ALL THAT STUFF!
FLUSH
AHH
MAN
WHAT DO I DO, HUH?
I'M AT A LOSS!
SERI-OUSLY, WHAT NOW?

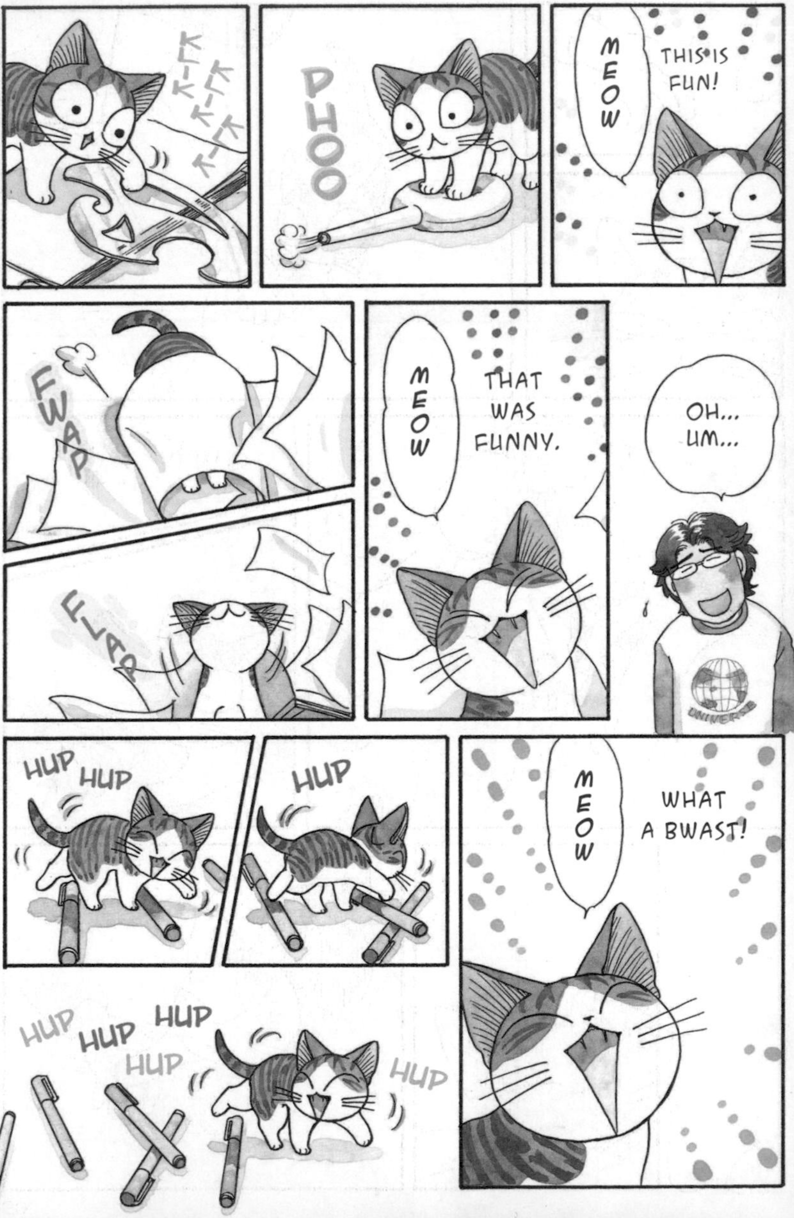
KLIK
KLIK KLIK
PHOO
MEOW
THIS IS FUN!
FWAP
FLAP
MEOW
THAT WAS FUNNY.
OH... UM...
UNIVERSE
HUP HUP
HUP
HUP HUP HUP HUP HUP
MEOW
WHAT A BWAST!

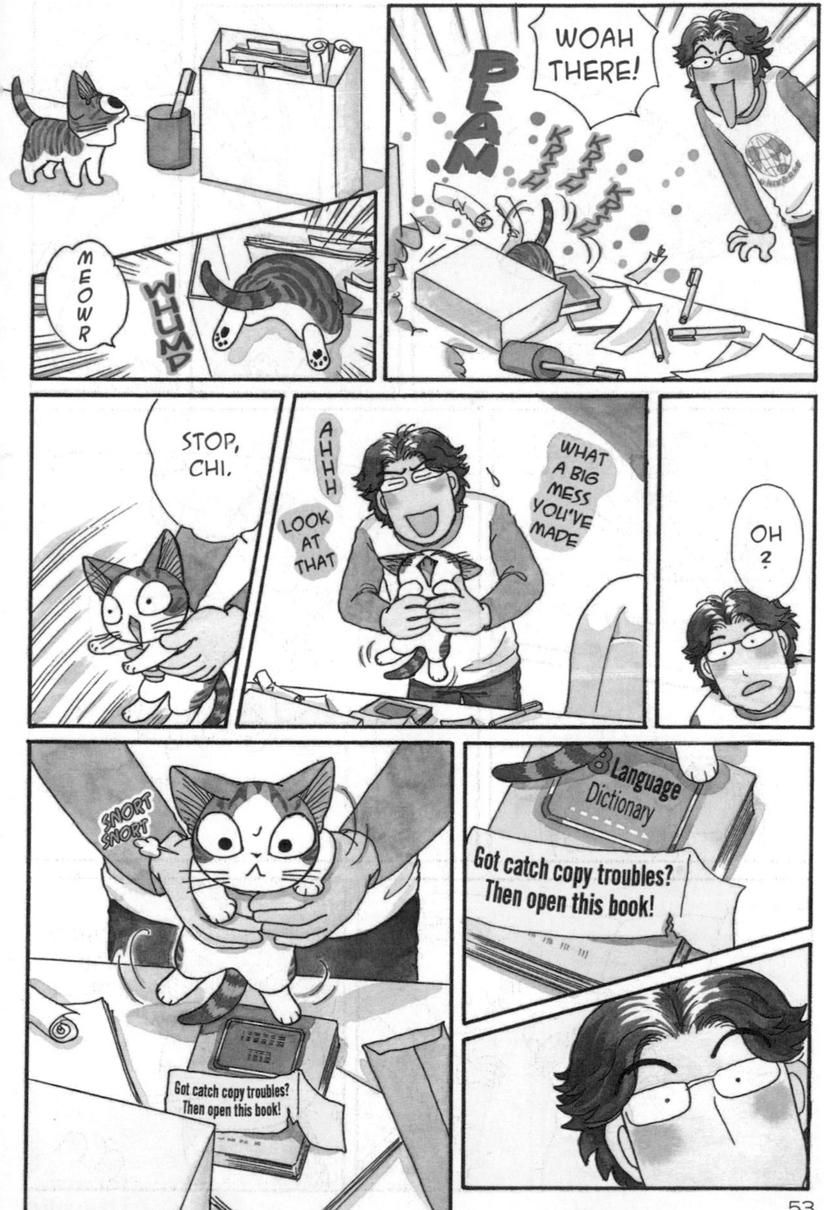
MEOWR
WHUMP
PLAM
KRSH KRSH KRSH
WOAH THERE!
STOP, CHI.
AHHH
LOOK AT THAT
WHAT A BIG MESS YOU'VE MADE
OH?
SNORT SNORT
Got catch copy troubles? Then open this book!
Language Dictionary
Got catch copy troubles? Then open this book!

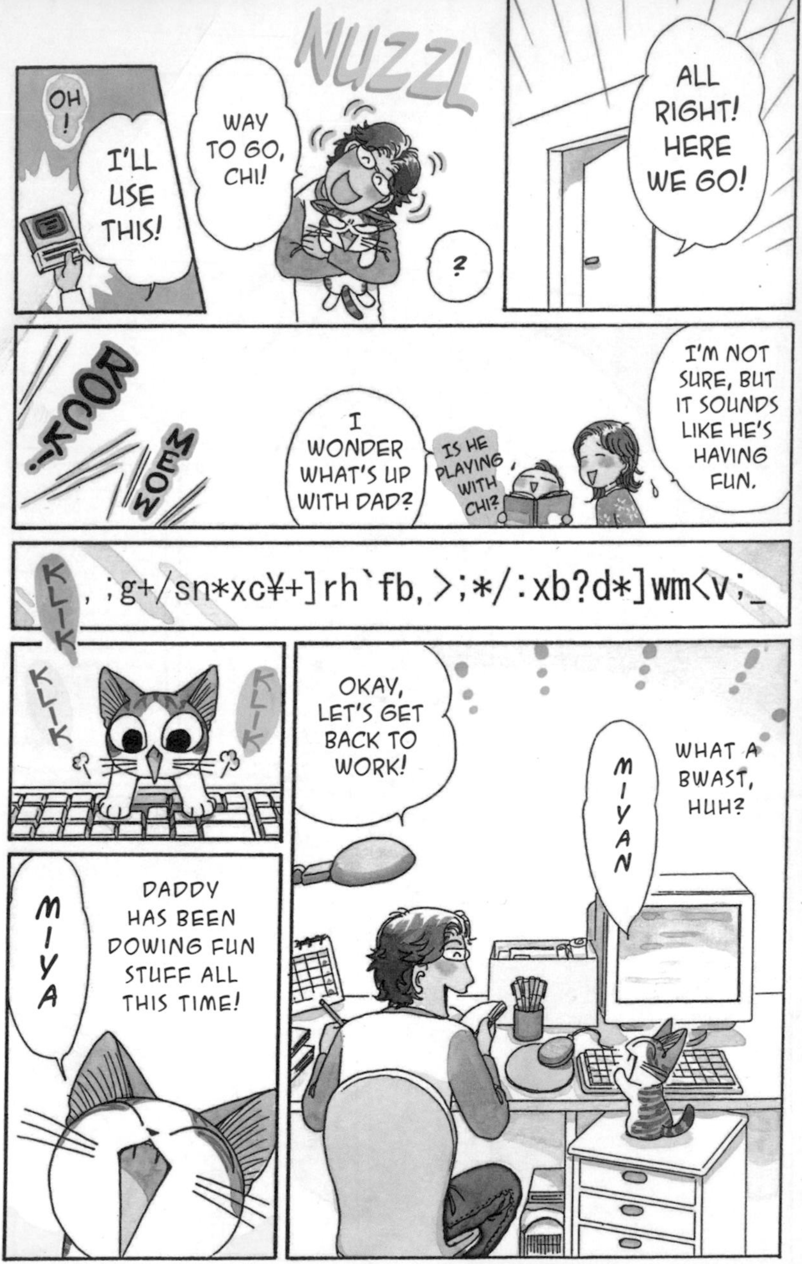
OH!
I'LL USE THIS!
WAY TO GO, CHI!
NUZZL
?
ALL RIGHT! HERE WE GO!
ROCK-!
MEOW
I WONDER WHAT'S UP WITH DAD?
IS HE PLAYING WITH CHI?
I'M NOT SURE, BUT IT SOUNDS LIKE HE'S HAVING FUN.
KLIK
, ;g+/sn*xc¥+]rh`fb,>;*/:xb?d*]wm<v;_
KLIK
KLIK
MIYA
DADDY HAS BEEN DOWING FUN STUFF ALL THIS TIME!
OKAY, LET'S GET BACK TO WORK!
MIYAN
WHAT A BWAST, HUH?

the end

homemade 28: a cat is robbed

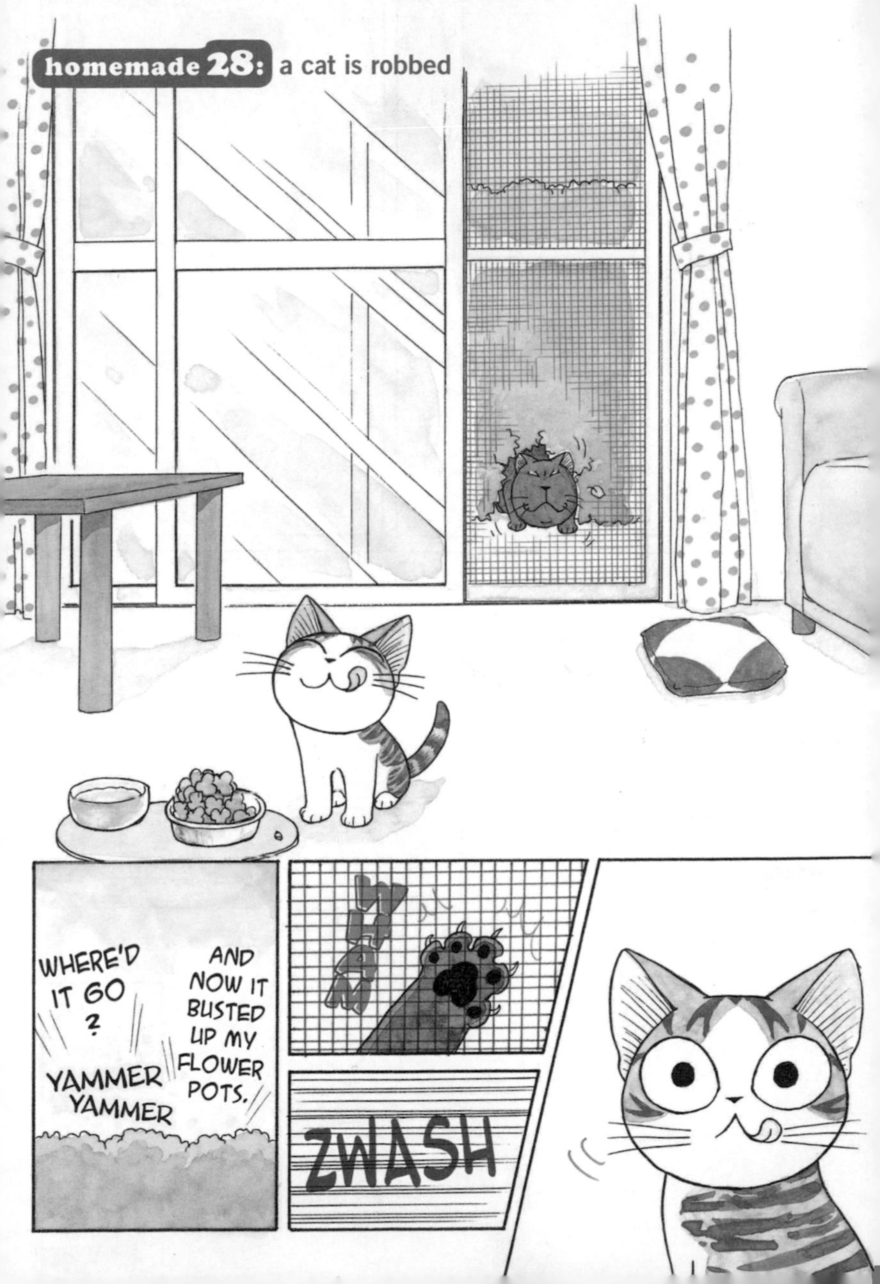
WHERE'D IT GO ?
AND NOW IT BUSTED UP MY FLOWER POTS.
YAMMER YAMMER
ZWASH

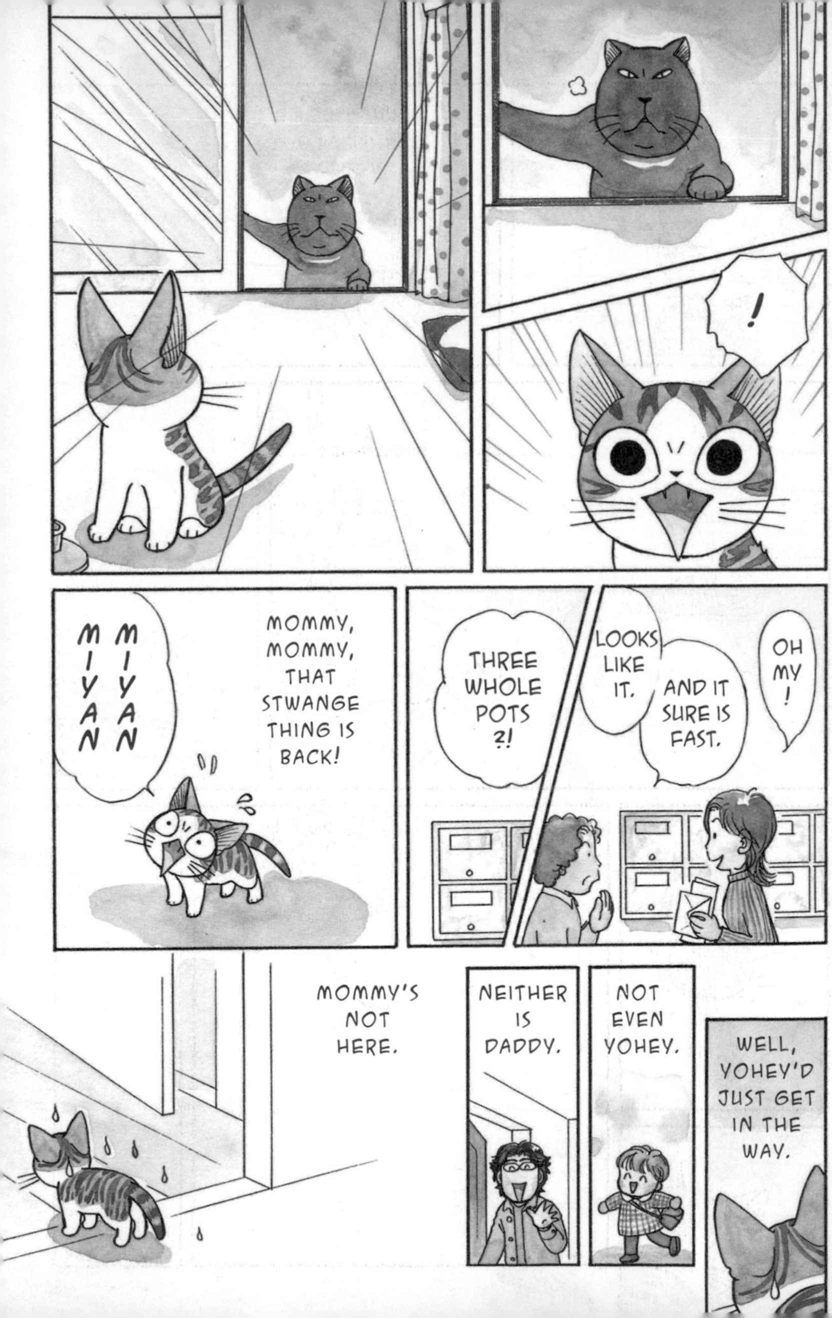
!
MIYAN MIYAN
MOMMY, MOMMY, THAT STWANGE THING IS BACK!
THREE WHOLE POTS ?!
LOOKS LIKE IT.
AND IT SURE IS FAST.
OH MY!
MOMMY'S NOT HERE.
NEITHER IS DADDY.
NOT EVEN YOHEY.
WELL, YOHEY'D JUST GET IN THE WAY.

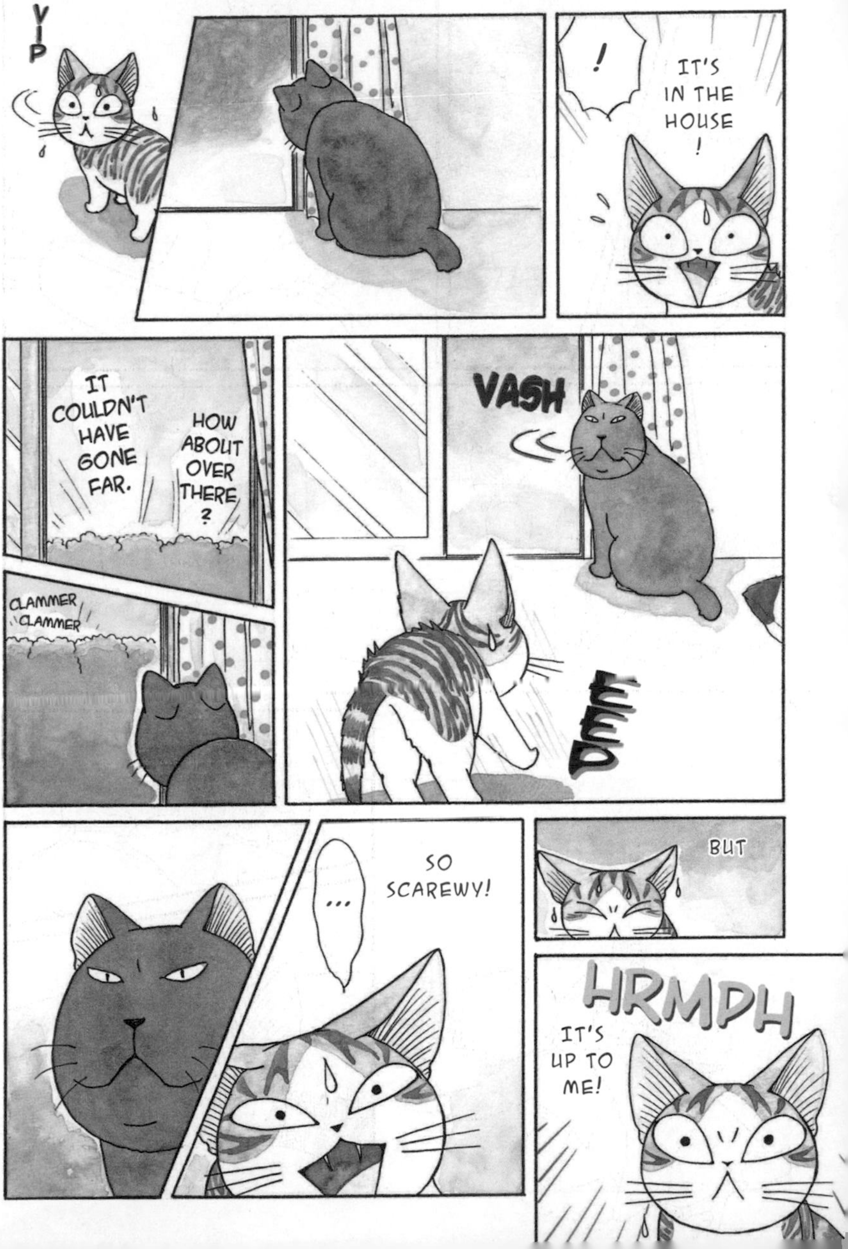
YIP
!
IT'S IN THE HOUSE !
IT COULDN'T HAVE GONE FAR.
HOW ABOUT OVER THERE ?
CLAMMER CLAMMER
VASH
...
SO SCAREWY!
BUT
HRMPH
IT'S UP TO ME!

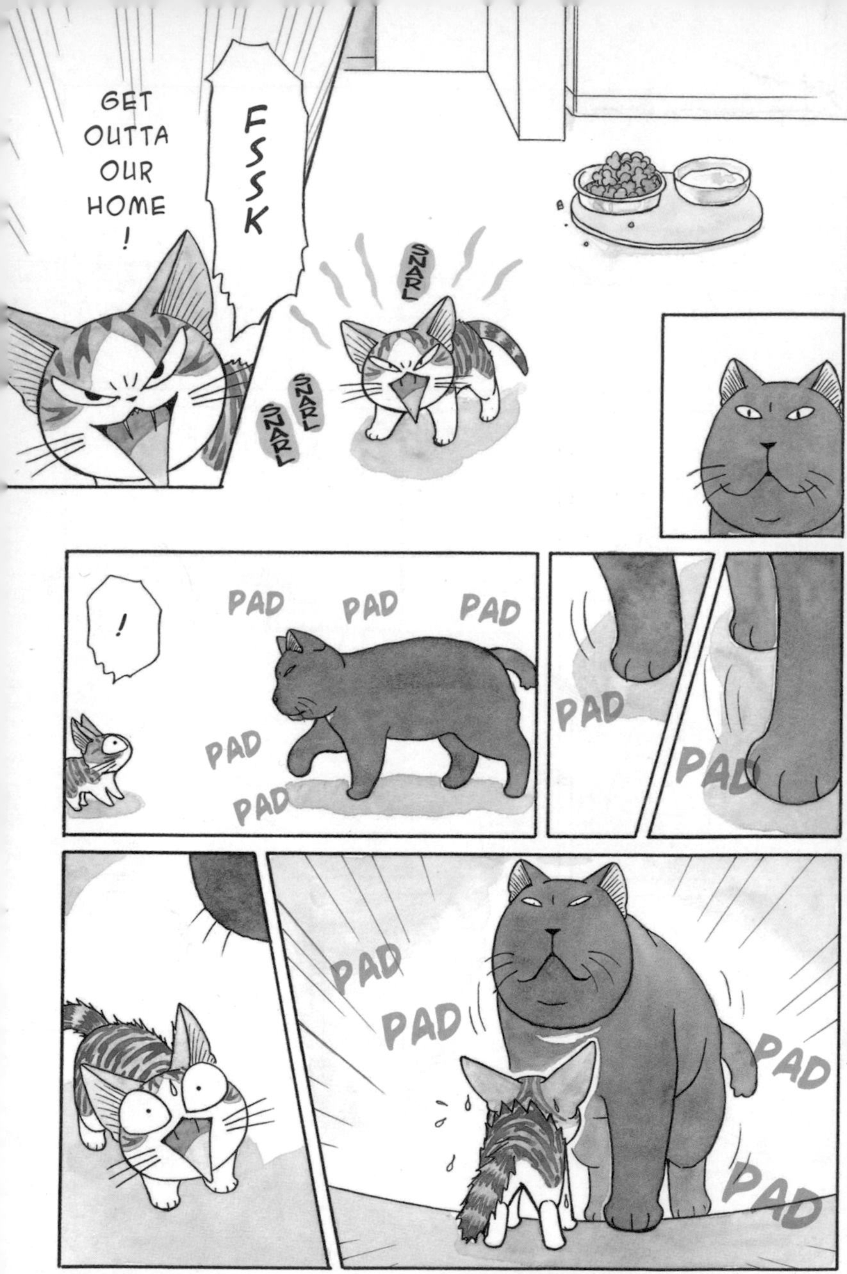
GET OUTTA OUR HOME!
FSSK
SNARL
SNARL
SNARL
!
PAD
PAD
PAD
PAD
PAD
PAD
PAD
PAD
PAD
PAD
PAD

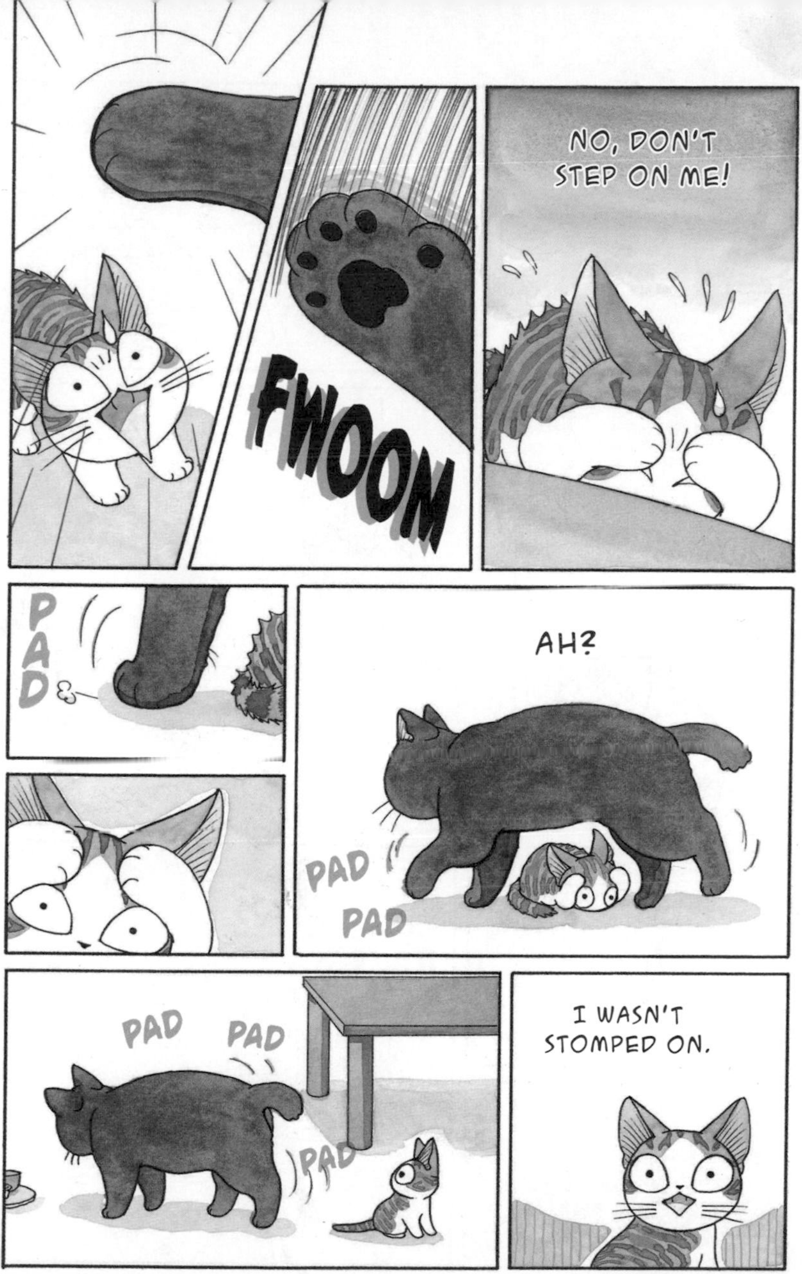
FWOOM
NO, DON'T STEP ON ME!
PAD
PAD
AH?
PAD
PAD
PAD
PAD
PAD
I WASN'T STOMPED ON.

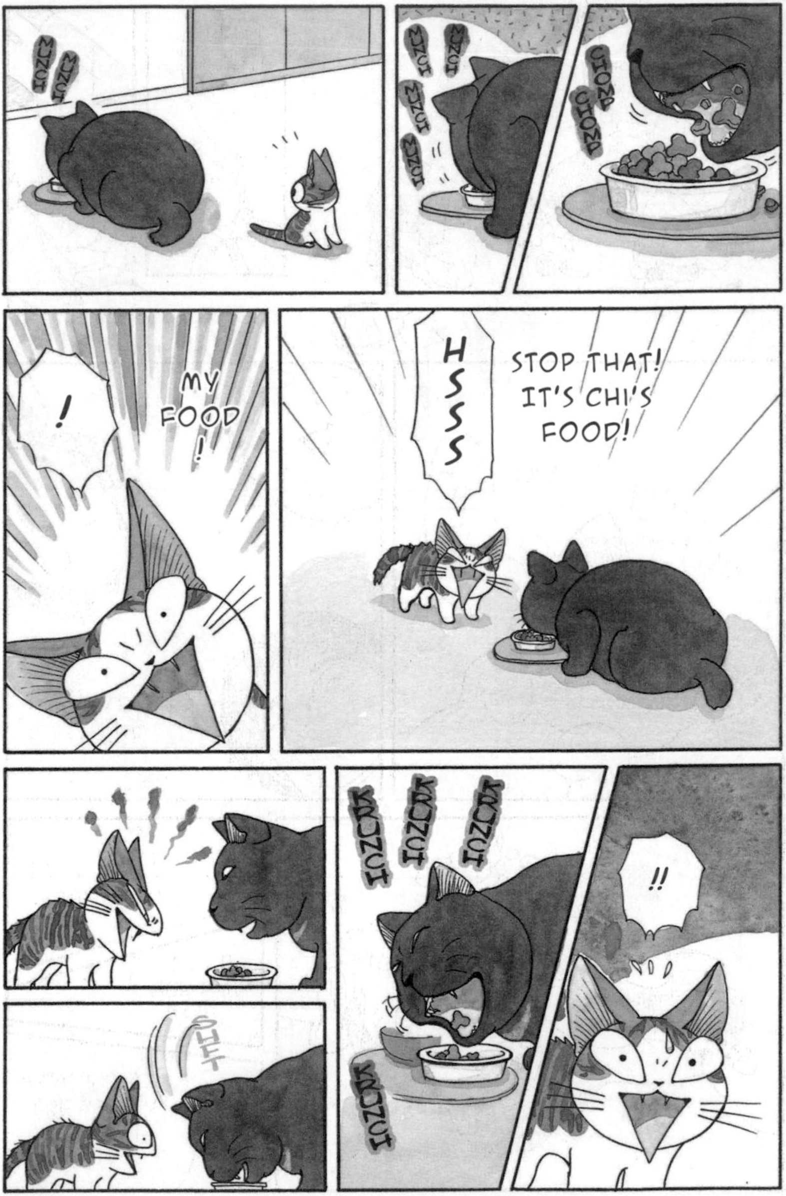
MUNCH MUNCH
MUNCH MUNCH
MUNCH
MUNCH
CHOMP CHOMP
!
MY FOOD !
HSSS
STOP THAT! IT'S CHI'S FOOD!
SHFT
KRUNCH KRUNCH KRUNCH
KRUNCH
!!

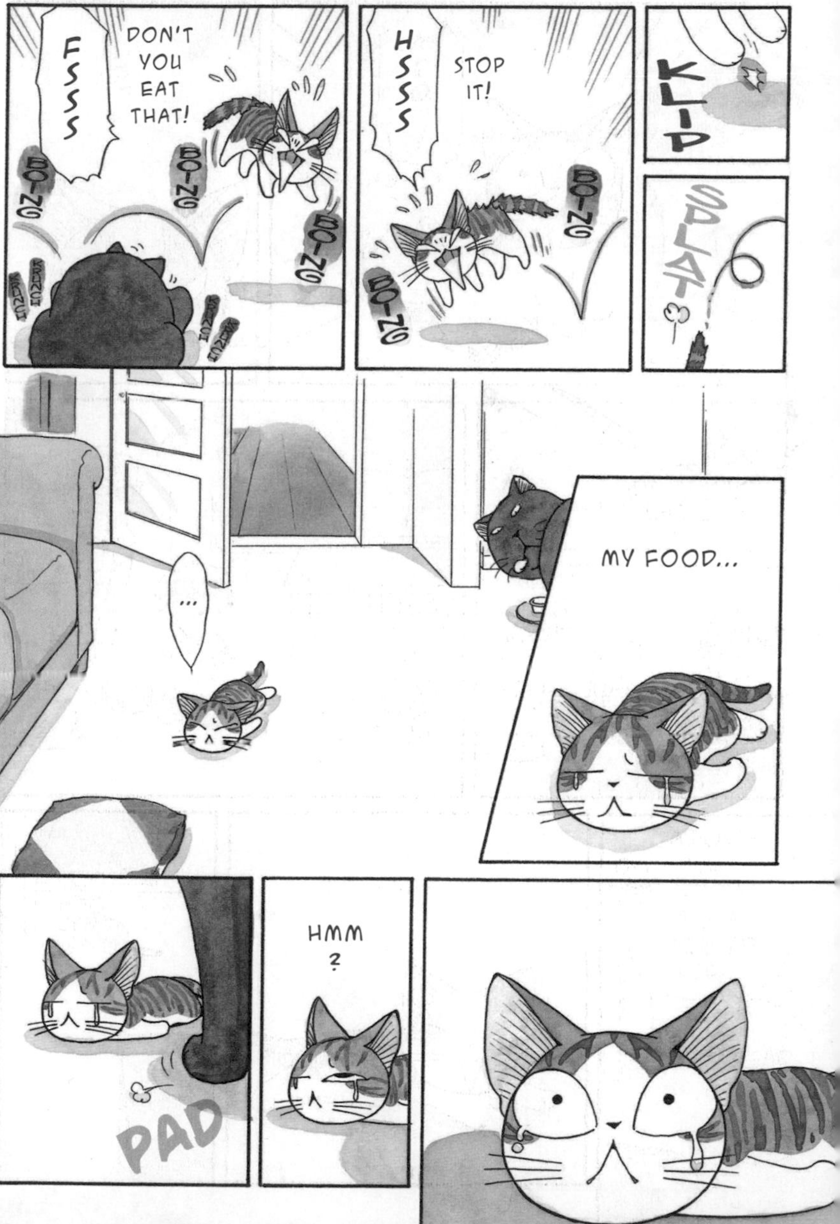
FSSS
DON'T YOU EAT THAT!
BOING
BOING
BOING
KRUNCH
KRUNCH
KRUNCH
KRUNCH
HSSS
STOP IT!
BOING
BOING
KLIP
SPLAT
...
MY FOOD...
PAD
HMM ?

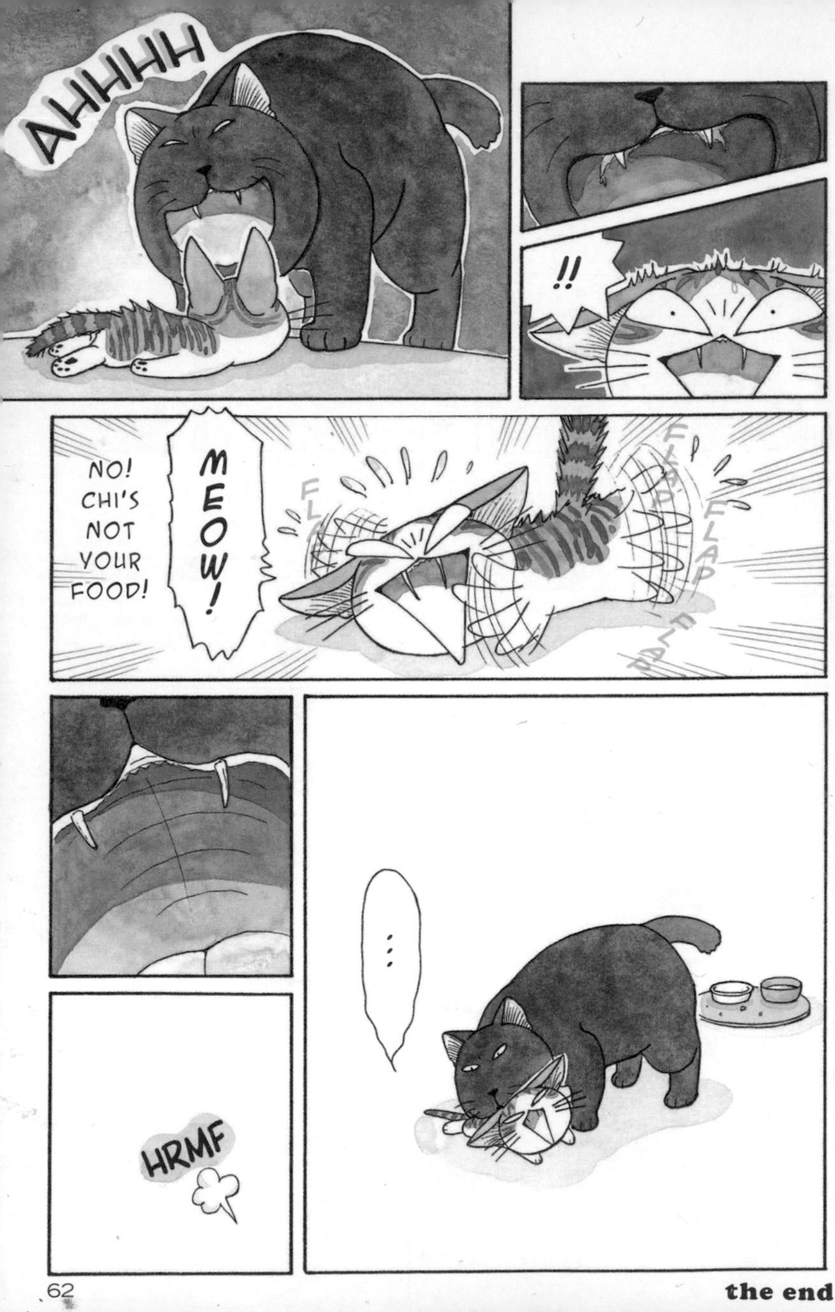
AHHHH
!!
NO! CHI'S NOT YOUR FOOD!
MEOW!
FLAP
FLAP
FLAP
FLAP
FLAP
HRMF
...

the end

homemade 29: a cat considers

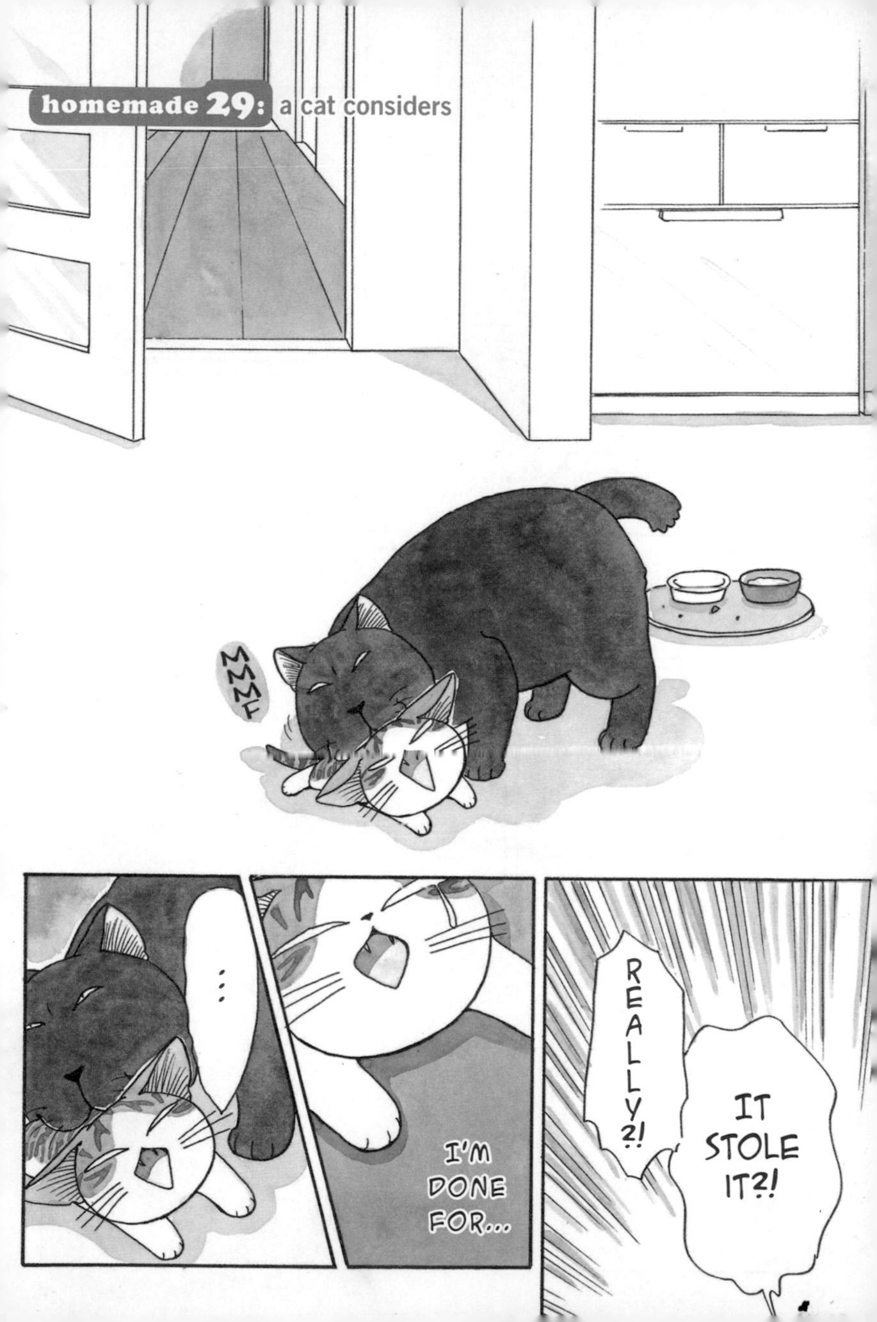
MMMF
...
I'M DONE FOR...
REALLY?!
IT STOLE IT?!

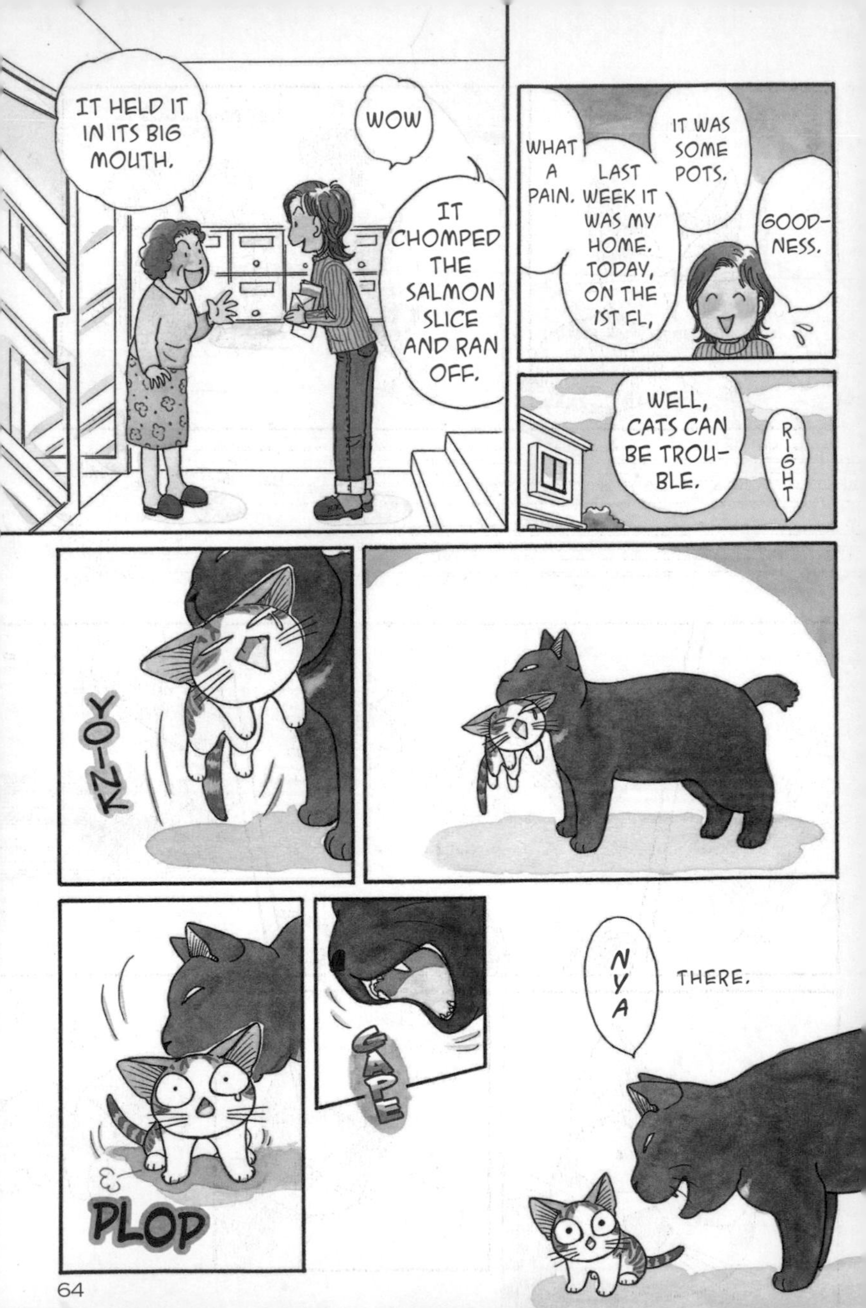
IT HELD IT IN ITS BIG MOUTH.
WOW
IT CHOMPED THE SALMON SLICE AND RAN OFF.
WHAT A PAIN. LAST WEEK IT WAS MY HOME. TODAY, ON THE 1ST FL,
IT WAS SOME POTS.
GOODNESS.
WELL, CATS CAN BE TROUBLE.
RIGHT
YOINK
PLOP
GAPE
NYA
THERE.

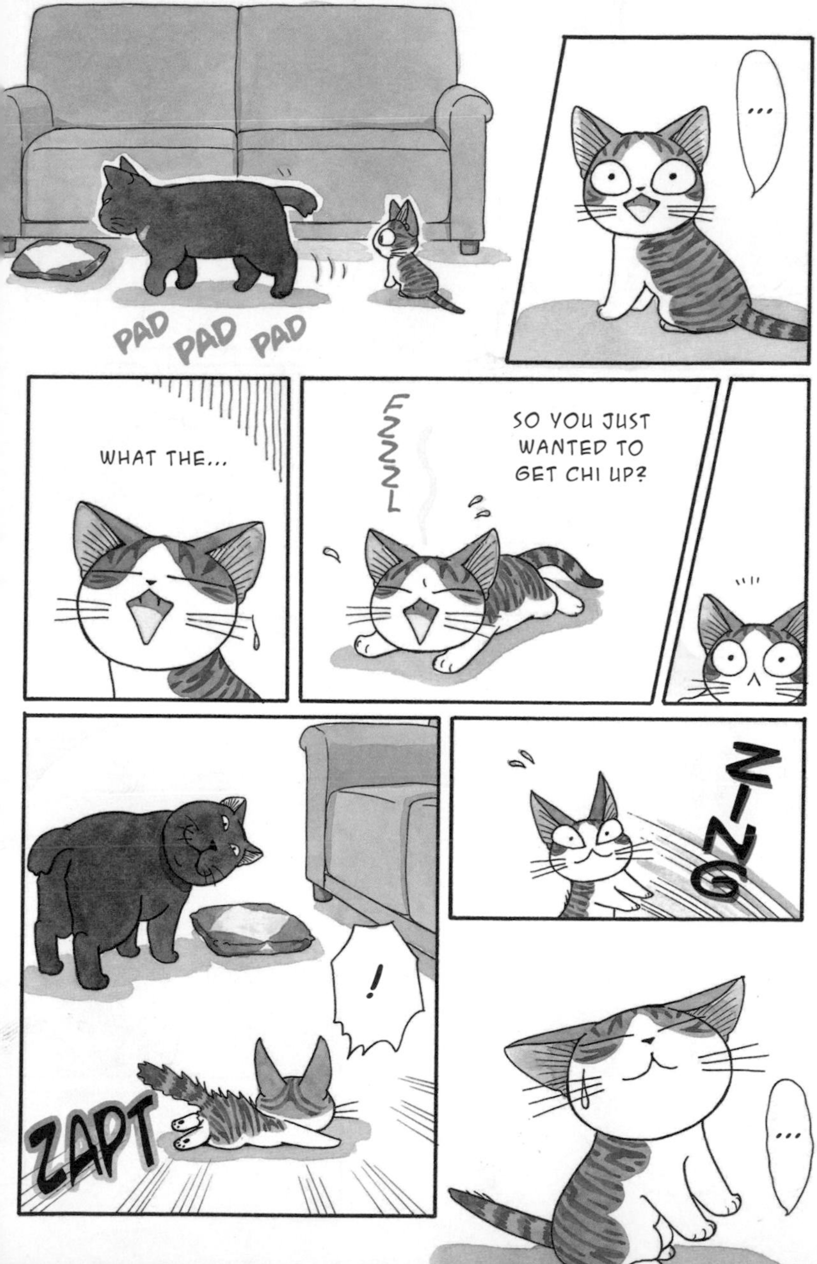
PAD PAD PAD
...
WHAT THE...
FZZZL
SO YOU JUST WANTED TO GET CHI UP?
!
ZAPT
ZING
...

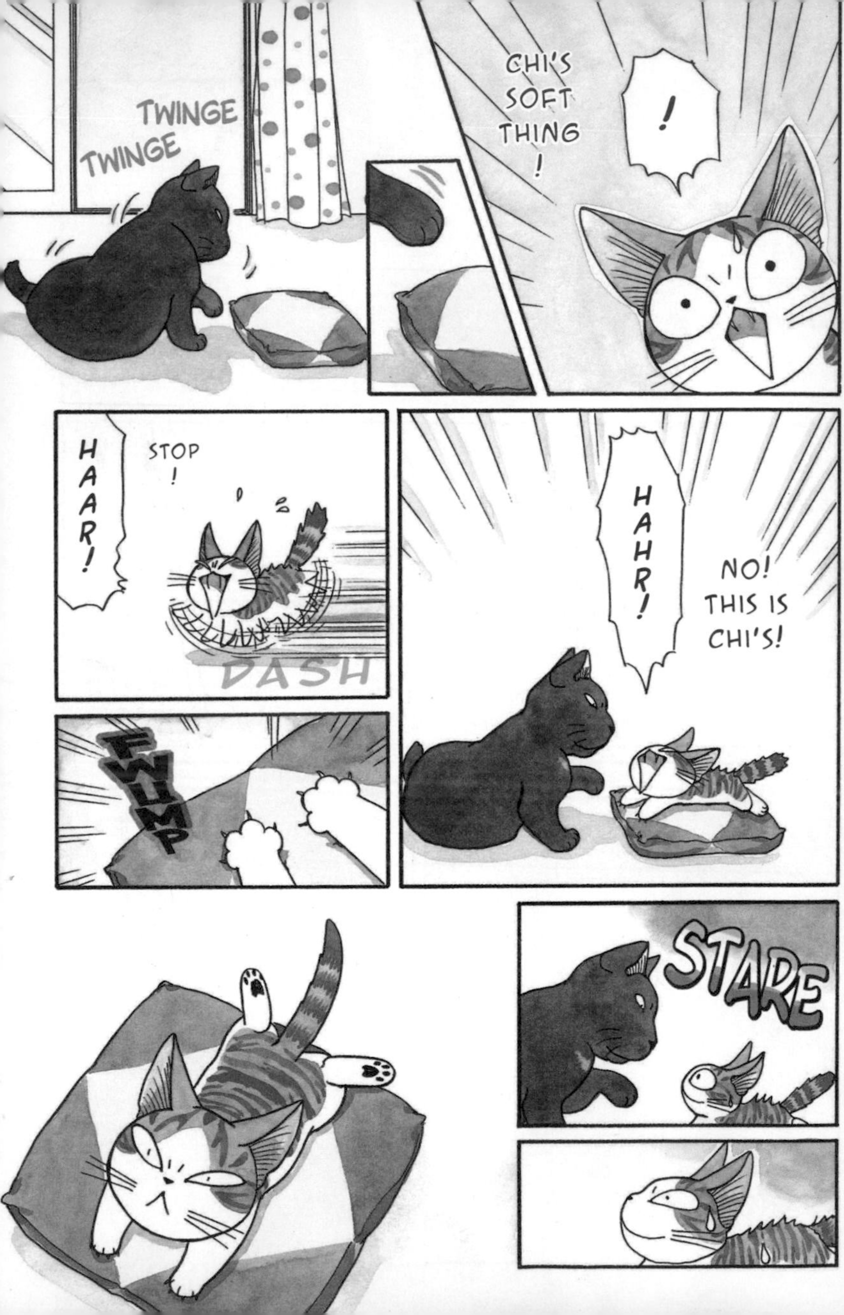
TWINGE
TWINGE
CHI'S SOFT THING!
!
HAAAR!
STOP!
DASH
FWUMP
HAHR!
NO! THIS IS CHI'S!
STARE

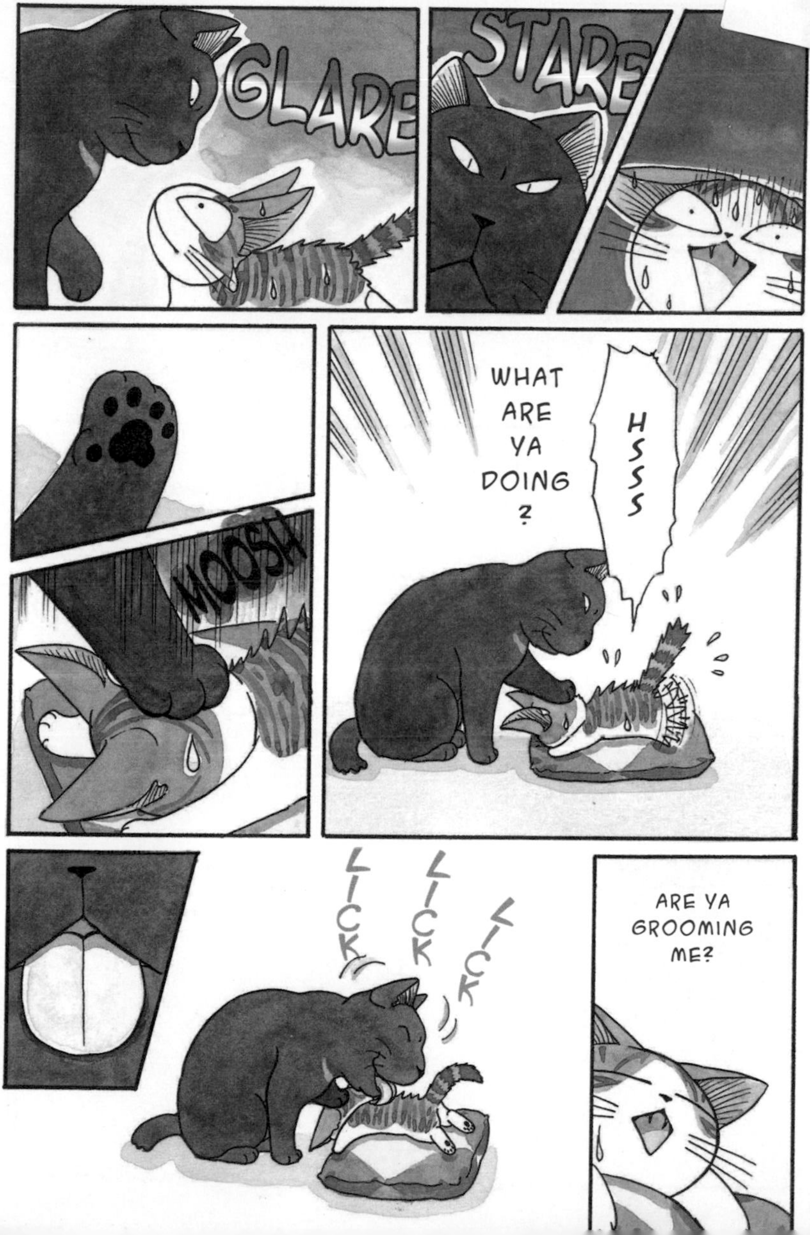
GLARE
STARE
MOOSH
WHAT ARE YA DOING?
HSSS
LICK
LICK
LICK
ARE YA GROOMING ME?

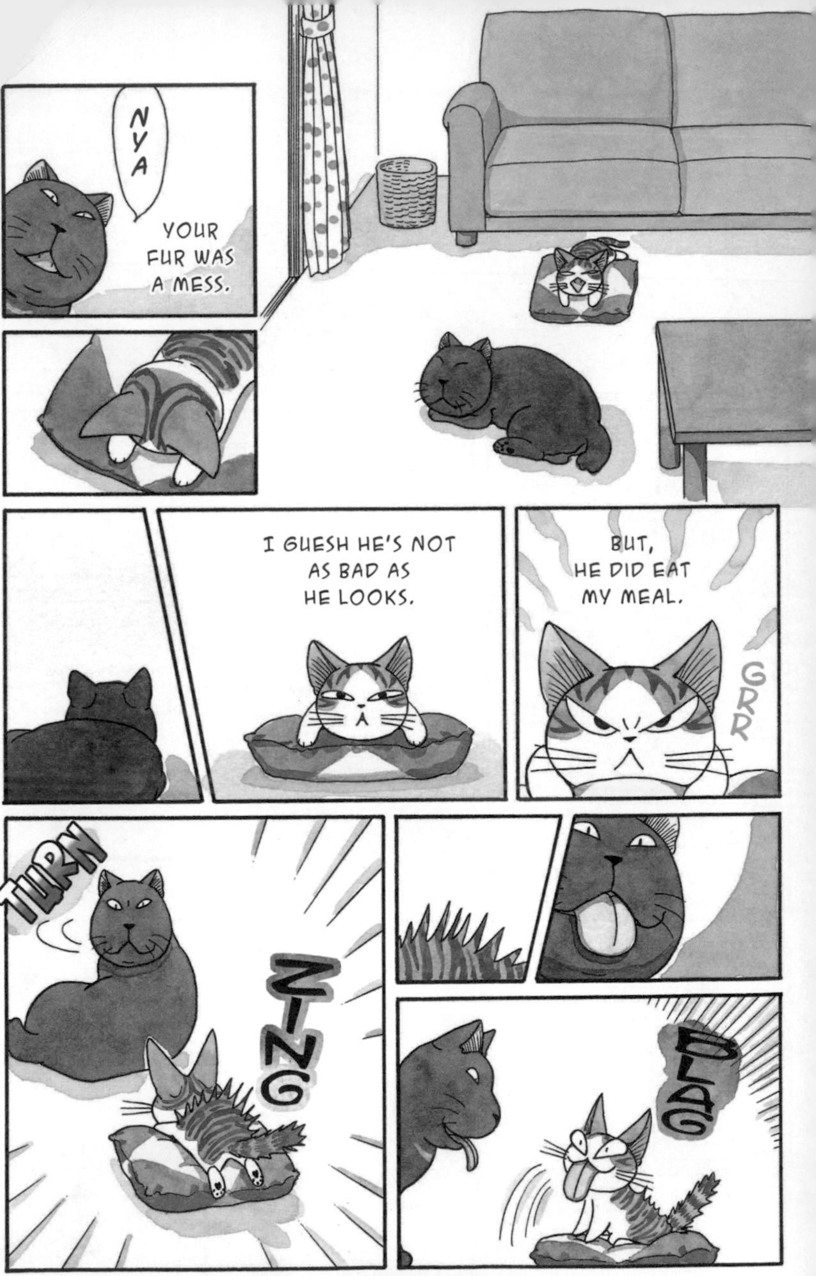
NYA
YOUR FUR WAS A MESS.
I GUESH HE'S NOT AS BAD AS HE LOOKS.
BUT, HE DID EAT MY MEAL.
GRR
TURN
ZING
BLAG

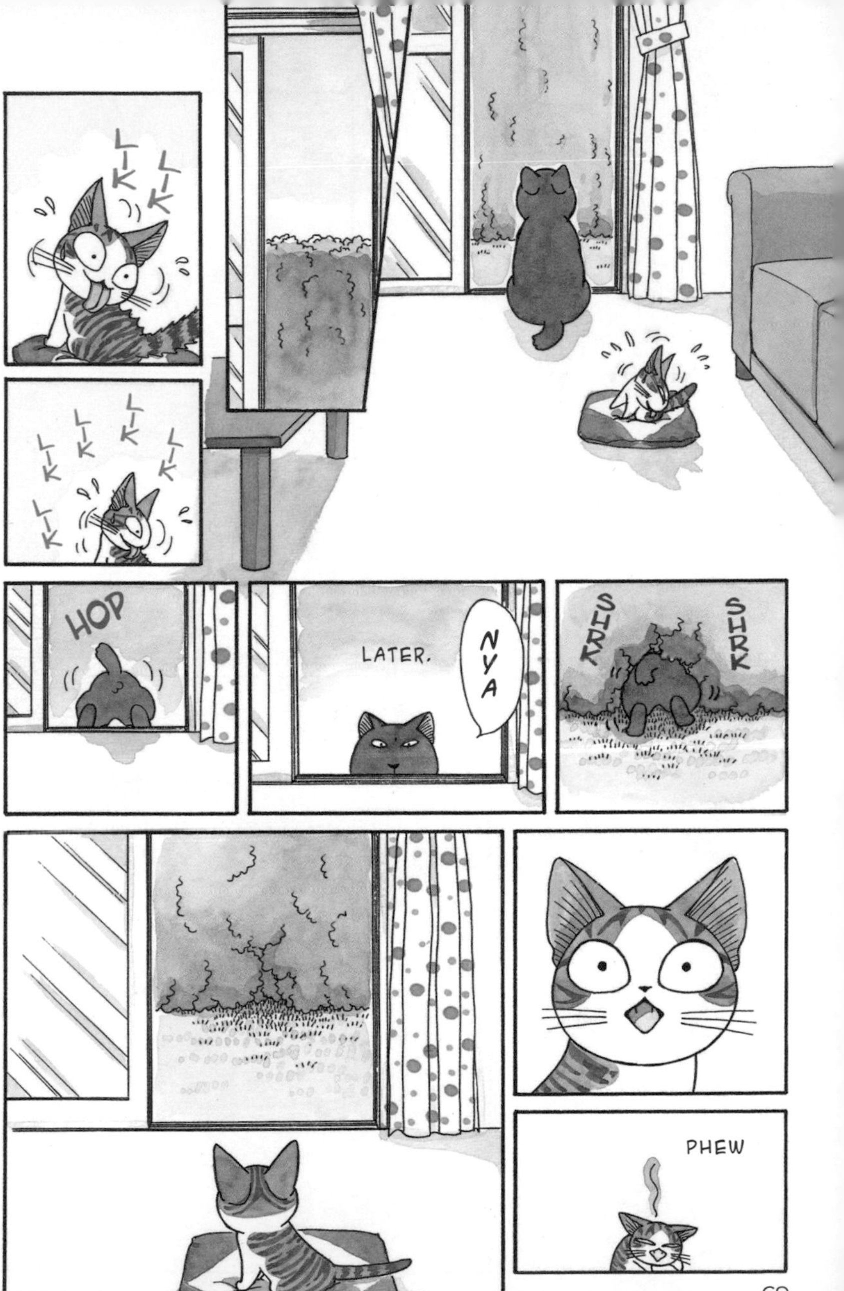
LIK LIK
LIK LIK LIK LIK
HOP
LATER.
NYA
SHRK SHRK
PHEW

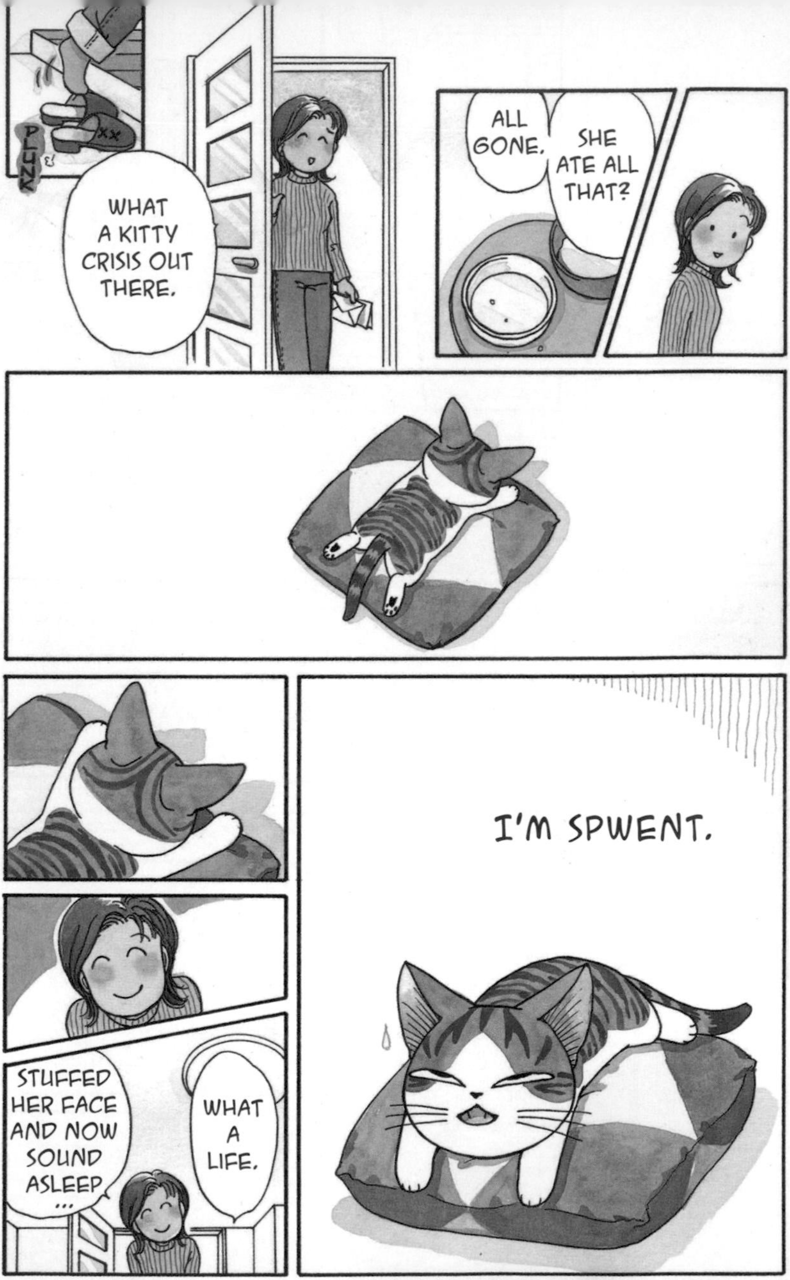
PLUNK
WHAT A KITTY CRISIS OUT THERE.
ALL GONE.
SHE ATE ALL THAT?
STUFFED HER FACE AND NOW SOUND ASLEEP...
WHAT A LIFE.
I'M SPWENT.

the end

homemade 30: a cat reports

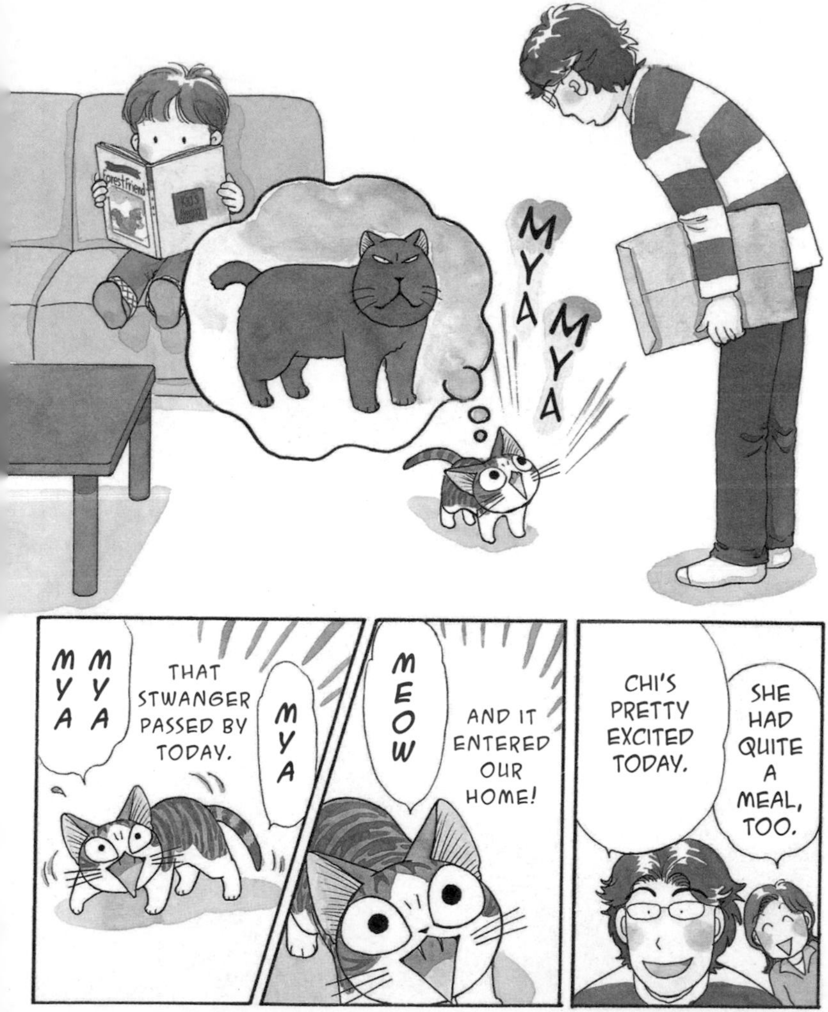
MYA
MYA
MYA MYA
THAT STWANGER PASSED BY TODAY.
MYA
MEOW
AND IT ENTERED OUR HOME!
CHI'S PRETTY EXCITED TODAY.
SHE HAD QUITE A MEAL, TOO.

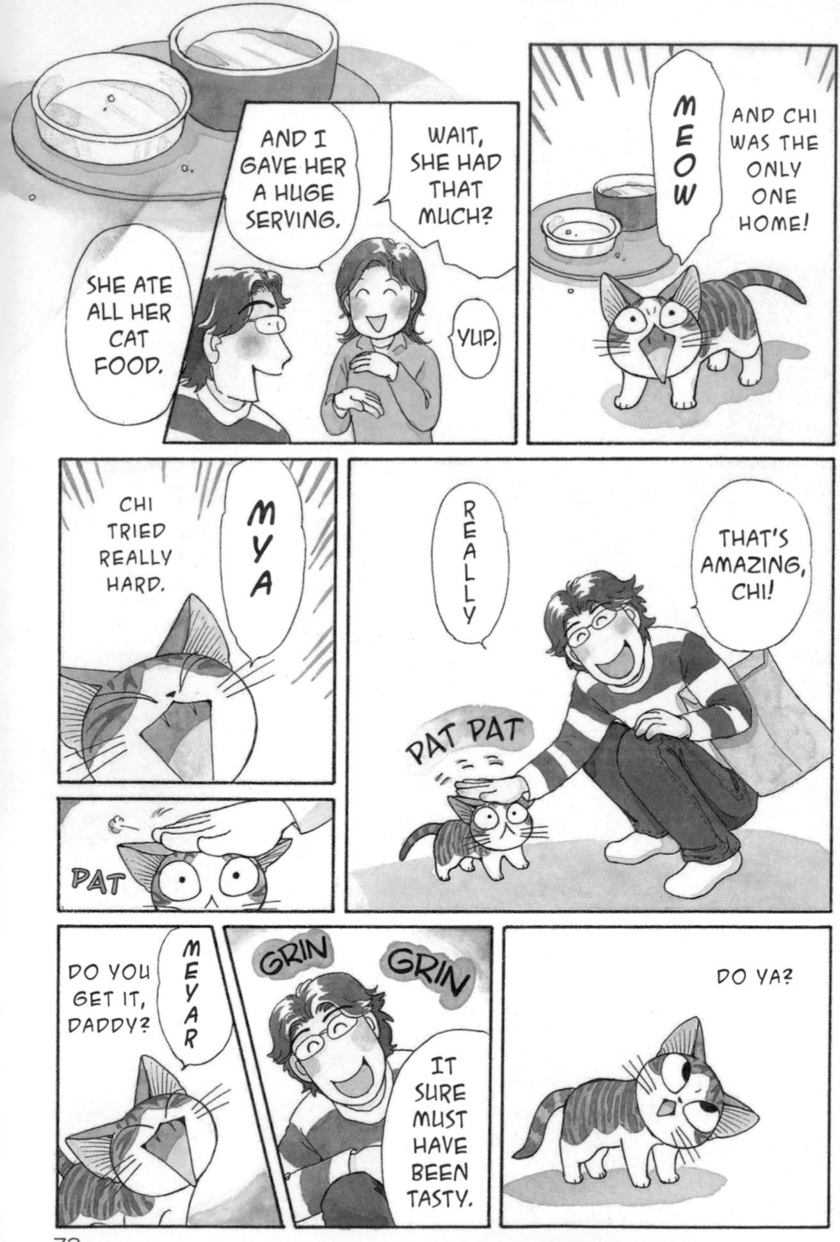
SHE ATE ALL HER CAT FOOD.
AND I GAVE HER A HUGE SERVING.
WAIT, SHE HAD THAT MUCH?
YUP.
MEOW
AND CHI WAS THE ONLY ONE HOME!
CHI TRIED REALLY HARD.
MYA
PAT
REALLY
THAT'S AMAZING, CHI!
PAT PAT
DO YOU GET IT, DADDY?
MEYAR
GRIN GRIN
IT SURE MUST HAVE BEEN TASTY.
DO YA?

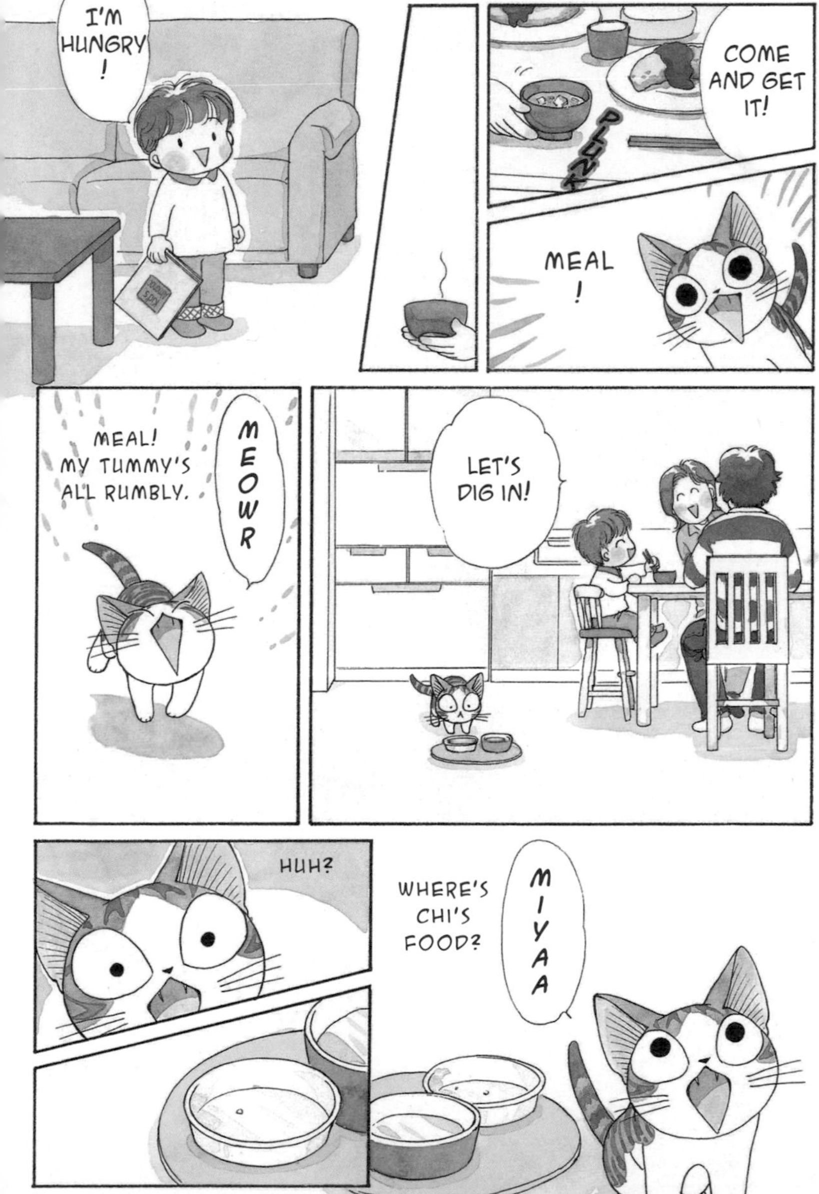
I'M HUNGRY!
COME AND GET IT!
PLUNK
MEAL!
MEAL! MY TUMMY'S ALL RUMBLY.
MEOWR
LET'S DIG IN!
HUH?
WHERE'S CHI'S FOOD?
MIYAA

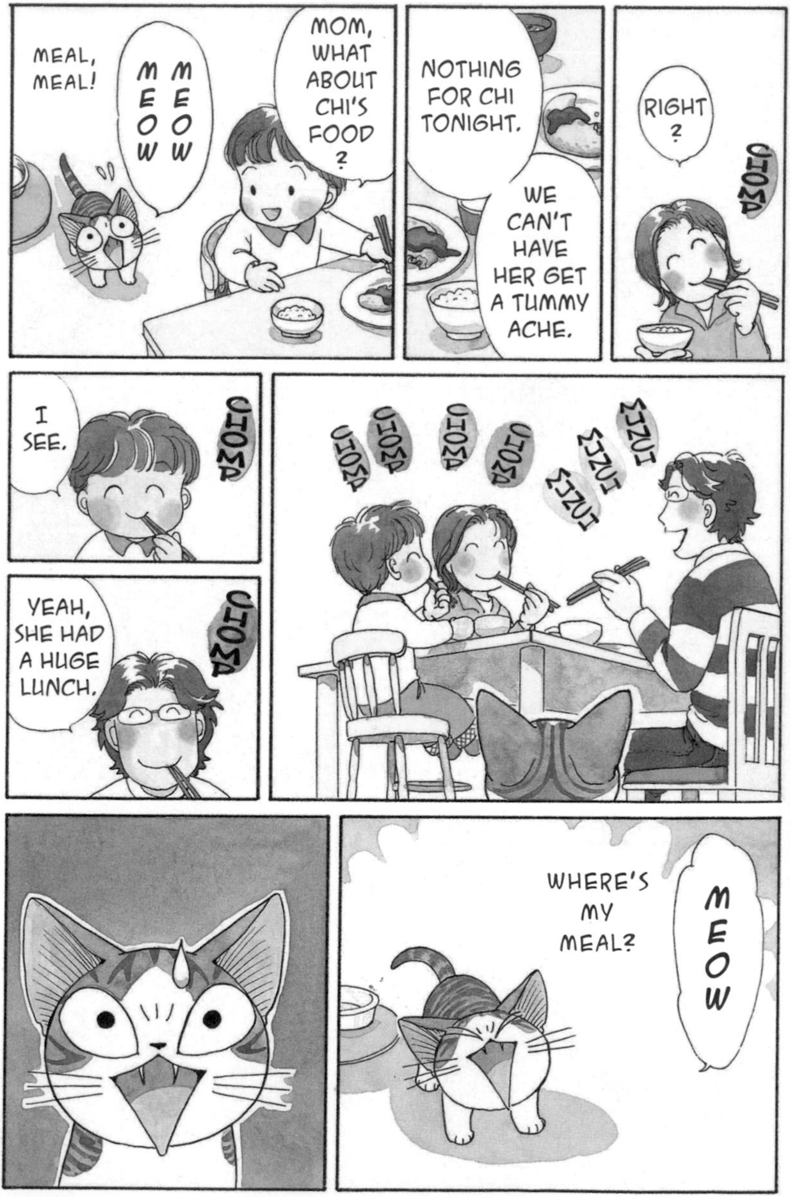
MEAL, MEAL!
MEOW MEOW
MOM, WHAT ABOUT CHI'S FOOD?
NOTHING FOR CHI TONIGHT.
WE CAN'T HAVE HER GET A TUMMY ACHE.
RIGHT?
CHOMP
I SEE.
CHOMP
YEAH, SHE HAD A HUGE LUNCH.
CHOMP
CHOMP
CHOMP
CHOMP
CHOMP
SLURP
SLURP
SLURP
WHERE'S MY MEAL?
MEOW

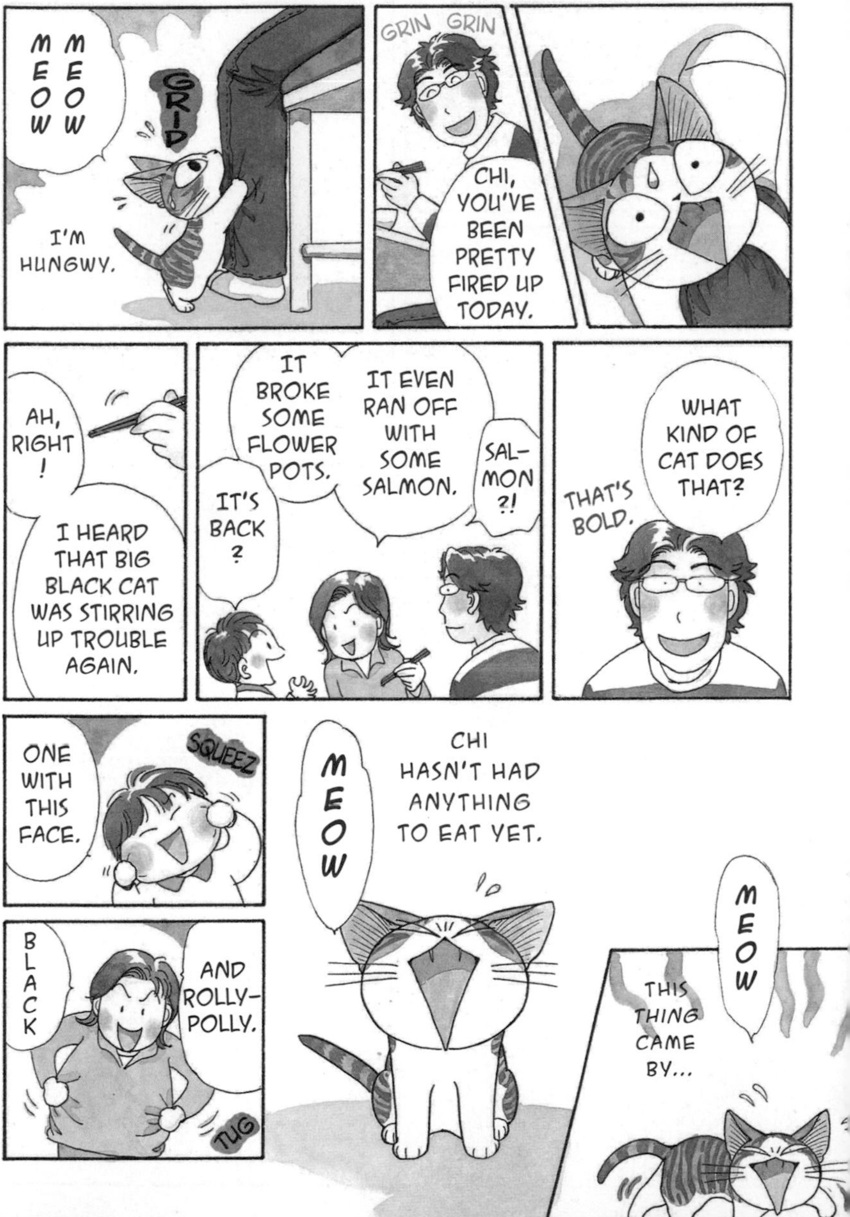

MEOW MEOW
GRID
I'M HUNGWY.
GRIN GRIN
CHI, YOU'VE BEEN PRETTY FIRED UP TODAY.
AH, RIGHT!
I HEARD THAT BIG BLACK CAT WAS STIRRING UP TROUBLE AGAIN.
IT BROKE SOME FLOWER POTS.
IT EVEN RAN OFF WITH SOME SALMON.
IT'S BACK?
SALMON?!
WHAT KIND OF CAT DOES THAT?
THAT'S BOLD.
ONE WITH THIS FACE.
SQUEEZ
BLACK
AND ROLLY-POLLY.
TUG
MEOW
CHI HASN'T HAD ANYTHING TO EAT YET.
MEOW
THIS THING CAME BY...

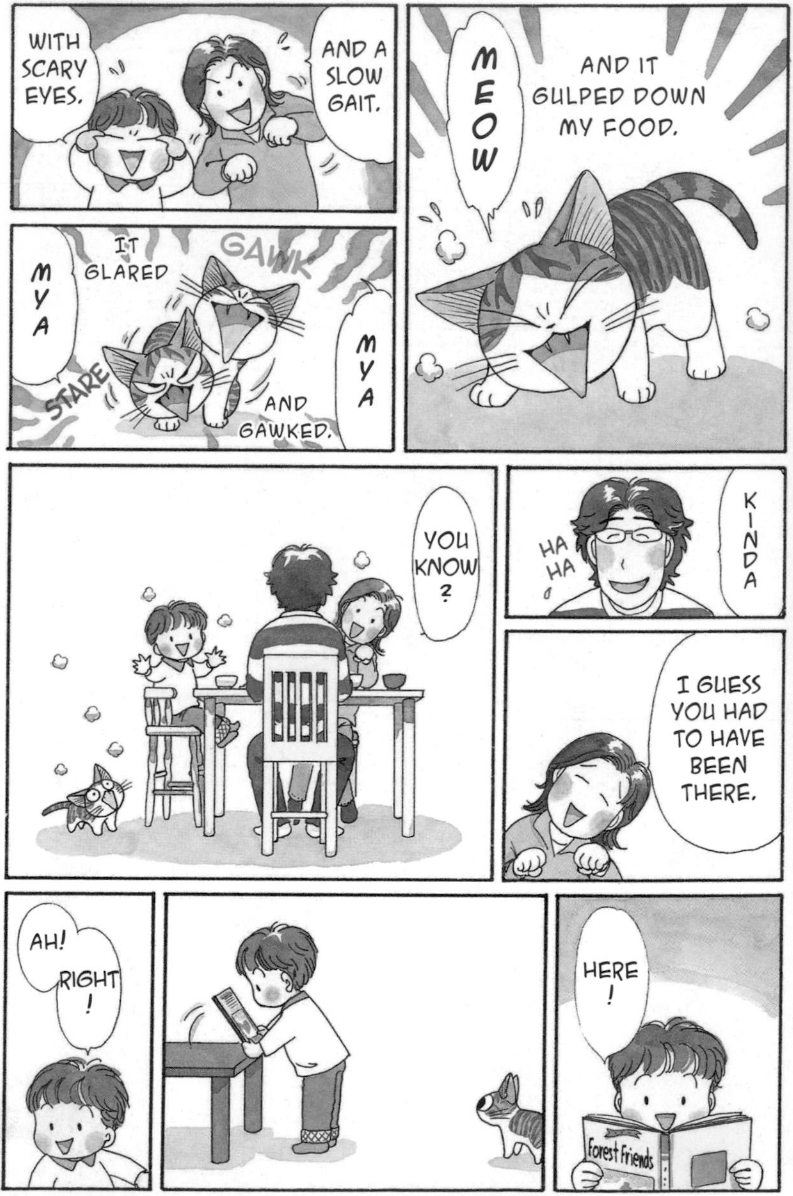
WITH SCARY EYES.
AND A SLOW GAIT.
MYA
IT GLARED
GAWK
STARE
MYA
AND GAWKED.
MEOW
AND IT GULPED DOWN MY FOOD.
YOU KNOW?
HA HA
KINDA
I GUESS YOU HAD TO HAVE BEEN THERE.
AH!
RIGHT!
HERE!
Forest Friends

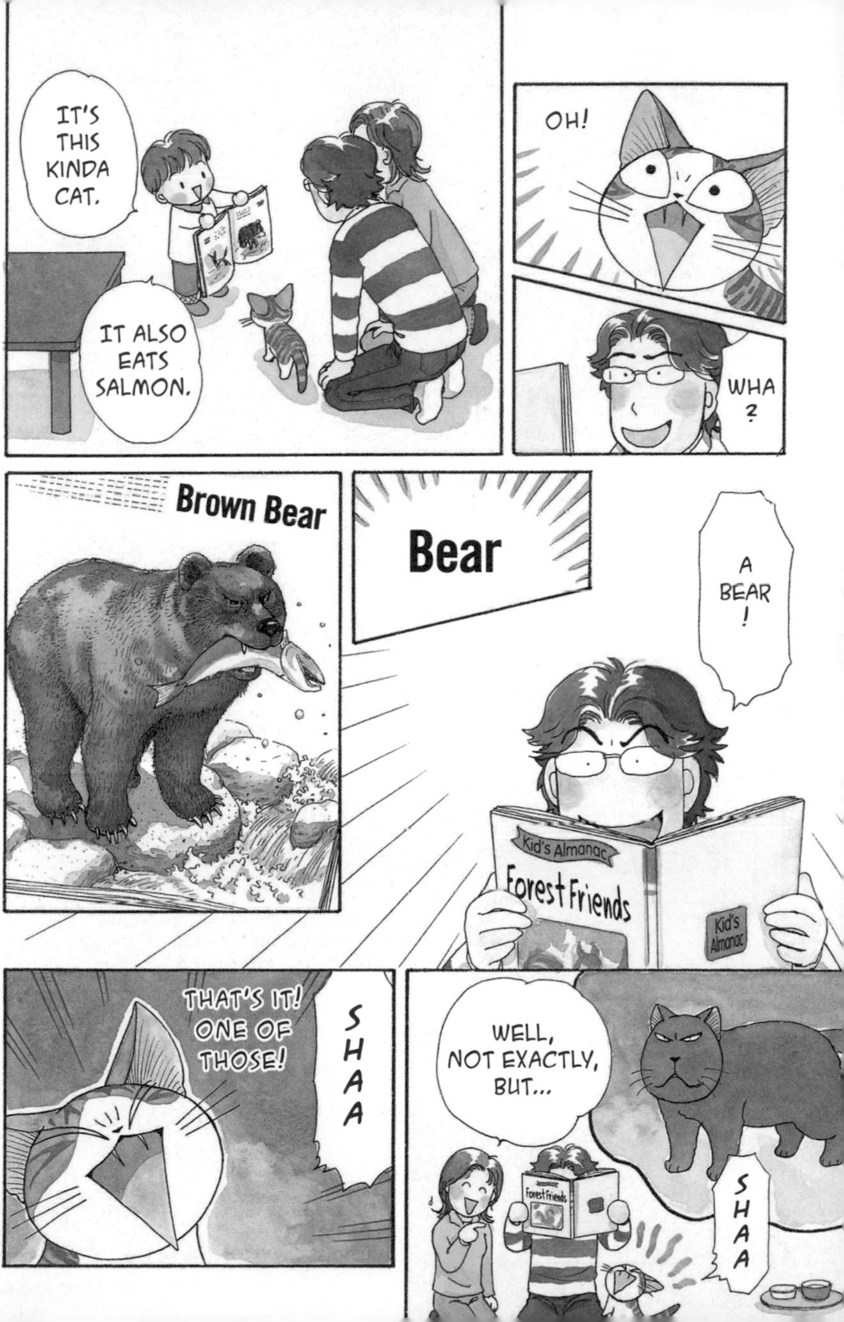
IT'S THIS KINDA CAT.
IT ALSO EATS SALMON.
OH!
WHA?
Brown Bear
Bear
A BEAR!
Kid's Almanac
Forest Friends
Kid's Almanac
THAT'S IT! ONE OF THOSE!
SHAA
WELL, NOT EXACTLY, BUT...
Forest Friends
SHAA

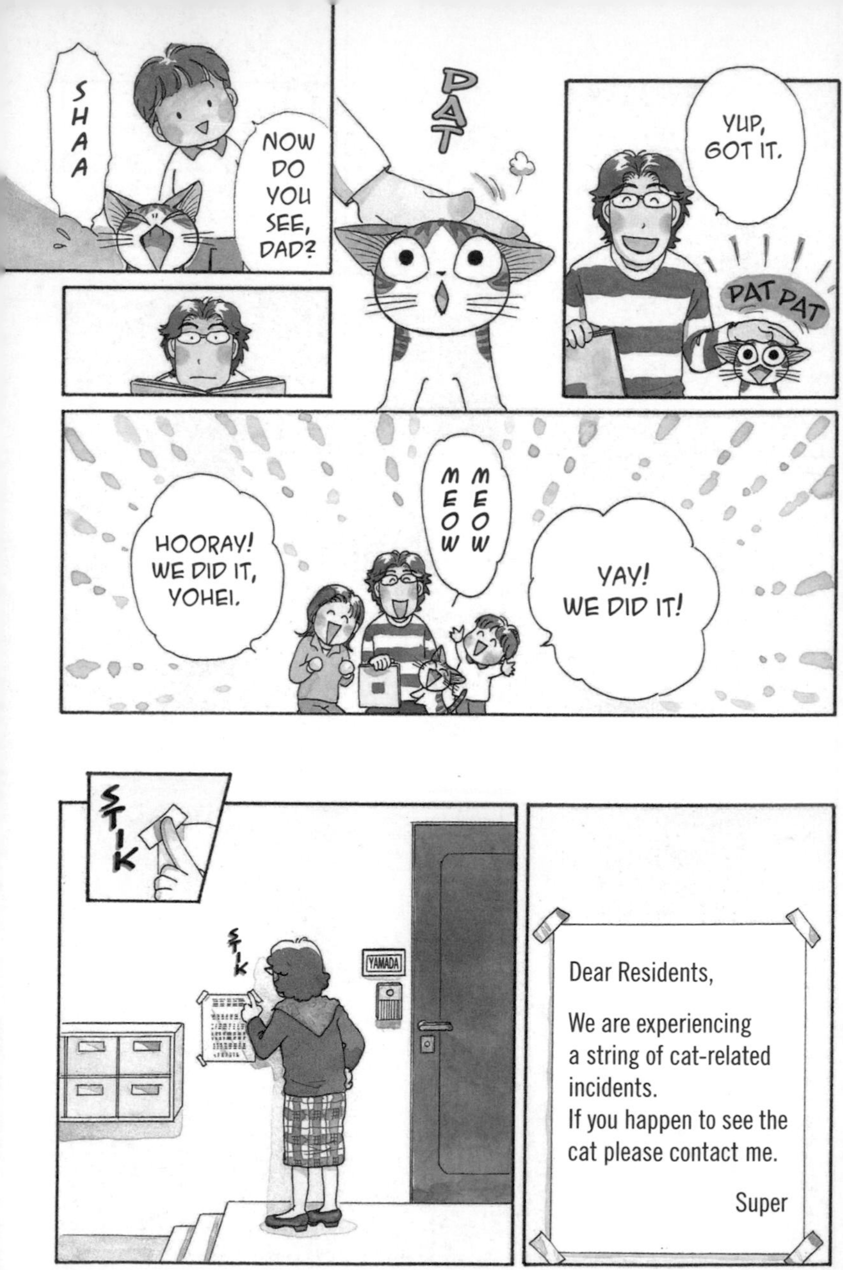
SHAA
NOW DO YOU SEE, DAD?
PAT
YUP, GOT IT.
PAT PAT
HOORAY! WE DID IT, YOHEI.
MEOW MEOW
YAY! WE DID IT!
STIK
STIK
YAMADA
Dear Residents,
We are experiencing a string of cat-related incidents.
If you happen to see the cat please contact me.
Super

the end

homemade 31: a cat uses her head

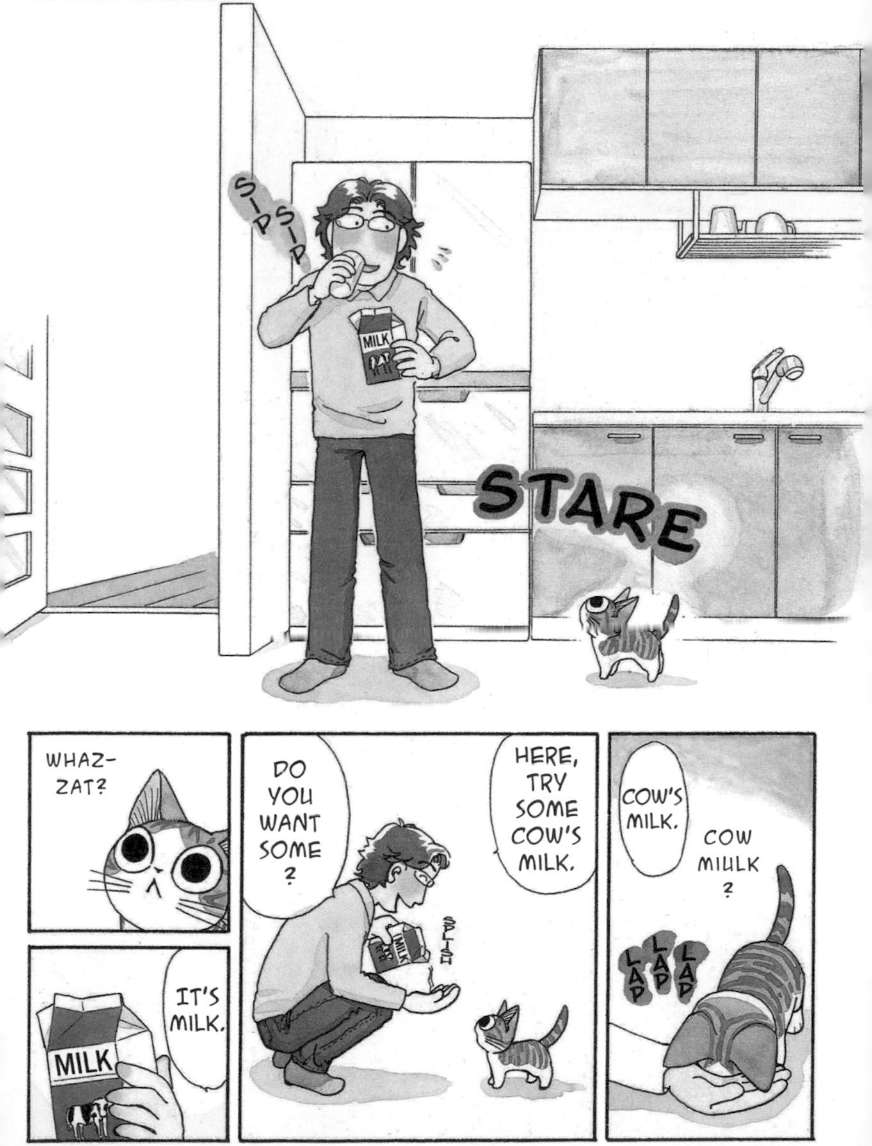
SIP SIP
MILK
STARE
WHAZ-ZAT?
IT'S MILK.
MILK
DO YOU WANT SOME?
HERE, TRY SOME COW'S MILK.
MILK
SPLISH
COW'S MILK.
COW MIULK?
LAP LAP LAP

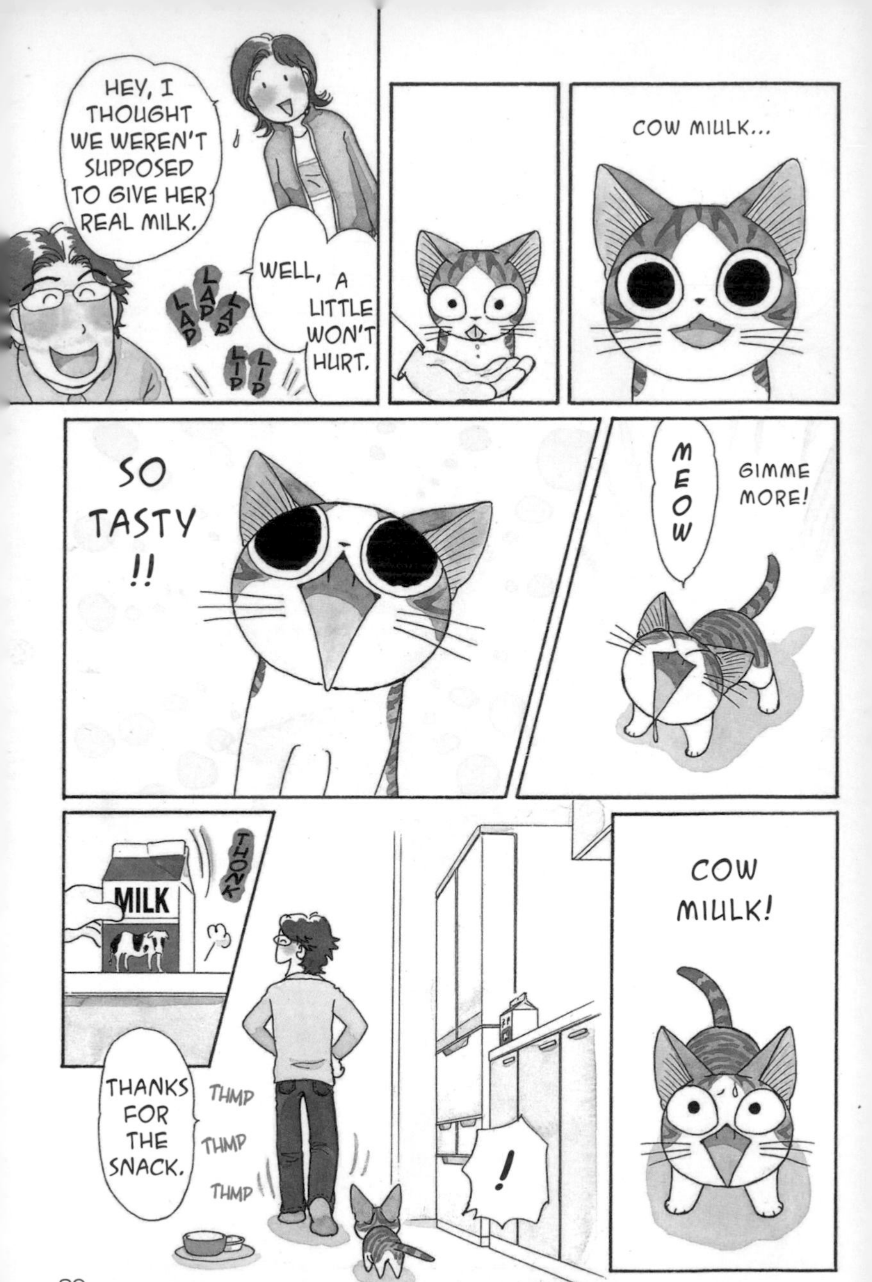
HEY, I THOUGHT WE WEREN'T SUPPOSED TO GIVE HER REAL MILK.
LAP LAP LAP
LIP LIP
WELL, A LITTLE WON'T HURT.
COW MIULK...
SO TASTY!!
MEOW
GIMME MORE!
MILK
THONK
THANKS FOR THE SNACK.
THMP
THMP
THMP
!
COW MIULK!

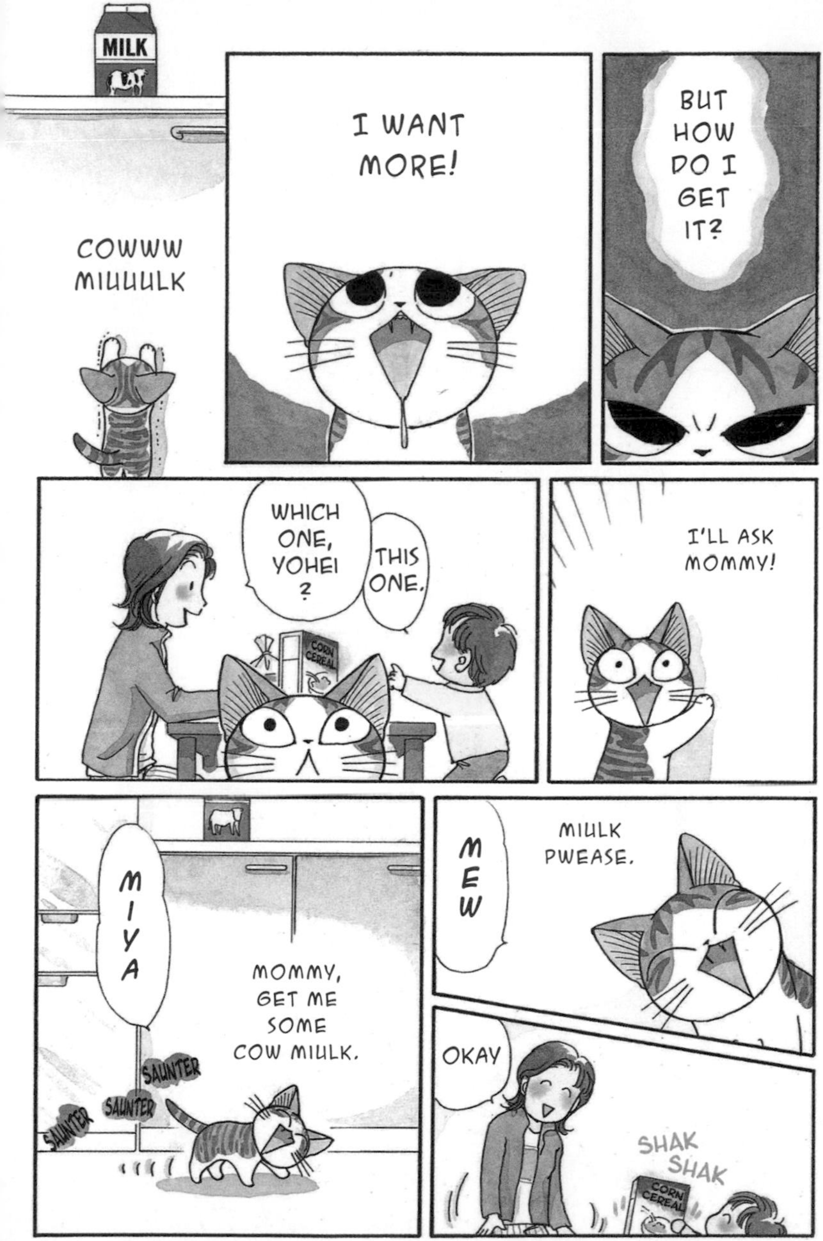
MILK
COWWW MIUUULK
I WANT MORE!
BUT HOW DO I GET IT?
WHICH ONE, YOHEI ?
THIS ONE.
CORN CEREAL
I'LL ASK MOMMY!
MIYA
MOMMY, GET ME SOME COW MIULK.
SAUNTER
SAUNTER
SAUNTER
MEW
MIULK PWEASE.
OKAY
SHAK SHAK
CORN CEREAL

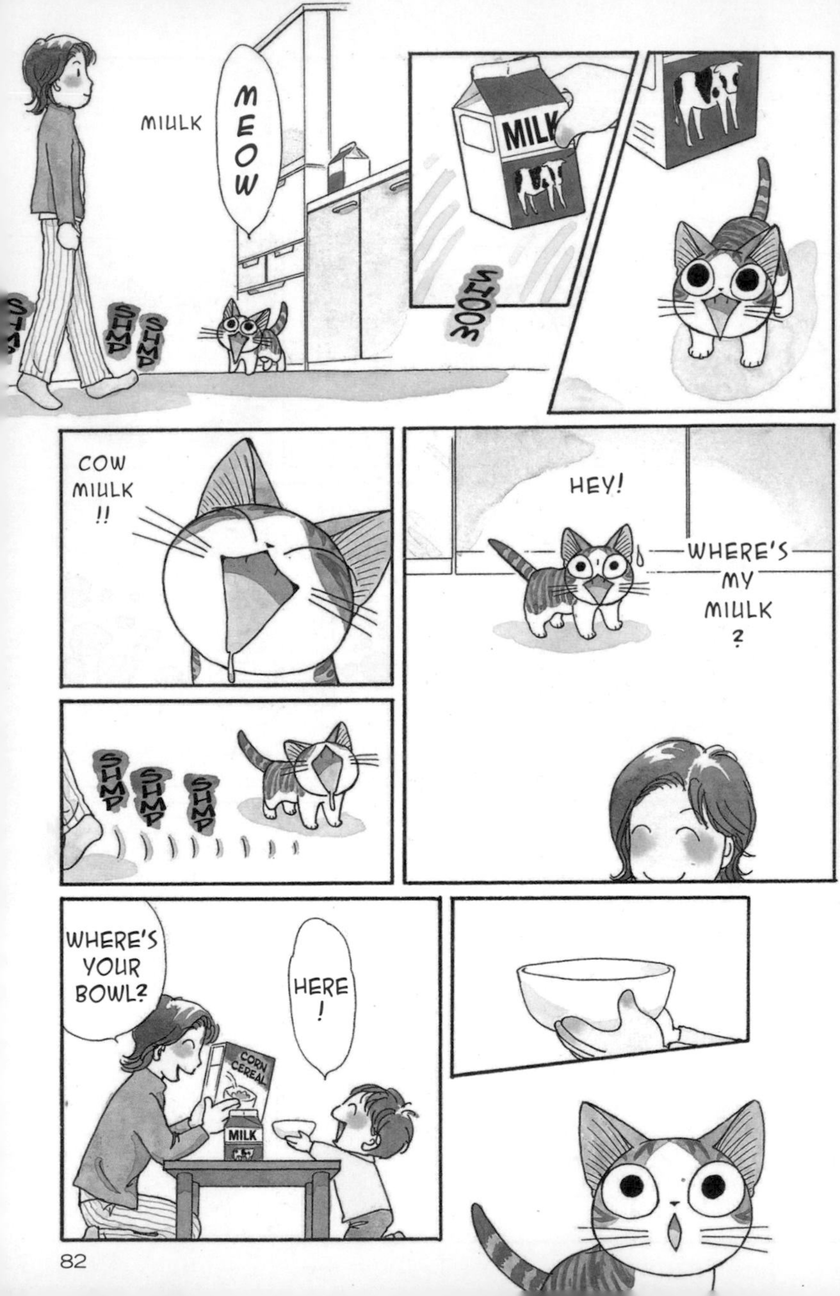
MIULK
MEOW
SHMP
SHMP
WOOSH
COW MIULK !!
SHMP
SHMP
SHMP
HEY!
WHERE'S MY MIULK ?
WHERE'S YOUR BOWL?
HERE !

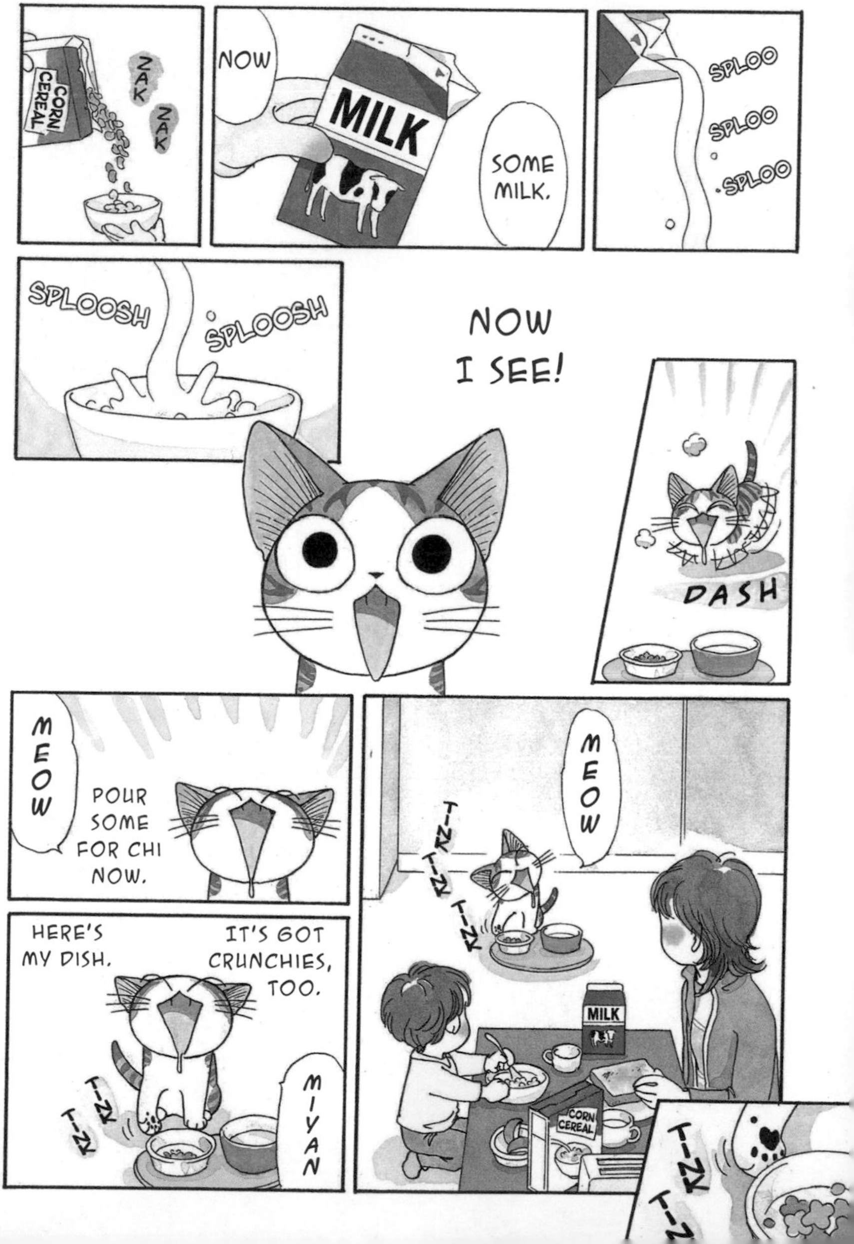

CORN CEREAL
ZAK
ZAK
NOW
MILK
SOME MILK.
SPLOO
SPLOO
SPLOO
SPLOOSH
SPLOOSH
NOW I SEE!
DASH
MEOW
POUR SOME FOR CHI NOW.
HERE'S MY DISH.
IT'S GOT CRUNCHIES, TOO.
TINK
TINK
MIYAN
MEOW
TINK
TINK
TINK
MILK
CORN CEREAL
TINK

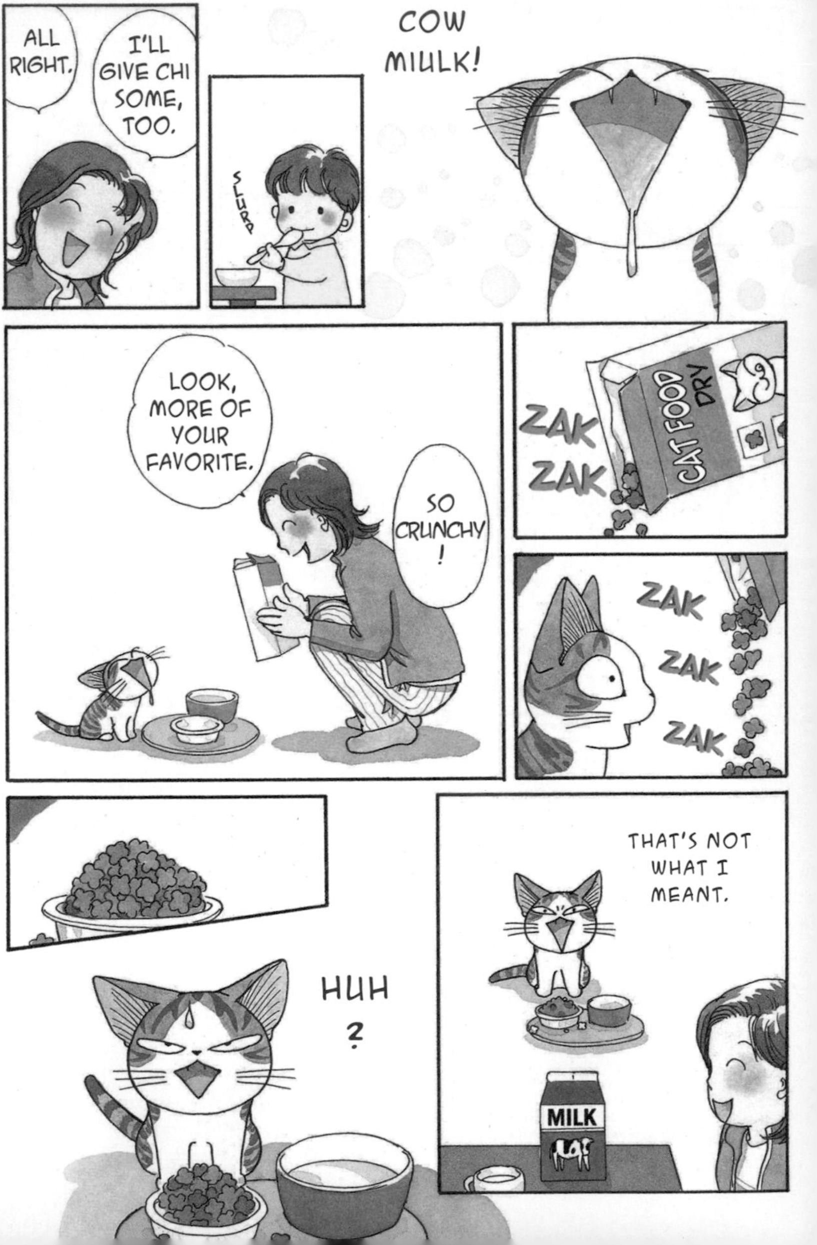
ALL RIGHT.
I'LL GIVE CHI SOME, TOO.
SLURP
COW MIULK!
LOOK, MORE OF YOUR FAVORITE.
SO CRUNCHY!
ZAK ZAK
CAT FOOD DRY
ZAK
ZAK
ZAK
HUH?
THAT'S NOT WHAT I MEANT.
MILK

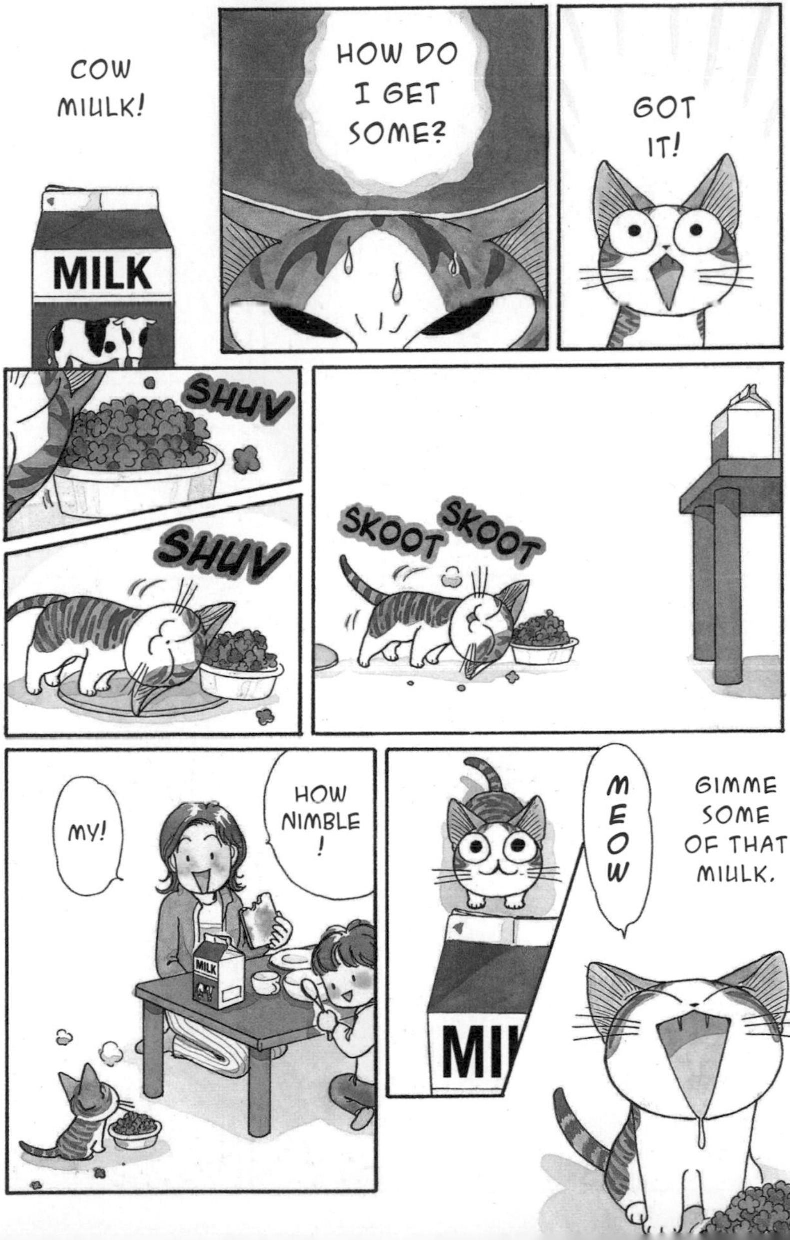

COW MIULK!
MILK
HOW DO I GET SOME?
GOT IT!
SHUV
SHUV
SKOOT SKOOT
MY!
HOW NIMBLE!
MILK
MEOW
GIMME SOME OF THAT MIULK.

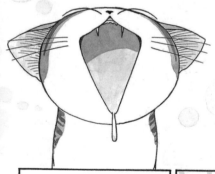

COW MIULK

WANNA JOIN US, CHI?

YOU DROPPED SOME.

THERE

SHMP SHMP SHMP

HEY?!

POP

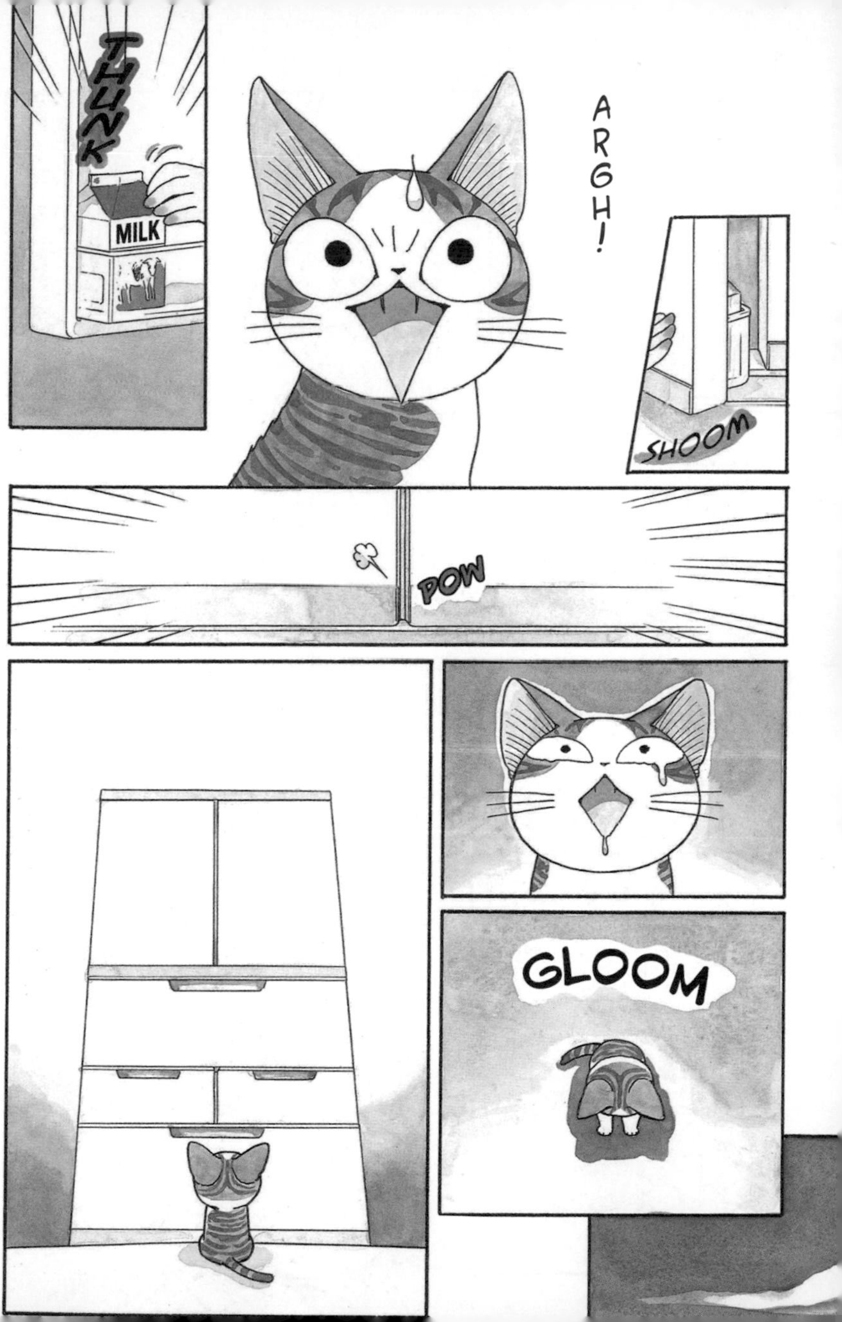
THUNK
MILK
ARGH!
SHOOM
POW
GLOOM

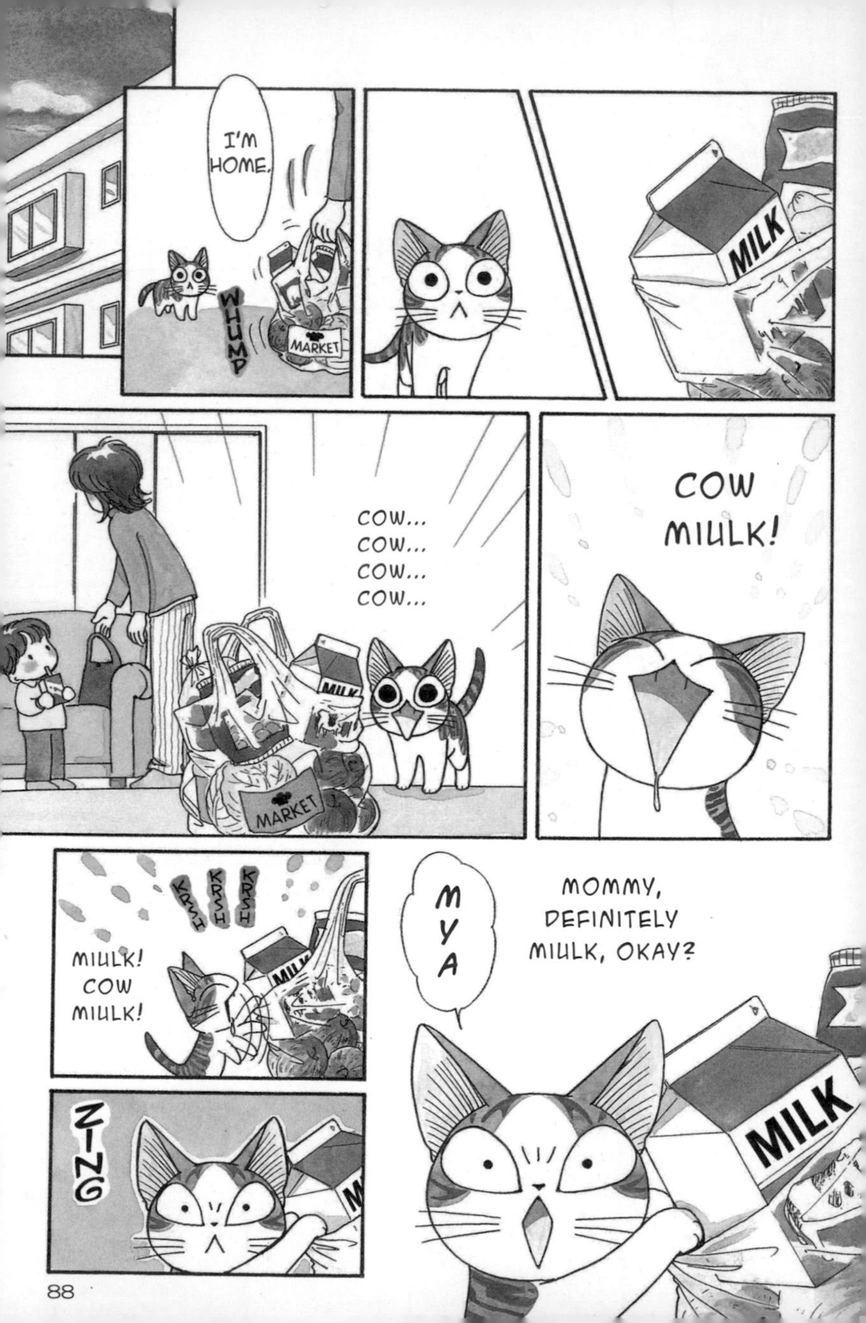
I'M HOME.
WHUMP
MARKET
MILK
COW...
COW...
COW...
COW...
MARKET
COW
MIULK!
KRSH KRSH KRSH
MIULK!
COW
MIULK!
ZING
MYA
MOMMY,
DEFINITELY
MIULK, OKAY?
MILK

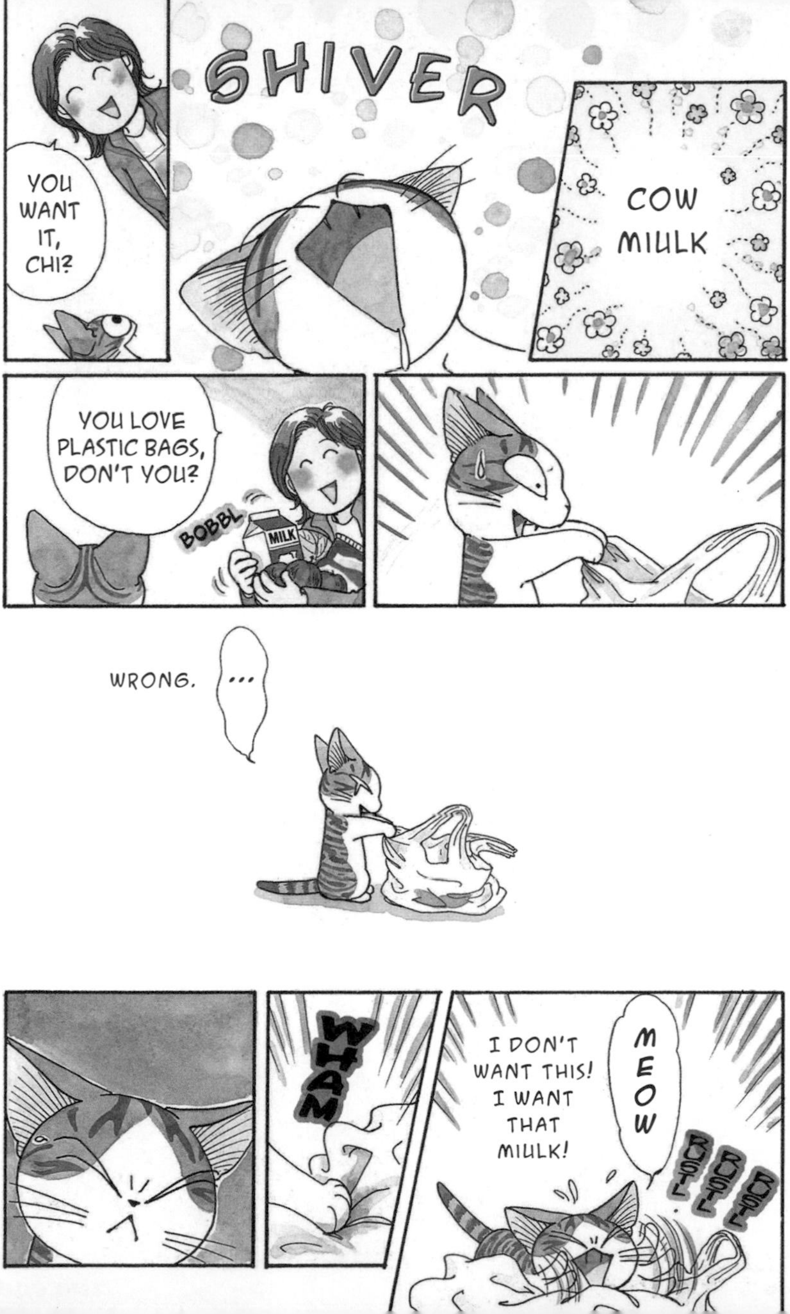
YOU WANT IT, CHI?
SHIVER
COW MIULK
YOU LOVE PLASTIC BAGS, DON'T YOU?
BOBBL
MILK
WRONG.
...
WHAM
I DON'T WANT THIS! I WANT THAT MIULK!
MEOW
RUSTL
RUSTL
RUSTL

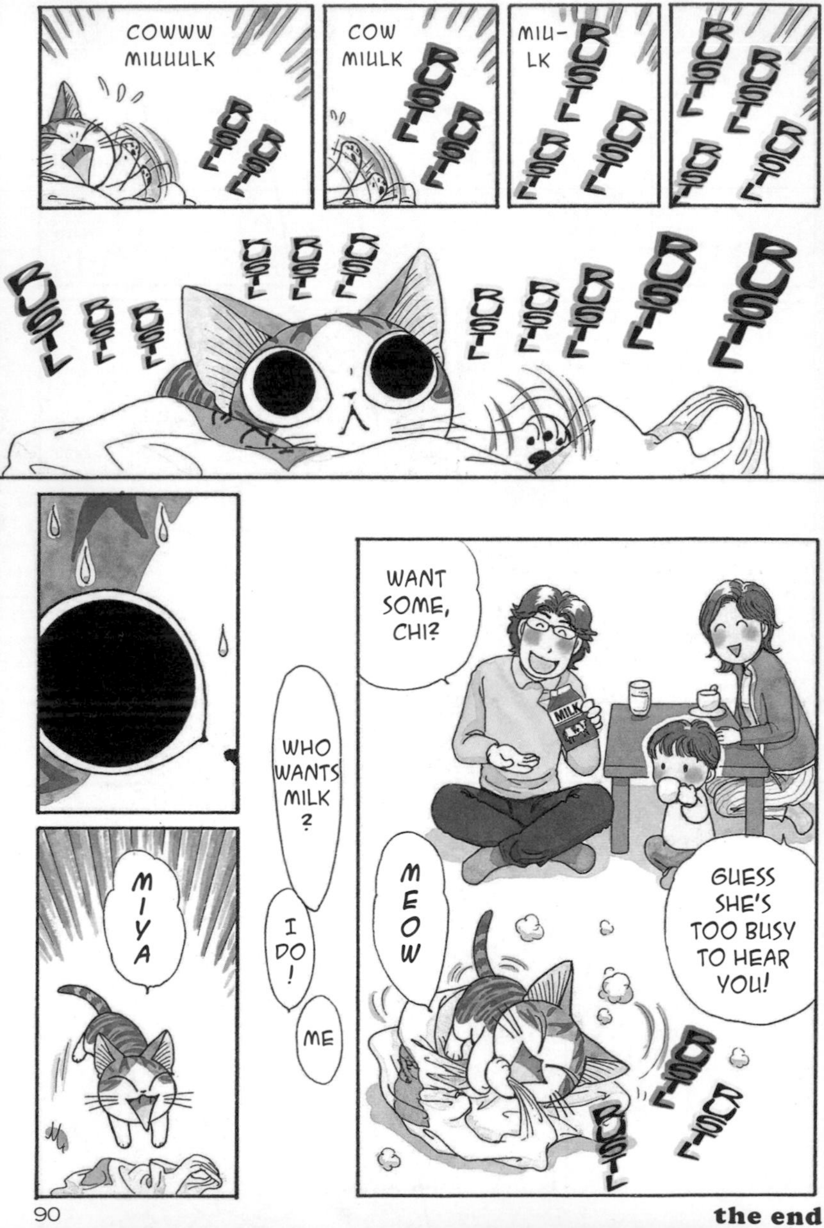
COWWW MIUUUULK
RUSTL RUSTL
COW MIULK
RUSTL RUSTL
MIU-LK
RUSTL RUSTL RUSTL
RUSTL RUSTL RUSTL RUSTL
RUSTL RUSTL RUSTL RUSTL RUSTL RUSTL RUSTL RUSTL RUSTL RUSTL RUSTL
MIYA
WANT SOME, CHI?
WHO WANTS MILK?
I DO!
ME
MEOW
MILK
GUESS SHE'S TOO BUSY TO HEAR YOU!
RUSTL RUSTL RUSTL

the end

homemade 32: a cat aggravates

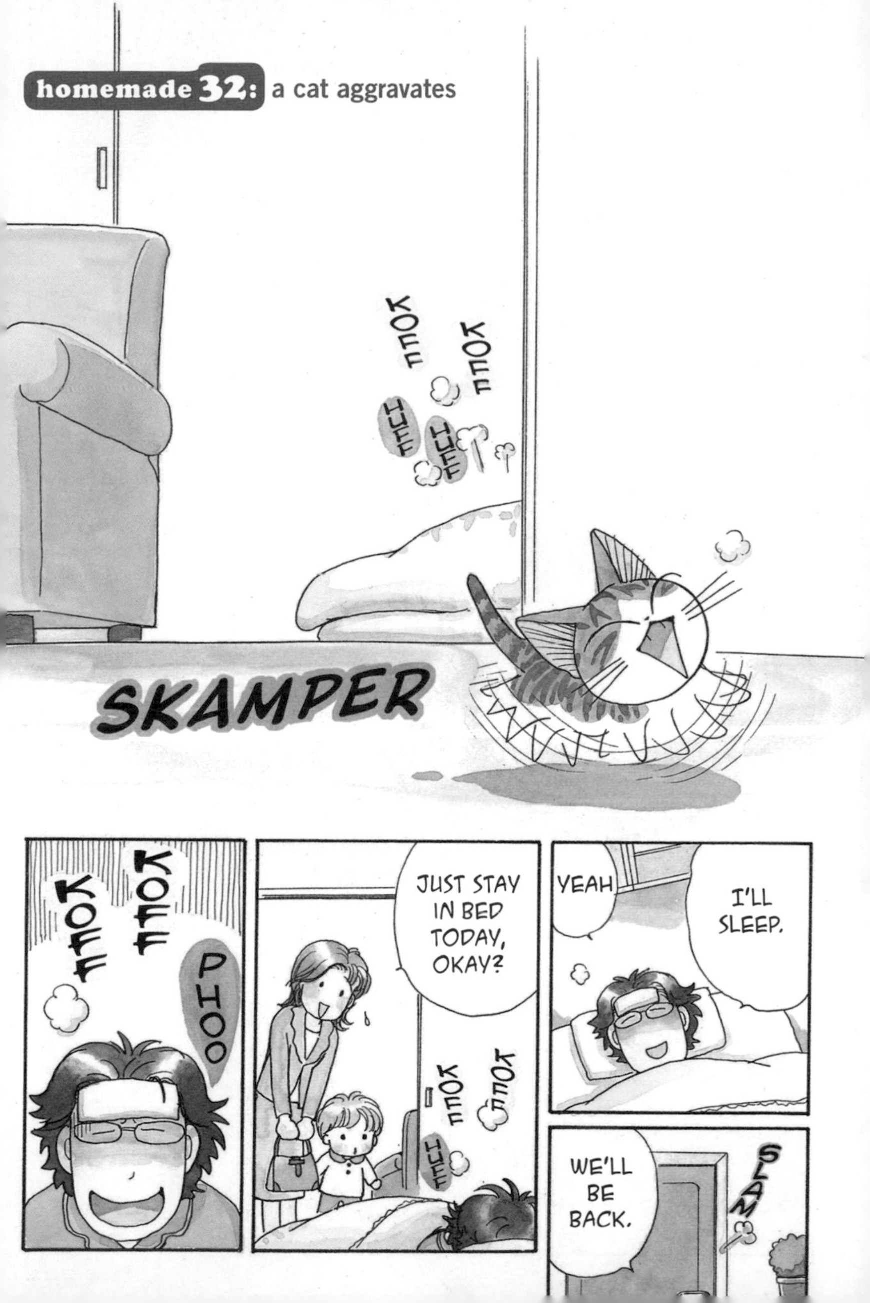

KOFF
KOFF
HUFF
HUFF
SKAMPER
KOFF
KOFF
PHOO
JUST STAY IN BED TODAY, OKAY?
KOFF
KOFF
HUFF
YEAH
I'LL SLEEP.
WE'LL BE BACK.
SLAM

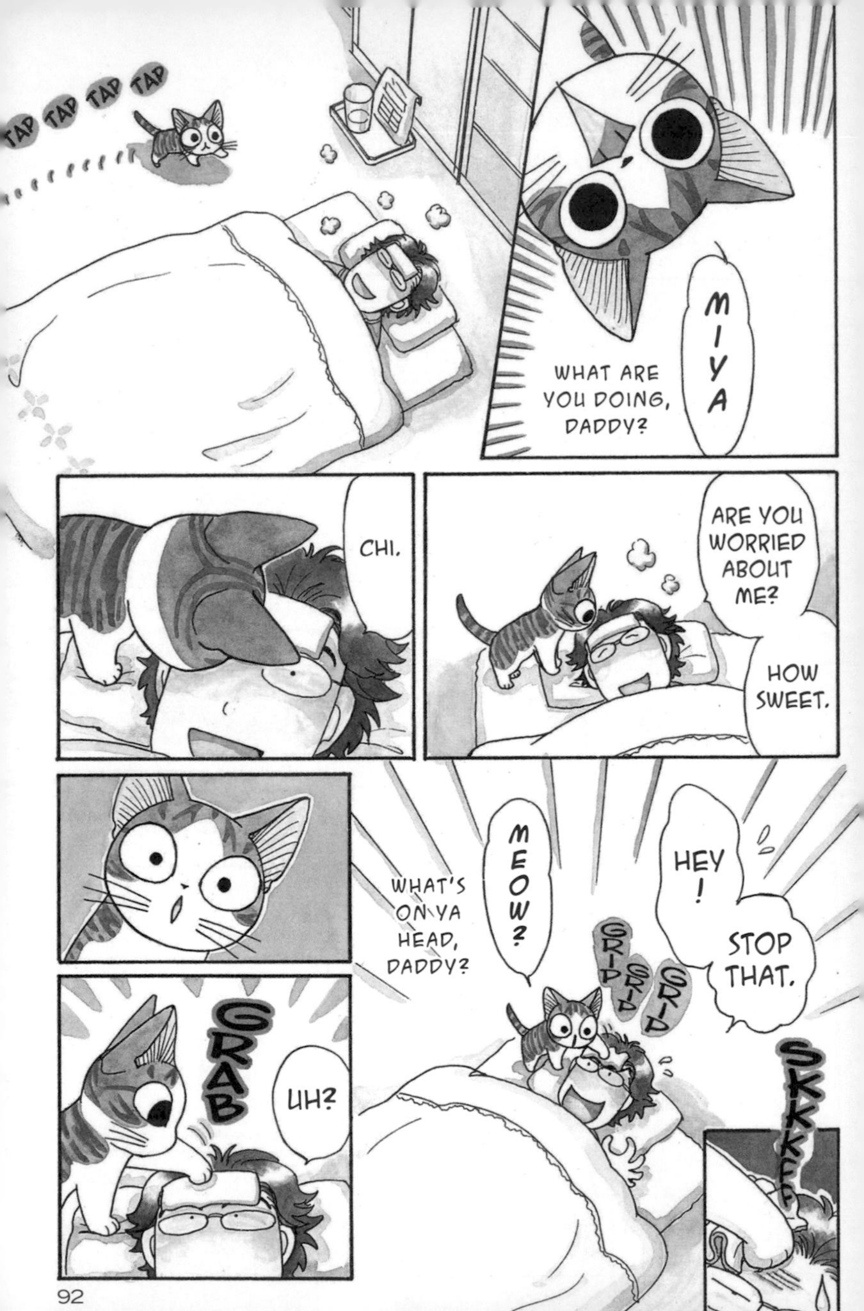

TAP TAP TAP TAP
MIYA
WHAT ARE YOU DOING, DADDY?
CHI.
ARE YOU WORRIED ABOUT ME?
HOW SWEET.
MEOW?
WHAT'S ON YA HEAD, DADDY?
GRAB
UH?
GRIP GRIP GRIP
HEY! STOP THAT.
SKKKE

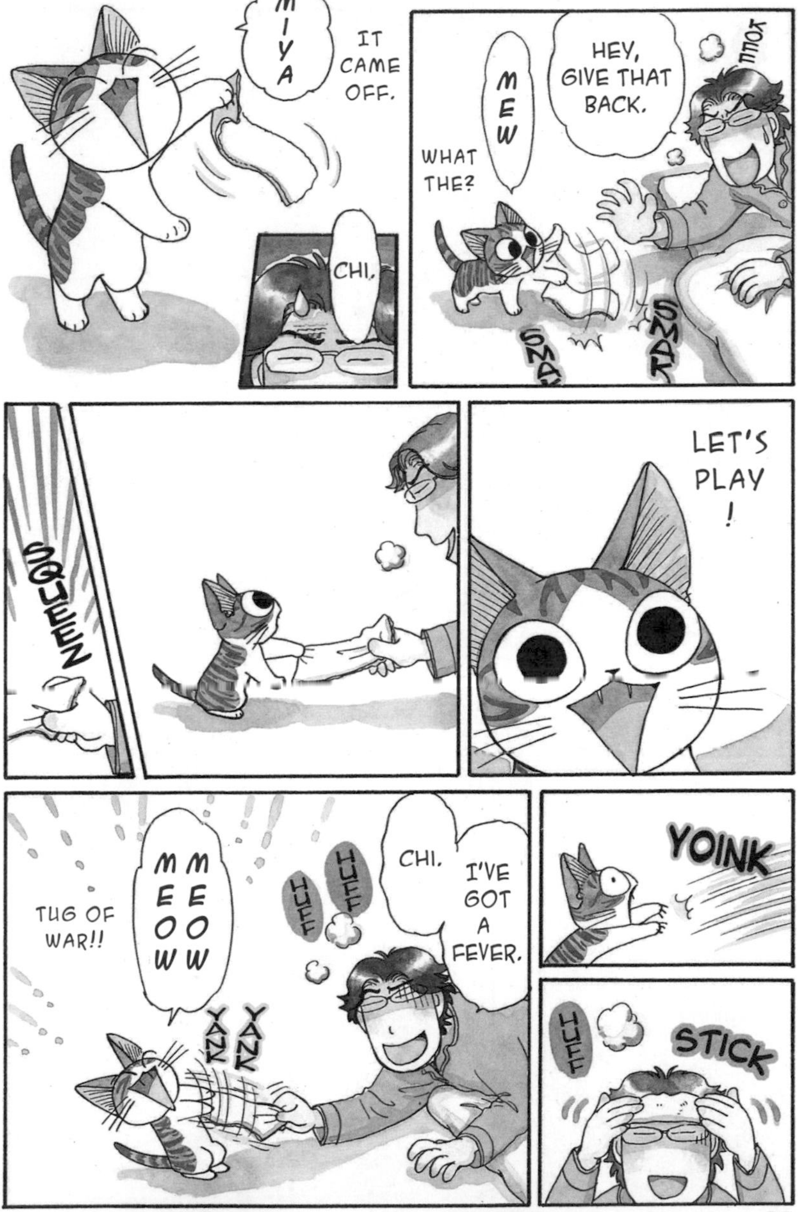

MIYA
IT CAME OFF.
CHI.
HEY, GIVE THAT BACK.
KOFF
MEW
WHAT THE?
SMAK
SMAK
SQUEEZ
LET'S PLAY!
TUG OF WAR!!
MEOW MEOW
HUFF HUFF
CHI.
I'VE GOT A FEVER.
YANK YANK
YOINK
HUFF
STICK

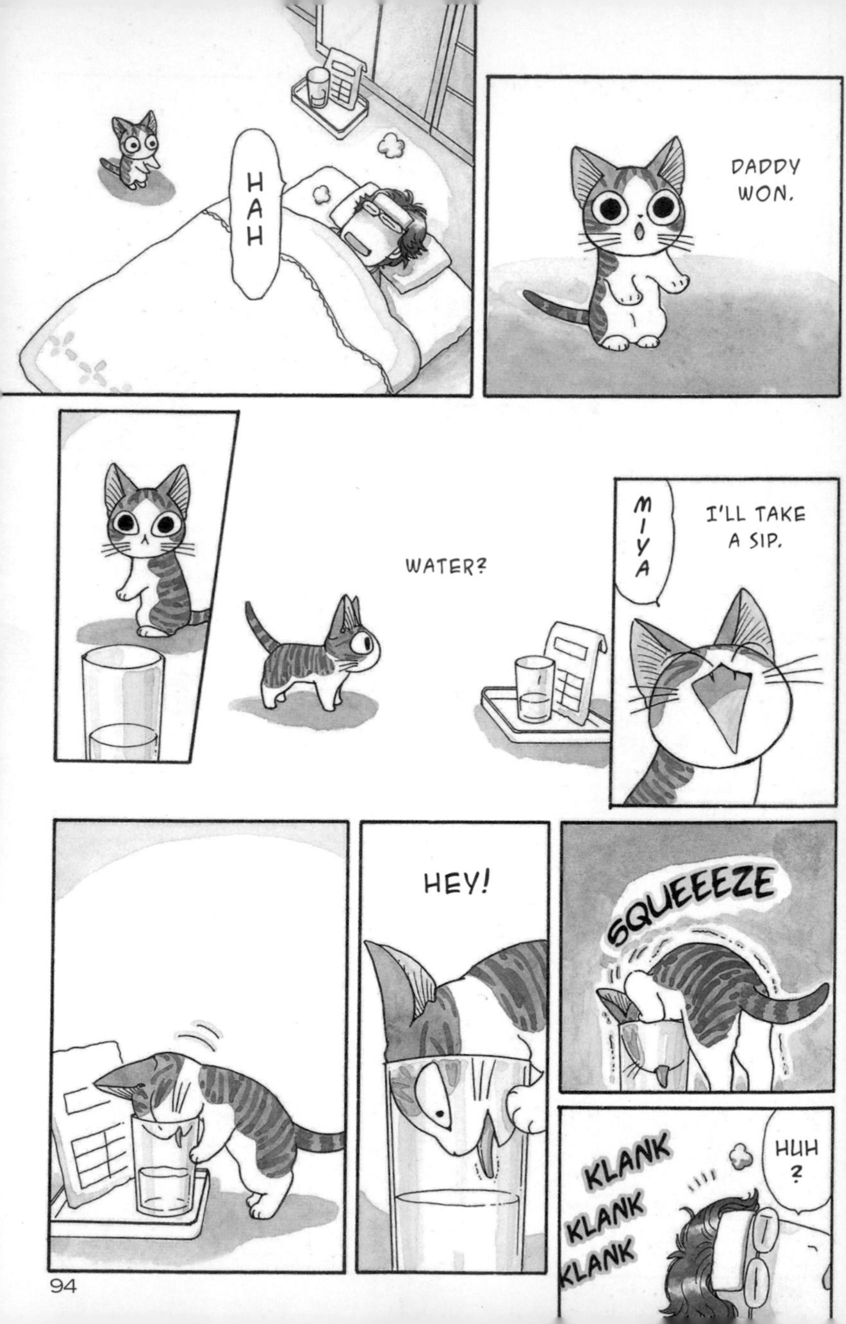
HAH
DADDY WON.
WATER?
MIYA
I'LL TAKE A SIP.
HEY!
SQUEEEZE
KLANK
KLANK
KLANK
KLANK
HUH?

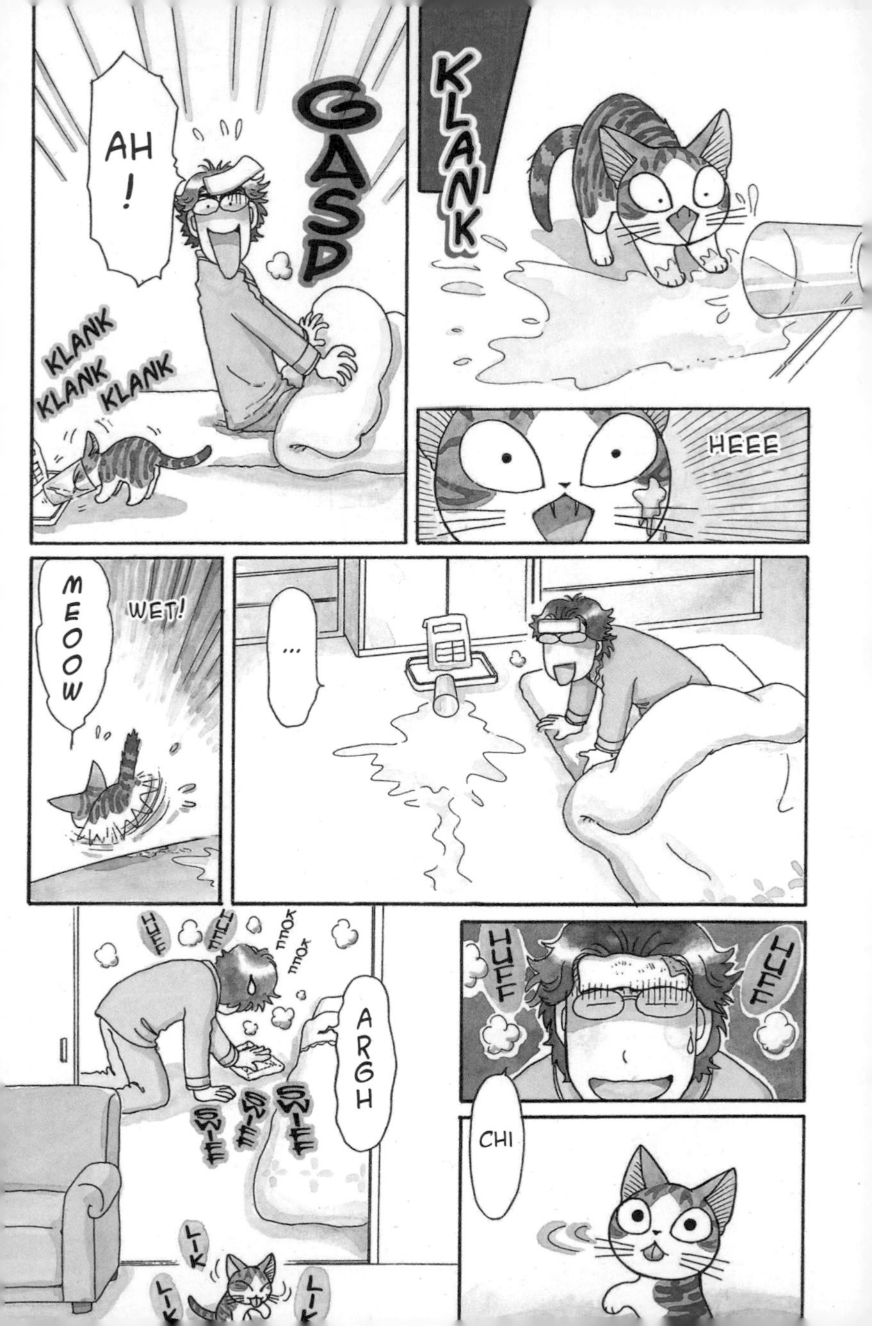
AH!
GASP
KLANK
KLANK
KLANK
KLANK
HEEE
MEOOW
WET!
...
HUFF
PUFF
TOK
TOK
ARGH
SWIF
SWIF
SWIF
LIK
LIK
HUFF
HUFF
CHI

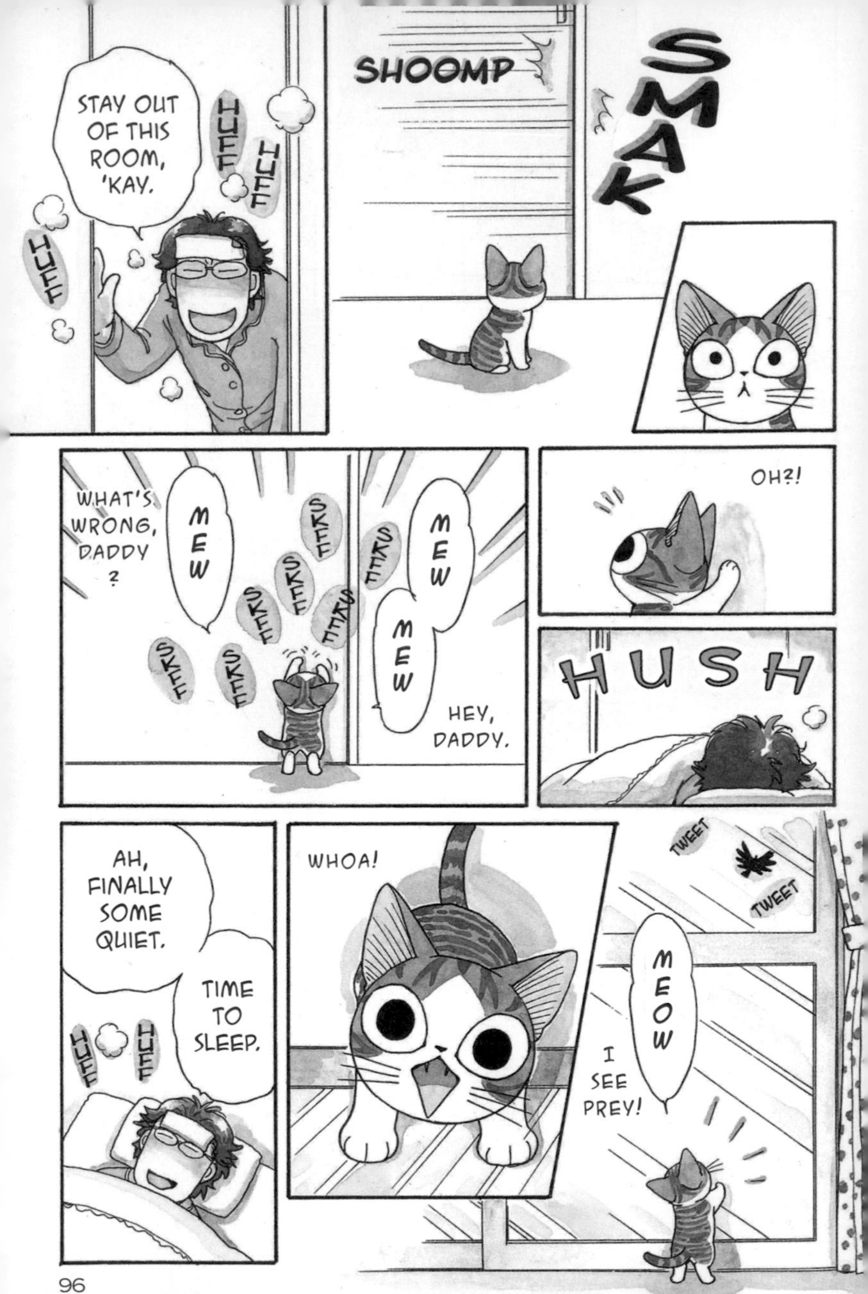
STAY OUT OF THIS ROOM, 'KAY.
HUFF
HUFF
HUFF
SHOOMP
SMAK
WHAT'S WRONG, DADDY?
MEW
SKFF
SKFF
SKFF
SKFF
SKFF
SKFF
SKFF
MEW
MEW
HEY, DADDY.
OH?!
HUSH
AH, FINALLY SOME QUIET.
TIME TO SLEEP.
HUFF
HUFF
WHOA!
TWEET
TWEET
MEOW
I SEE PREY!

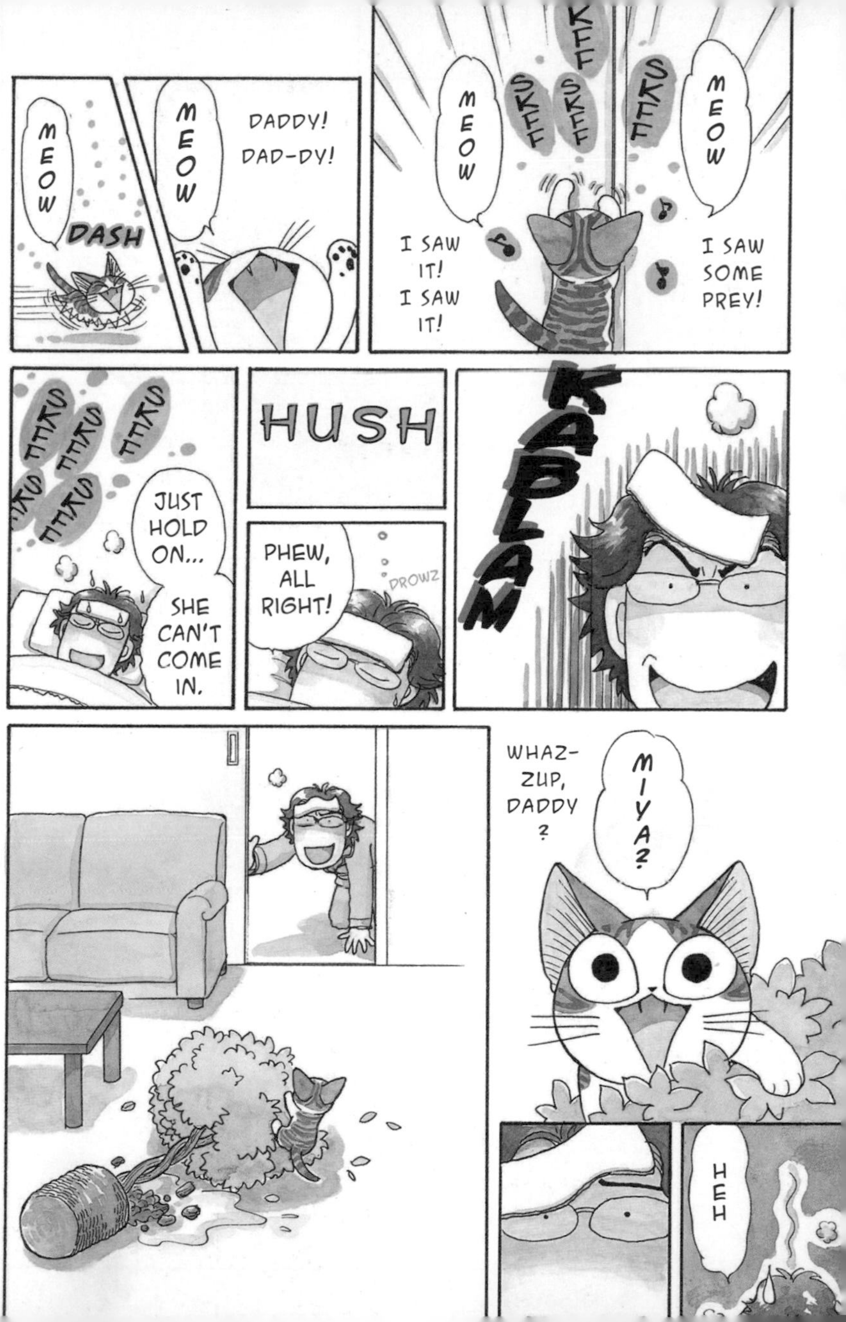

MEOW
DASH
MEOW
DADDY! DAD-DY!
MEOW
SKFF SKFF
KFF
SKFF
MEOW
I SAW IT! I SAW IT!
I SAW SOME PREY!
SKTTKS
JUST HOLD ON...
SHE CAN'T COME IN.
HUSH
PHEW, ALL RIGHT!
DROWZ
KABLAM
WHAZ-ZUP, DADDY?
MIYA?
HEH

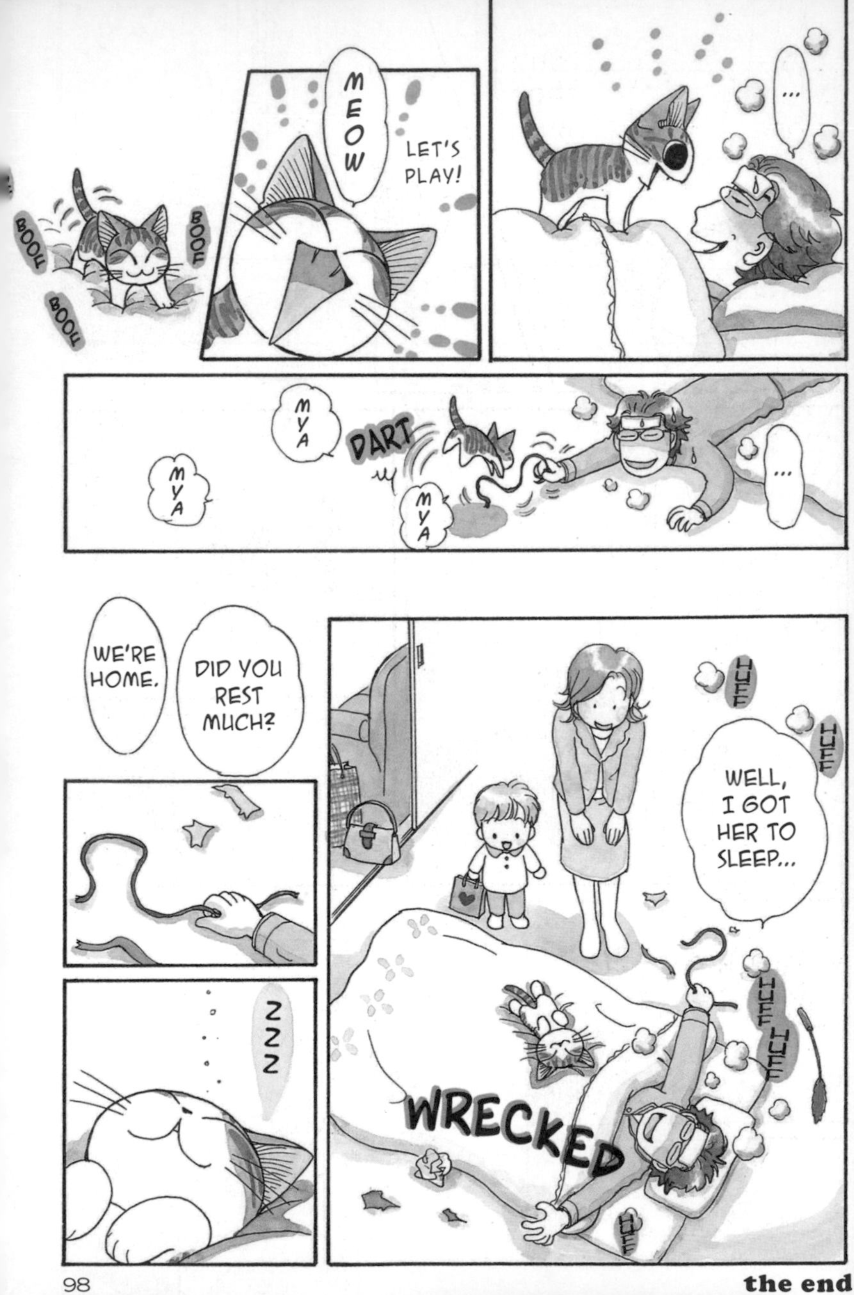
BOOF
BOOF
BOOF
MEOW
LET'S PLAY!
...
MYA
MYA
DART
MYA
...
WE'RE HOME.
DID YOU REST MUCH?
ZZZ
HUFF
HUFF
WELL, I GOT HER TO SLEEP...
HUFF HUFF
WRECKED
HUFF

the end

homemade 33: a cat searches

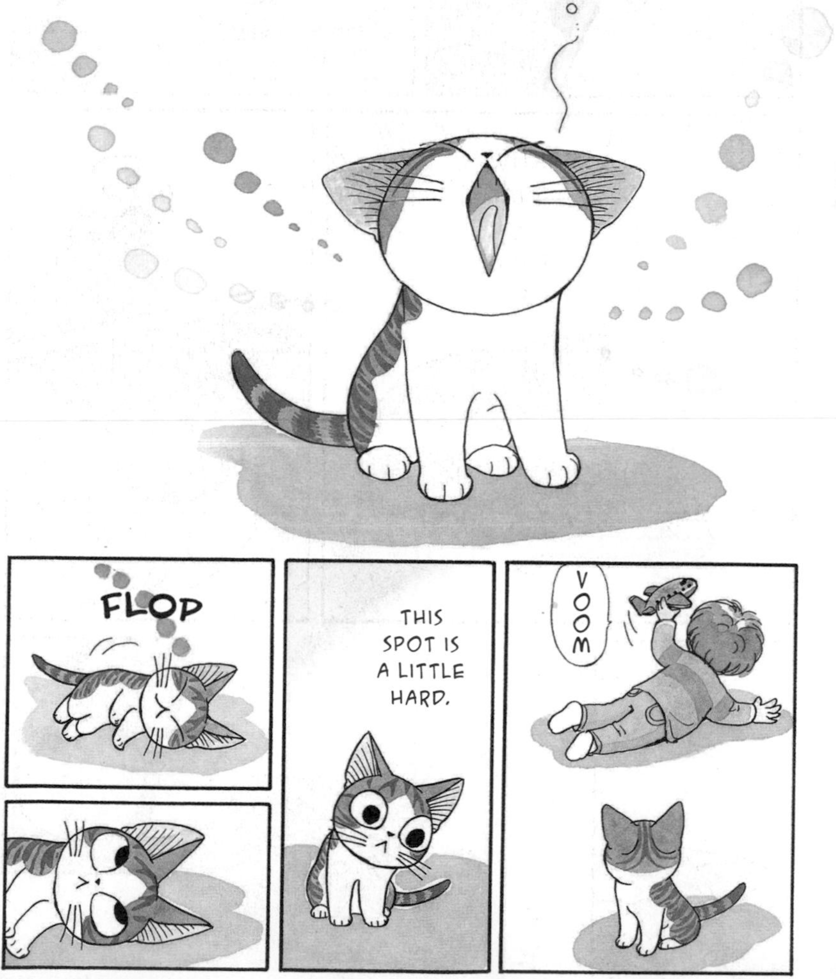

FLOP
THIS SPOT IS A LITTLE HARD.
VOOM

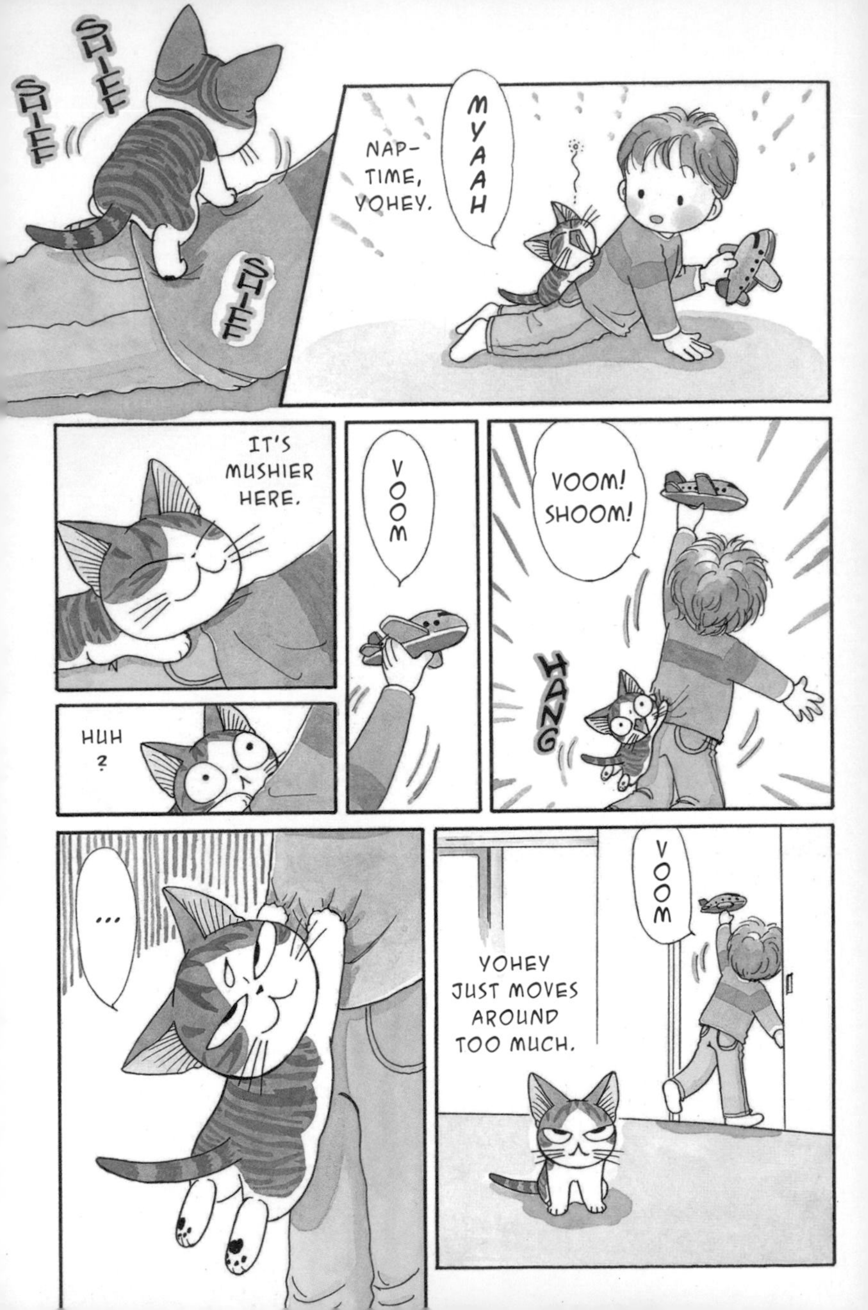
SNIFF
SNIFF
SNIFF
NAP-TIME, YOHEY.
MYAAH
IT'S MUSHIER HERE.
HUH ?
VOOM
VOOM! SHOOM!
HANG
...
VOOM
YOHEY JUST MOVES AROUND TOO MUCH.

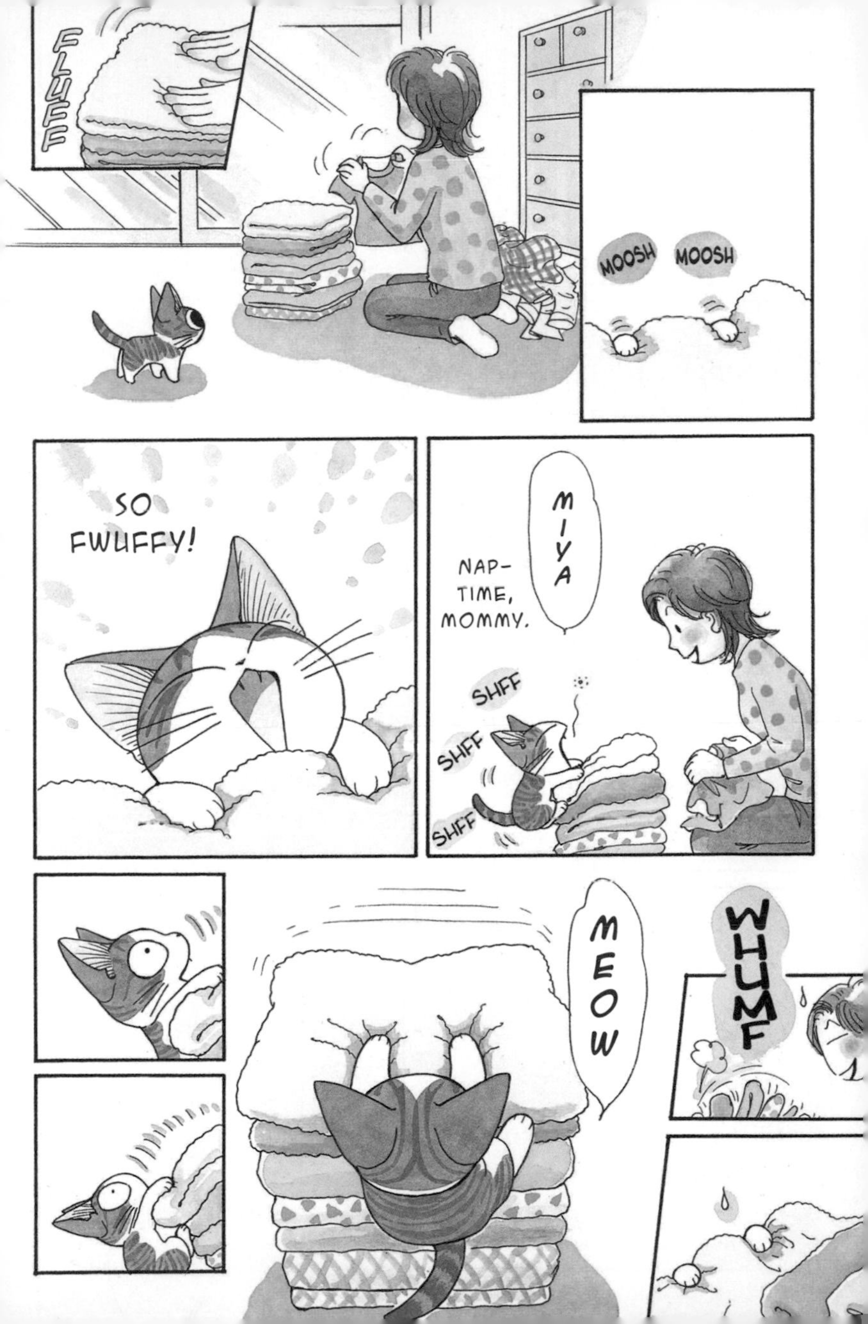
FLUFF
MOOSH
MOOSH
SO FWUFFY!
MIYA
NAP-TIME, MOMMY.
SHFF
SHFF
SHFF
MEOW
WHUMF

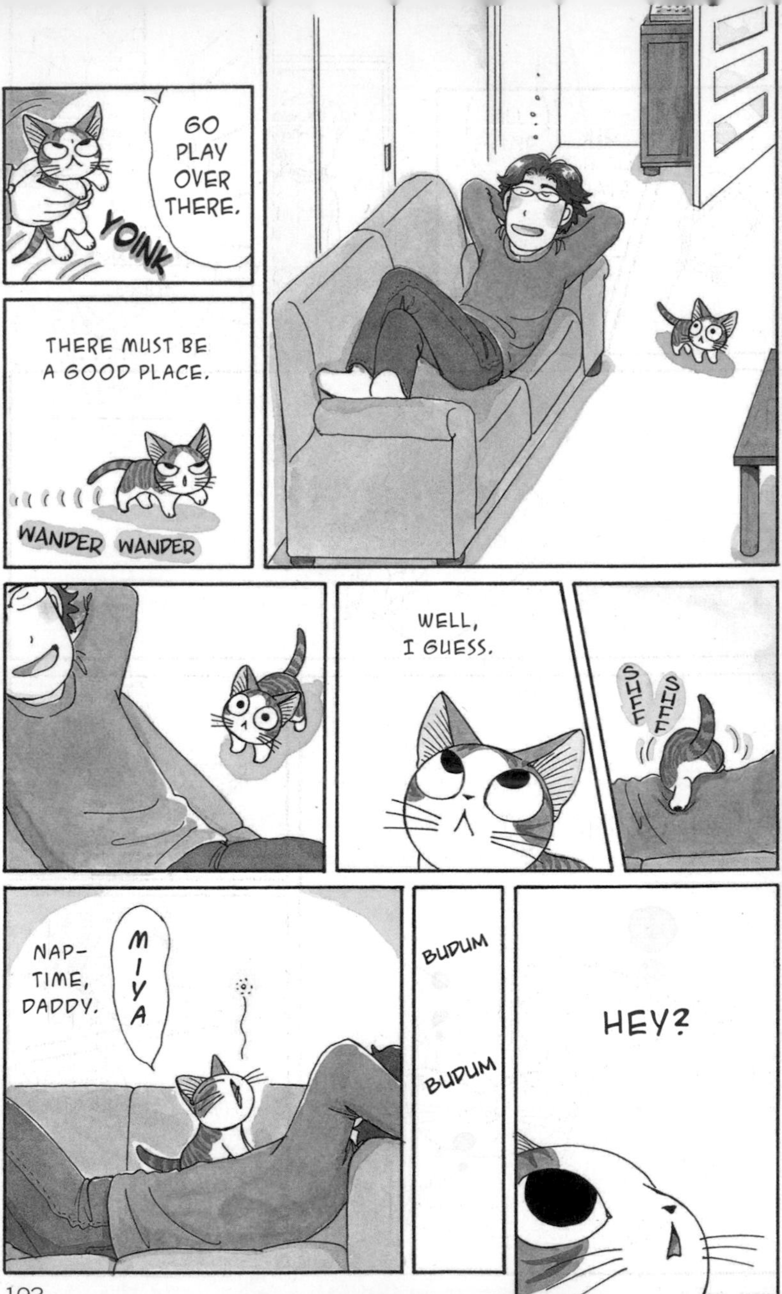
GO PLAY OVER THERE.
YOINK
THERE MUST BE A GOOD PLACE.
WANDER WANDER
WELL, I GUESS.
SHUFF SHUFF
NAP-TIME, DADDY.
MIYA
BUDUM
BUDUM
HEY?

BUDUM
BUDUM
BUDUM
BUDUM

BUDUM
WHAZ-
ZAT?
BUDUM
BUDUM

WHAT
?
BUDUM
BUDUM
BUDUM

BUDUM
BUDUM

I
WONDER.

BUDUM
BUDUM

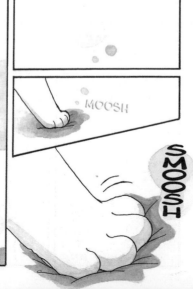

MOOSH

SMOOSH

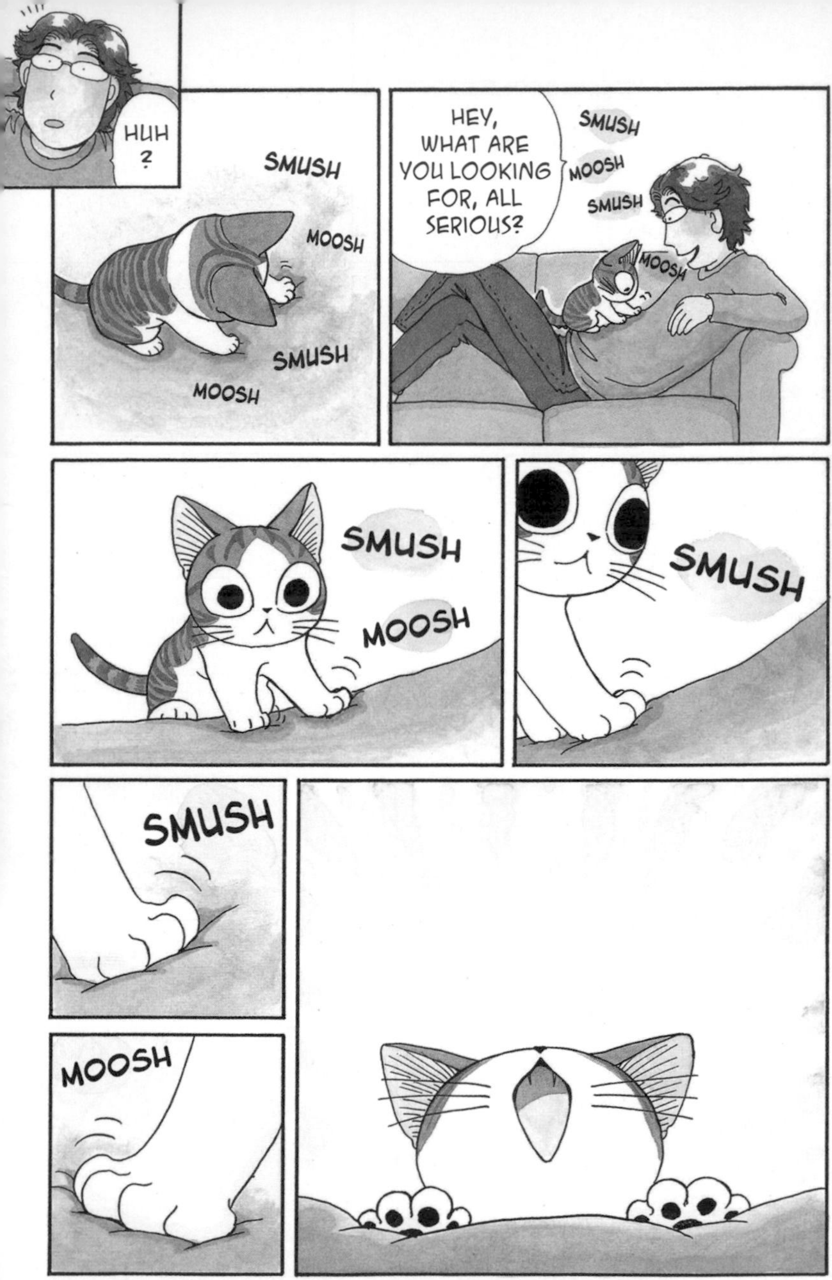
HUH?
SMUSH
MOOSH
SMUSH
MOOSH
HEY, WHAT ARE YOU LOOKING FOR, ALL SERIOUS?
SMUSH
MOOSH
SMUSH
MOOSH
SMUSH
MOOSH
SMUSH
SMUSH
MOOSH

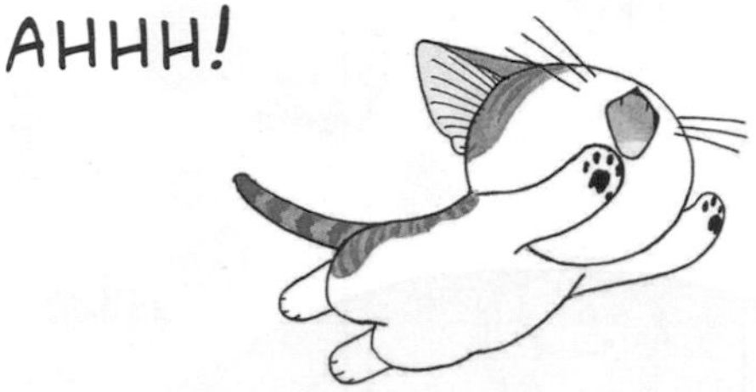
AHHH!

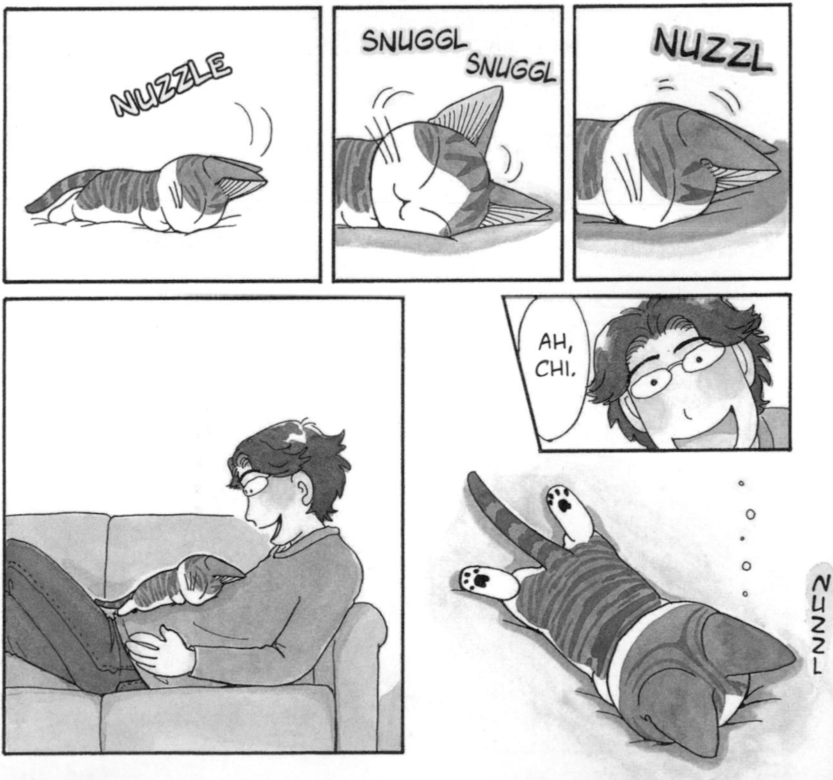
NUZZLE
SNUGGL
SNUGGL
NUZZL
AH, CHI.
NUZZL

SHE JUST DUG IN,

BURIED HER HEAD AND CONKED OUT.

MAKES ME THINKS THAT SHE REALLY LIKES ME, HEH.

HA HA HA

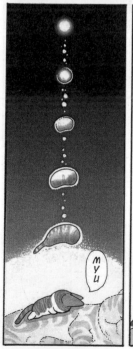

MYU

I WONDER WHAT THIS FEELWING IS?

106

the end

homemade 34: a cat stalks

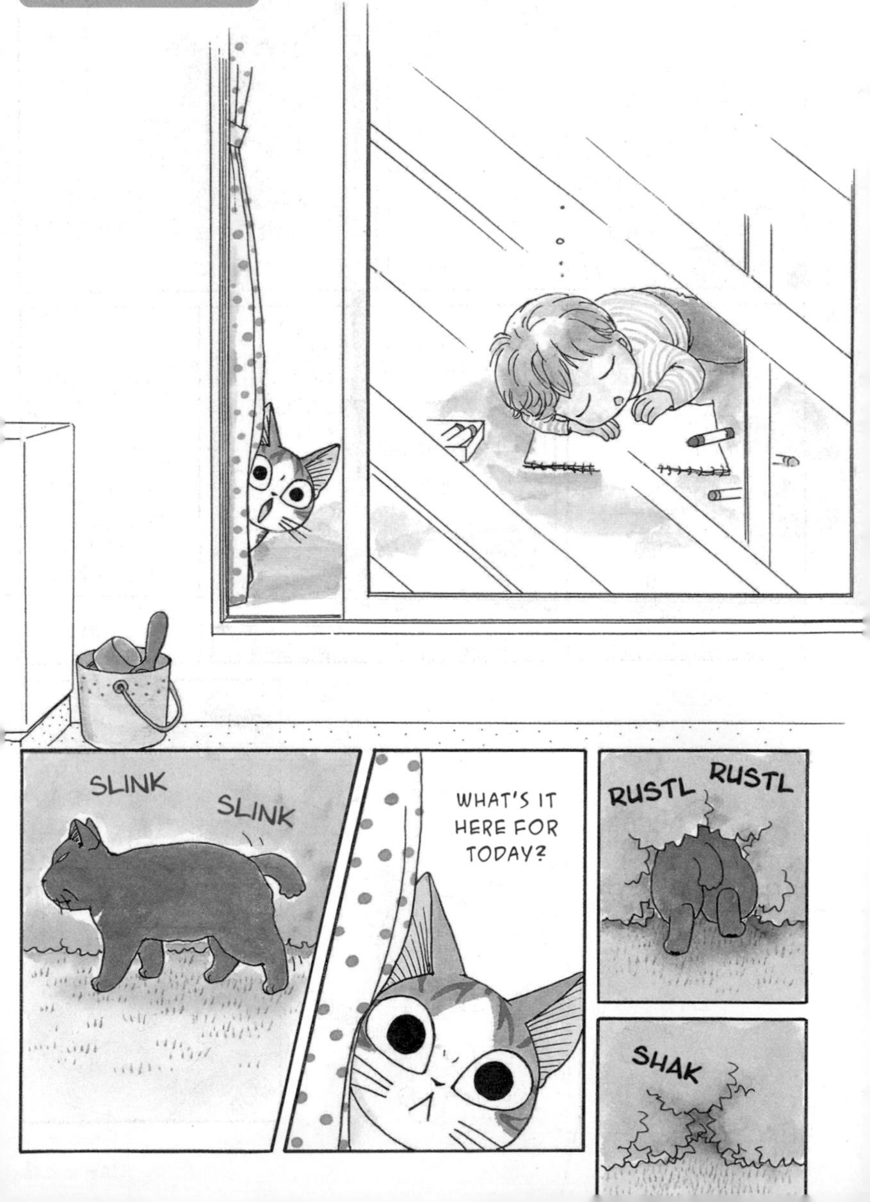
SLINK
SLINK
WHAT'S IT HERE FOR TODAY?
RUSTL
RUSTL
SHAK

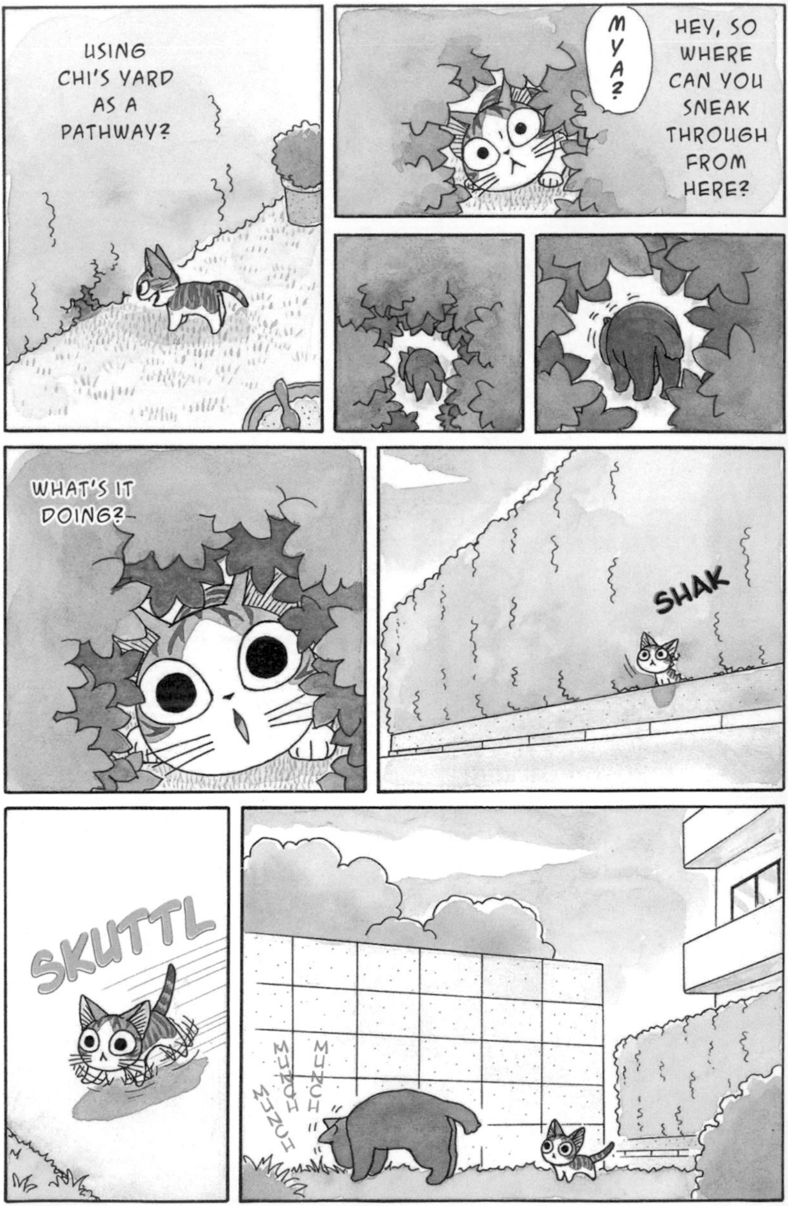
USING CHI'S YARD AS A PATHWAY?
MYA?
HEY, SO WHERE CAN YOU SNEAK THROUGH FROM HERE?
WHAT'S IT DOING?
SHAK
SKUTTL
MUNCH
MUNCH
MUNCH

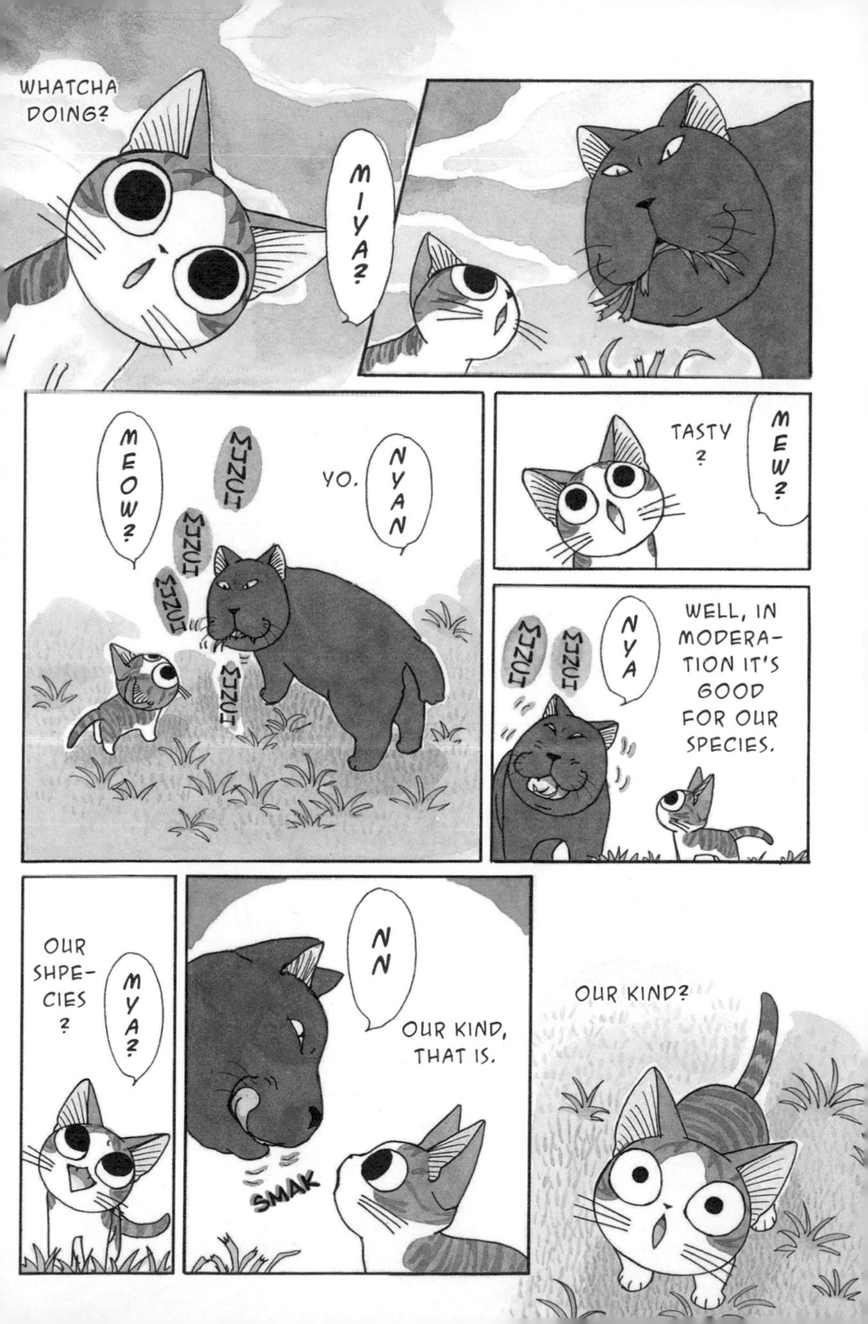
WHATCHA DOING?
MIYA?
MEOW?
MUNCH
MUNCH
MUNCH
MUNCH
YO.
NYAN
TASTY?
MEW?
MUNCH
MUNCH
NYA
WELL, IN MODERATION IT'S GOOD FOR OUR SPECIES.
OUR SHPECIES?
MYA?
NN
OUR KIND, THAT IS.
SMAK
OUR KIND?

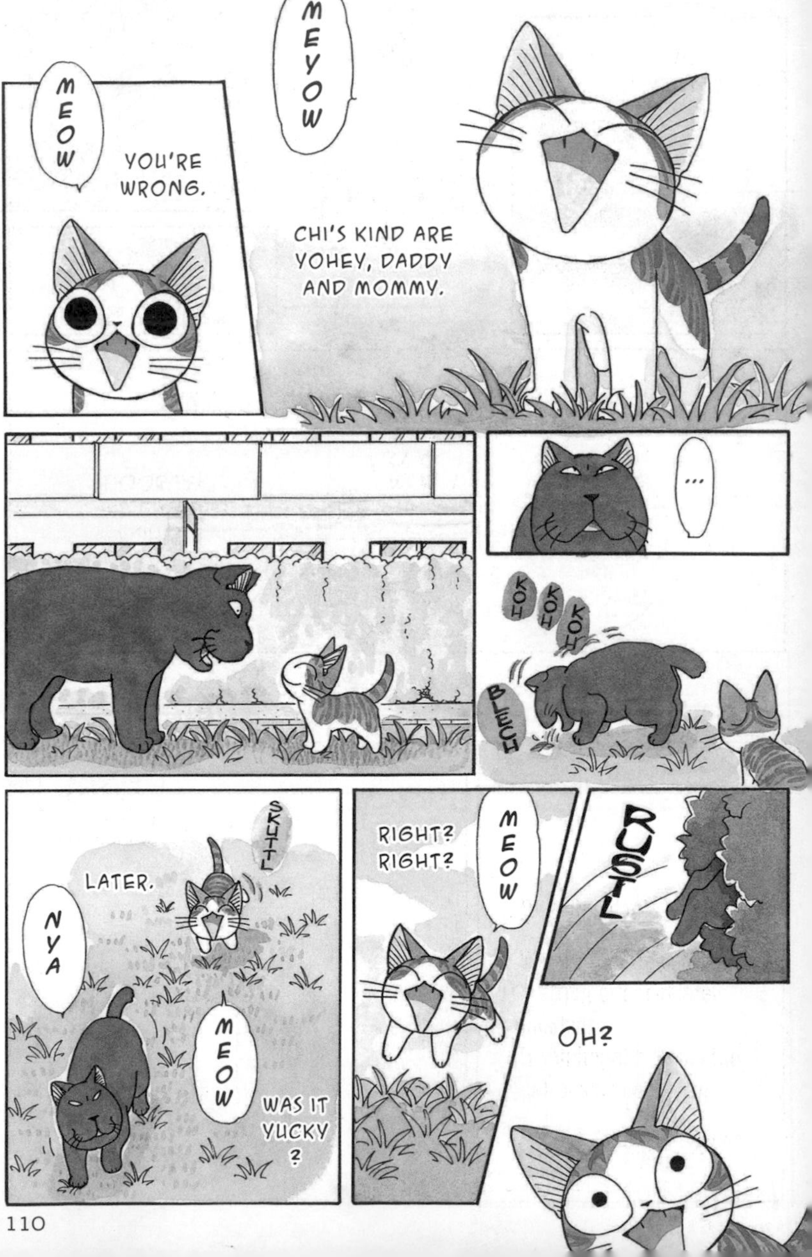
MEOW
YOU'RE WRONG.
MEYOW
CHI'S KIND ARE YOHEY, DADDY AND MOMMY.
...
KOH
KOH
KOH
BLECH
SKUTTL
LATER.
NYA
MEOW
WAS IT YUCKY?
RIGHT? RIGHT?
MEOW
RUSTL
OH?

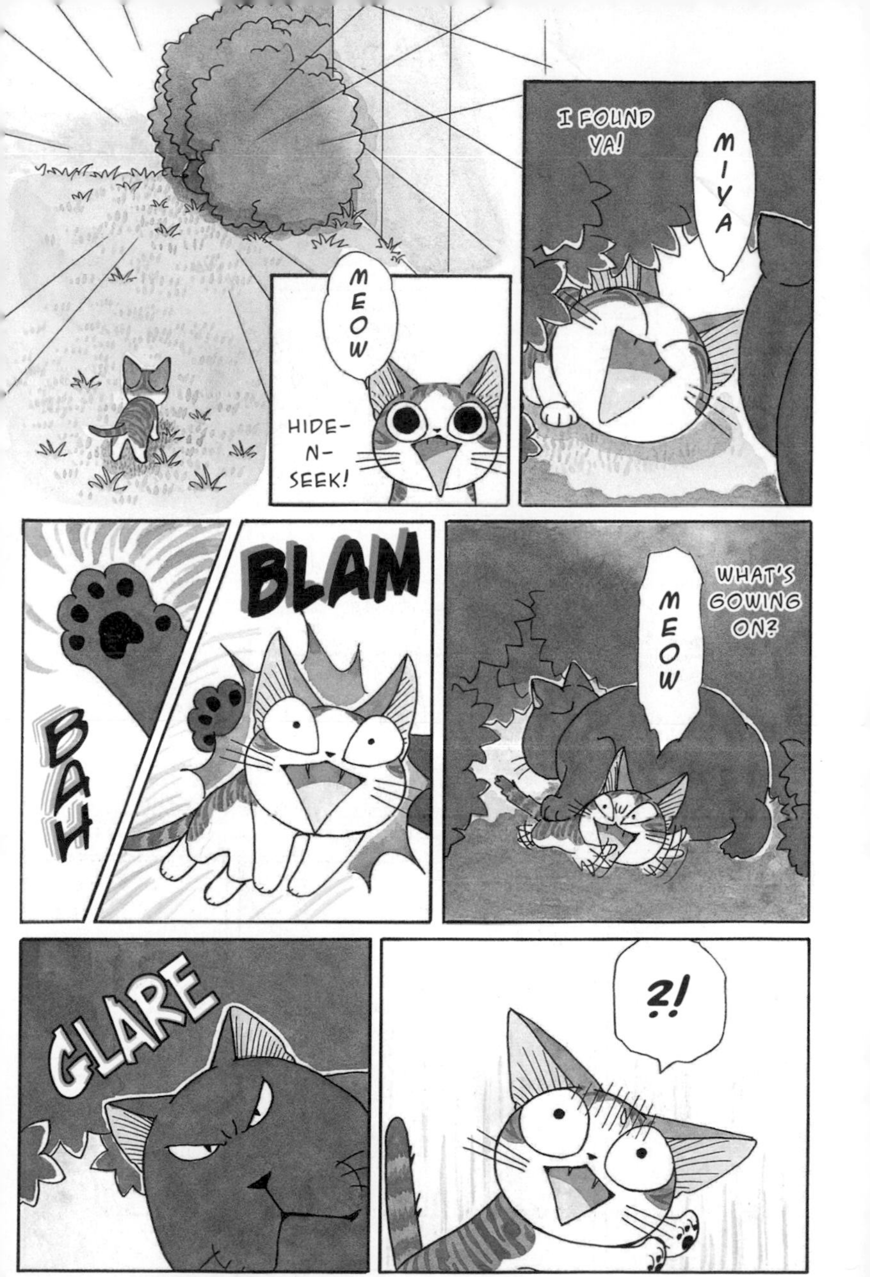
MEOW
HIDE-N-SEEK!
I FOUND YA!
MIYA
BAH
BLAM
WHAT'S GOWING ON?
MEOW
GLARE
?!

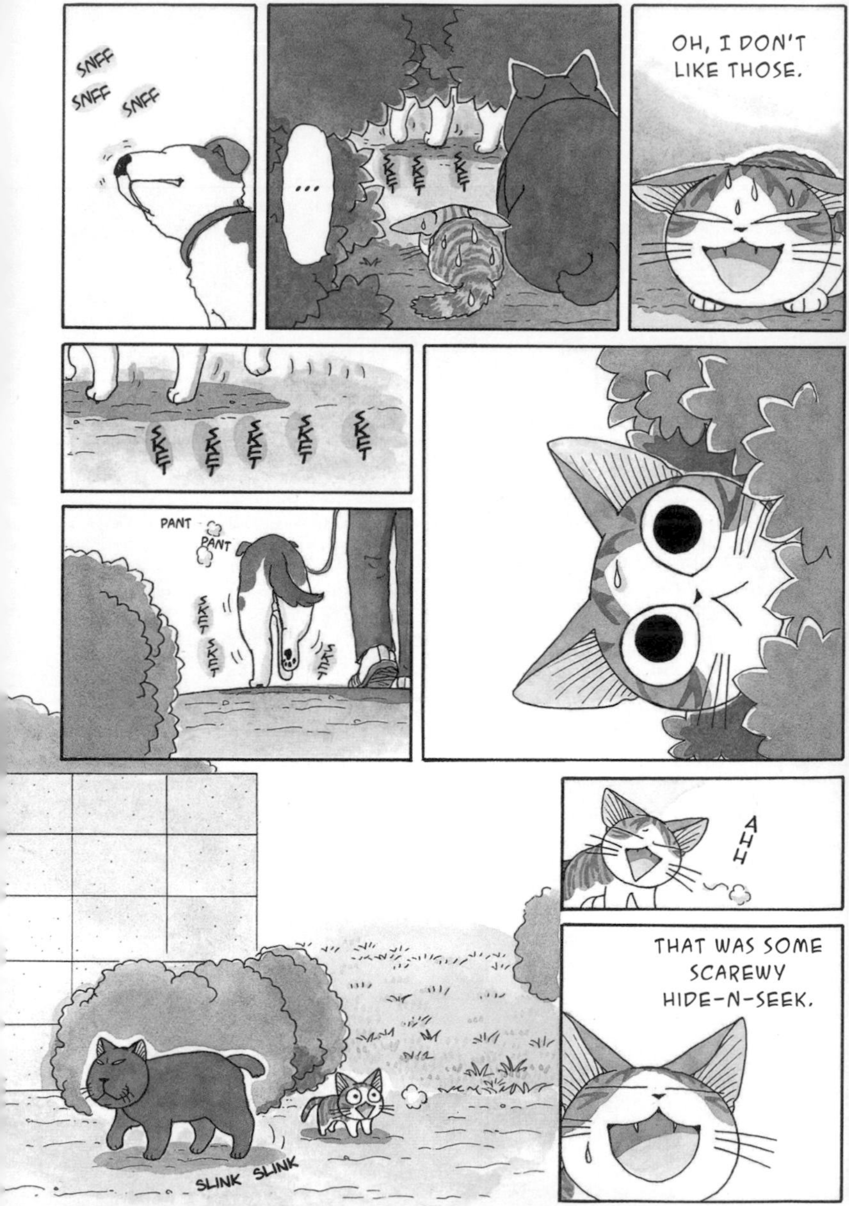
SNFF
SNFF
SNFF
...
SKET
SKET
SKET
OH, I DON'T LIKE THOSE.
SKET
SKET
SKET
SKET
SKET
PANT
PANT
SKET
SKET
SKET
AHH
THAT WAS SOME SCAREWY HIDE-N-SEEK.
SLINK SLINK

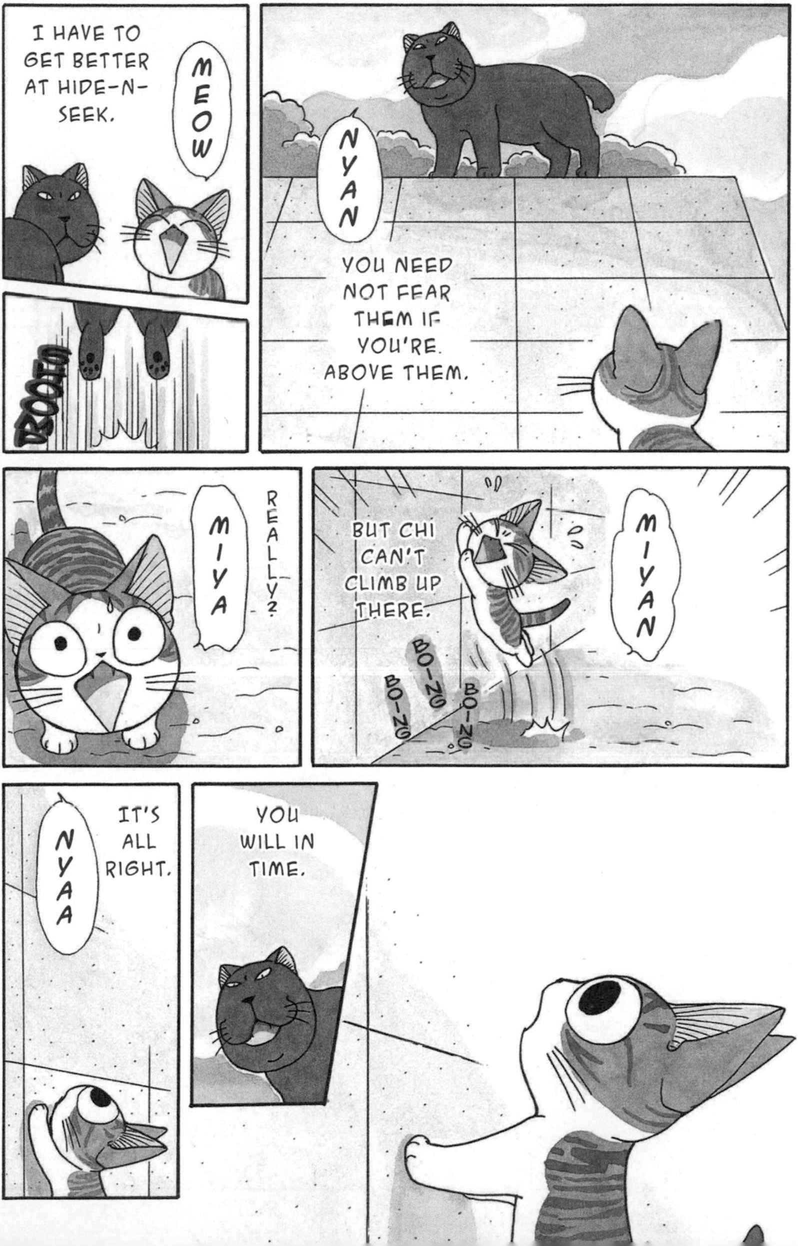
I HAVE TO GET BETTER AT HIDE-N-SEEK.
MEOW
NYAN
YOU NEED NOT FEAR THEM IF YOU'RE ABOVE THEM.
MIYA
REALLY?
BUT CHI CAN'T CLIMB UP THERE.
MIYAN
BOING
BOING
BOING
NYAA
IT'S ALL RIGHT.
YOU WILL IN TIME.

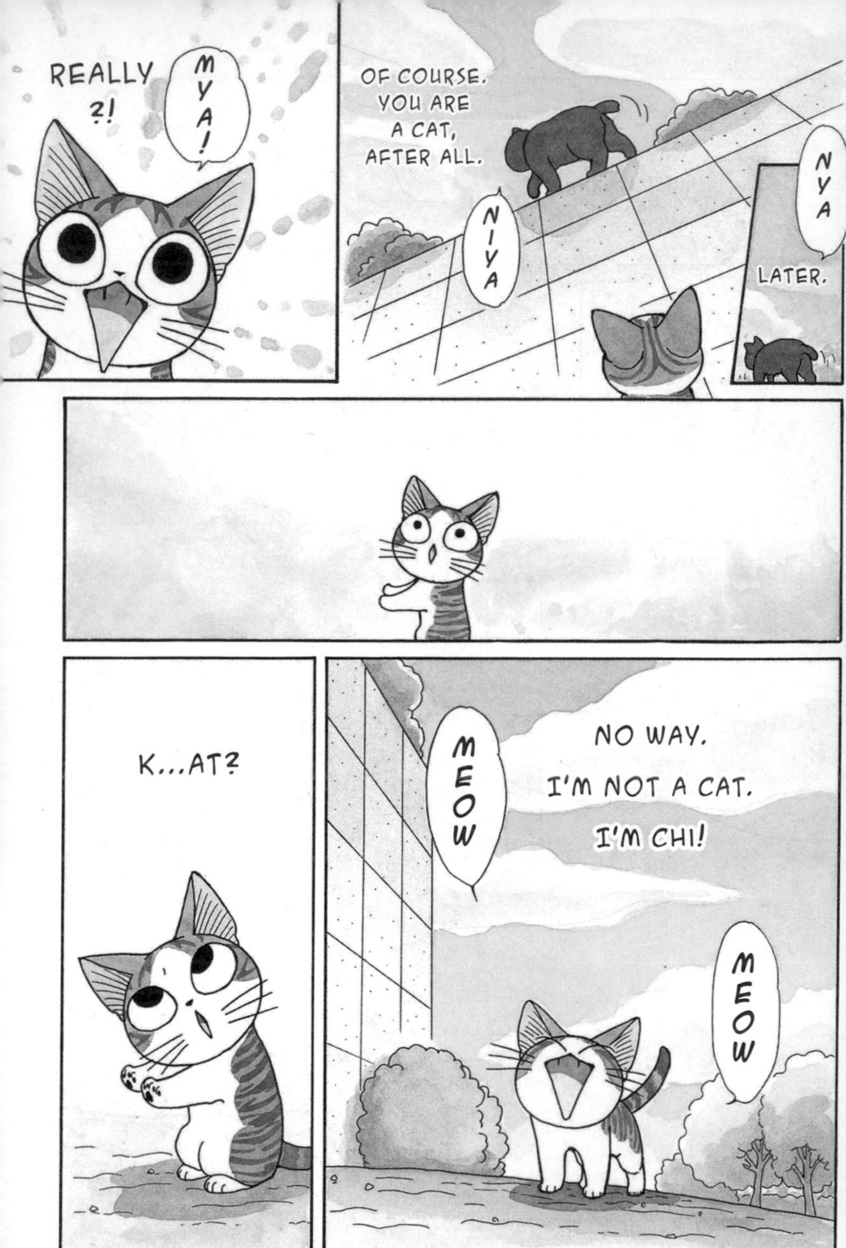

REALLY ?!
MYA!
OF COURSE. YOU ARE A CAT, AFTER ALL.
NIYA
NYA
LATER.
K...AT?
MEOW
NO WAY. I'M NOT A CAT. I'M CHI!
MEOW

the end

homemade 35: a cat goes home

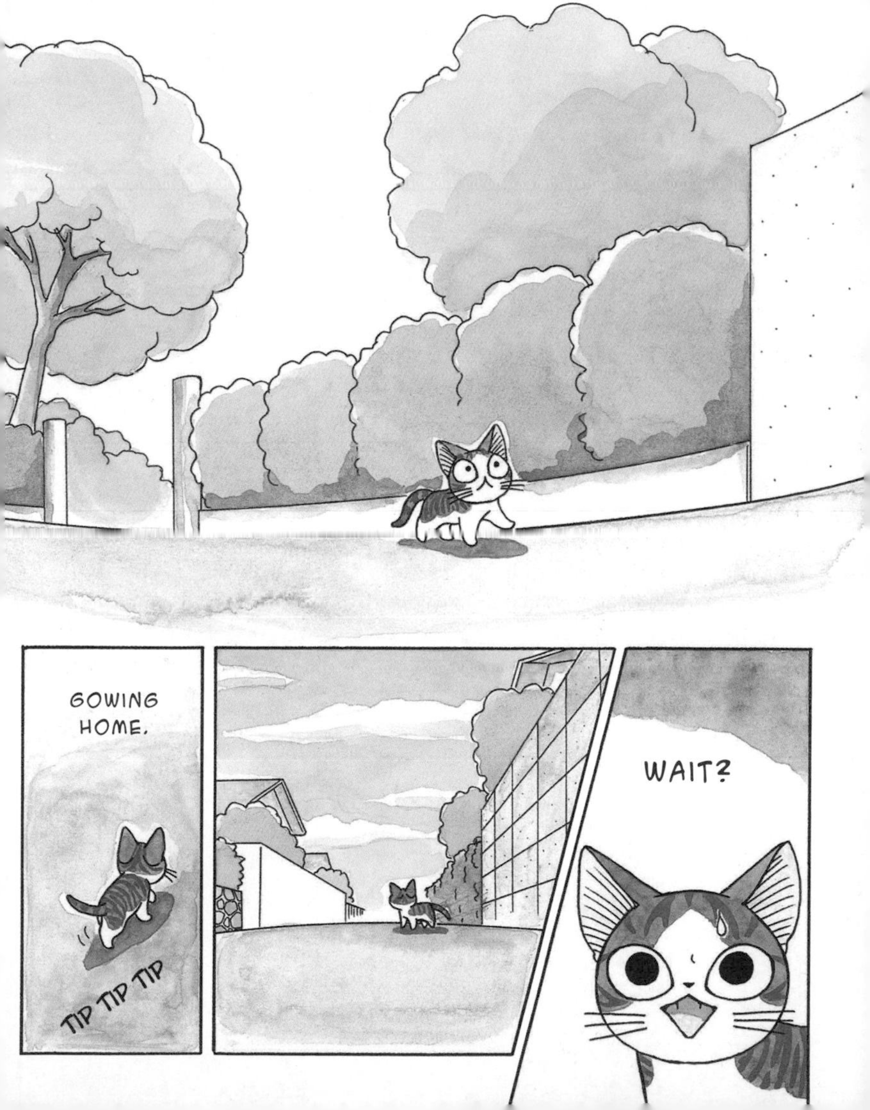
GOWING HOME.
TIP TIP TIP
WAIT?

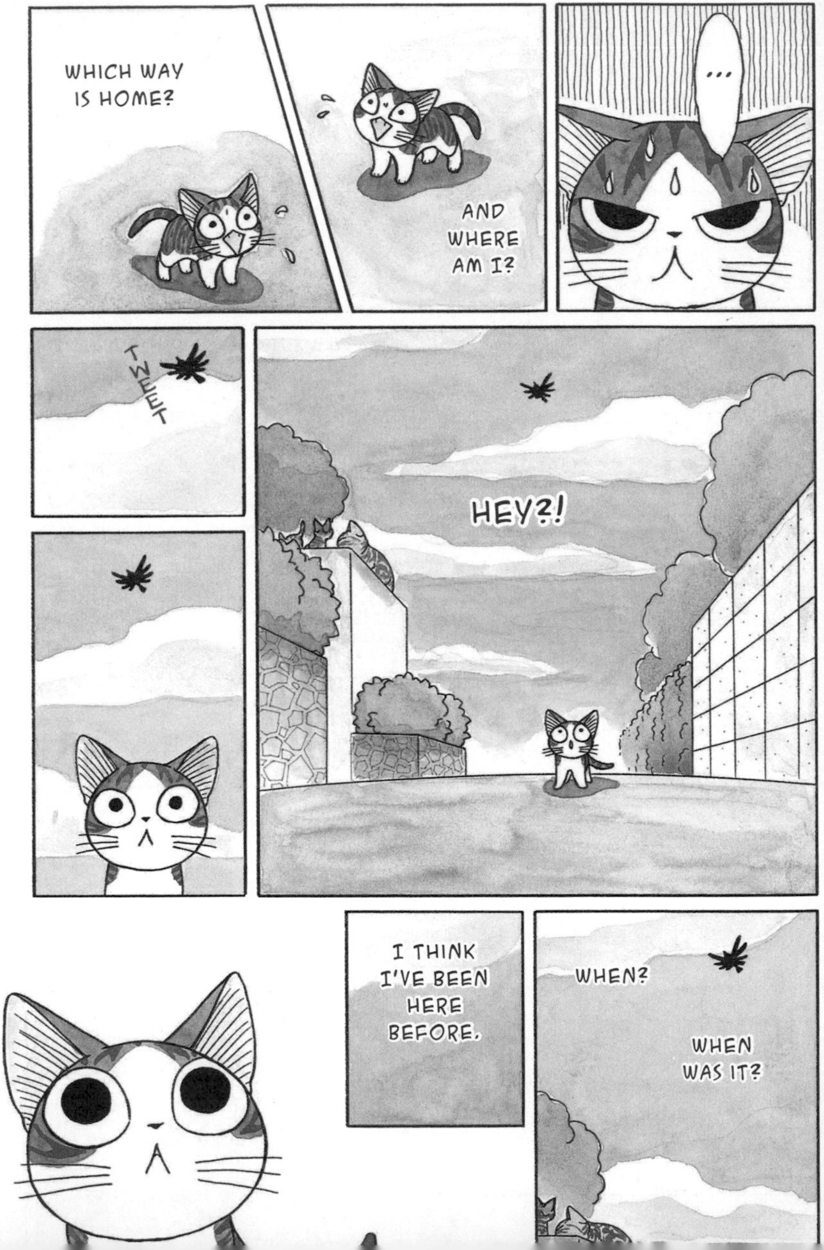
WHICH WAY IS HOME?
AND WHERE AM I?
...
TWEET
HEY?!
I THINK I'VE BEEN HERE BEFORE.
WHEN?
WHEN WAS IT?

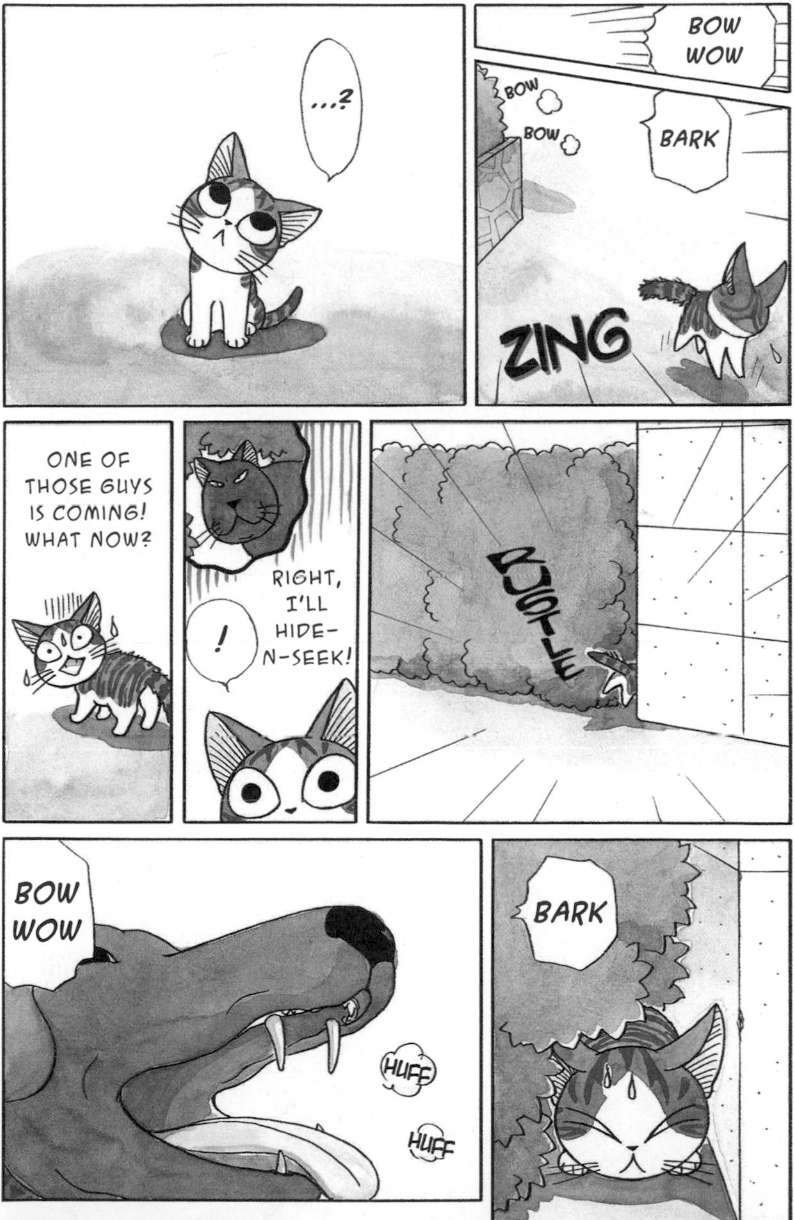
...?
BOW WOW
BOW
BOW
BARK
ZING
ONE OF THOSE GUYS IS COMING! WHAT NOW?
!
RIGHT, I'LL HIDE-N-SEEK!
RUSTLE
BOW WOW
HUFF
HUFF
BARK

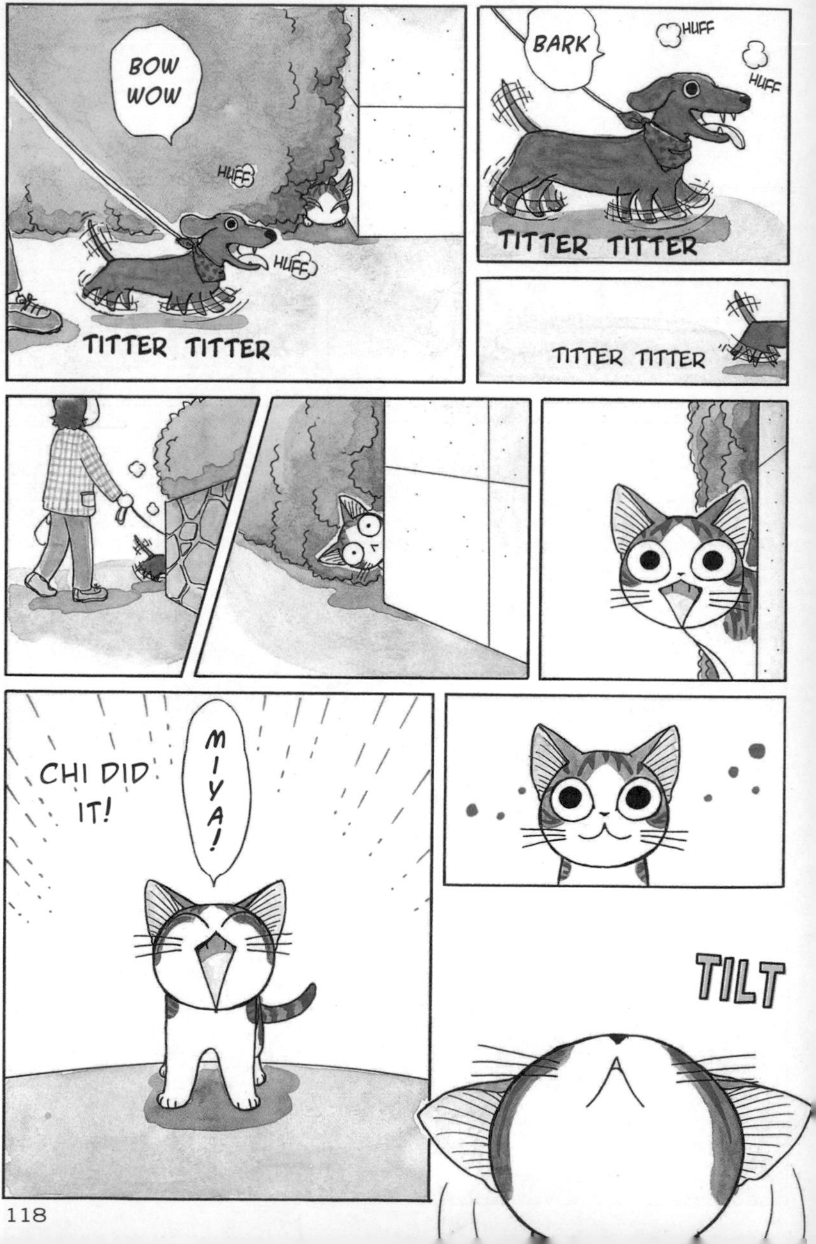
BOW WOW
HUFF
HUFF
TITTER TITTER
BARK
HUFF
HUFF
TITTER TITTER
TITTER TITTER
CHI DID IT!
MIYA!
TILT

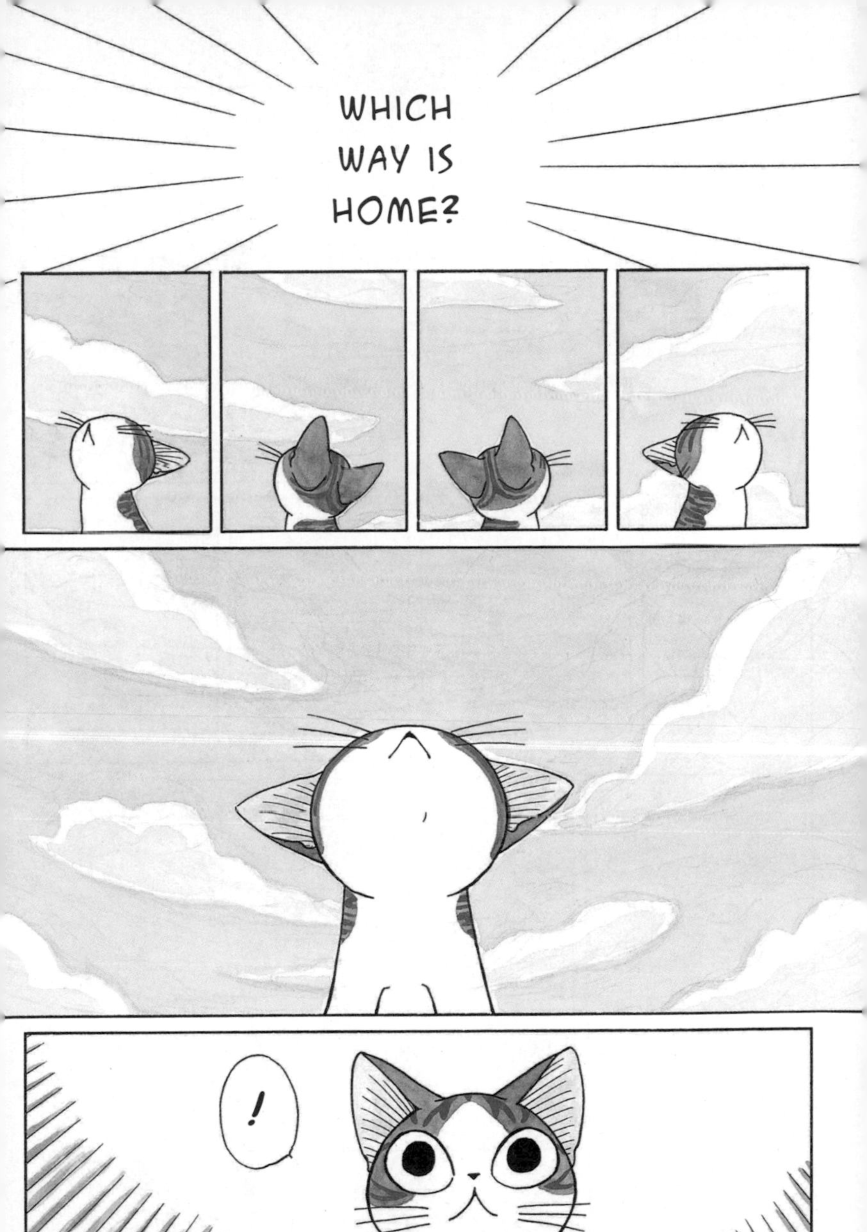
WHICH WAY IS HOME?
!

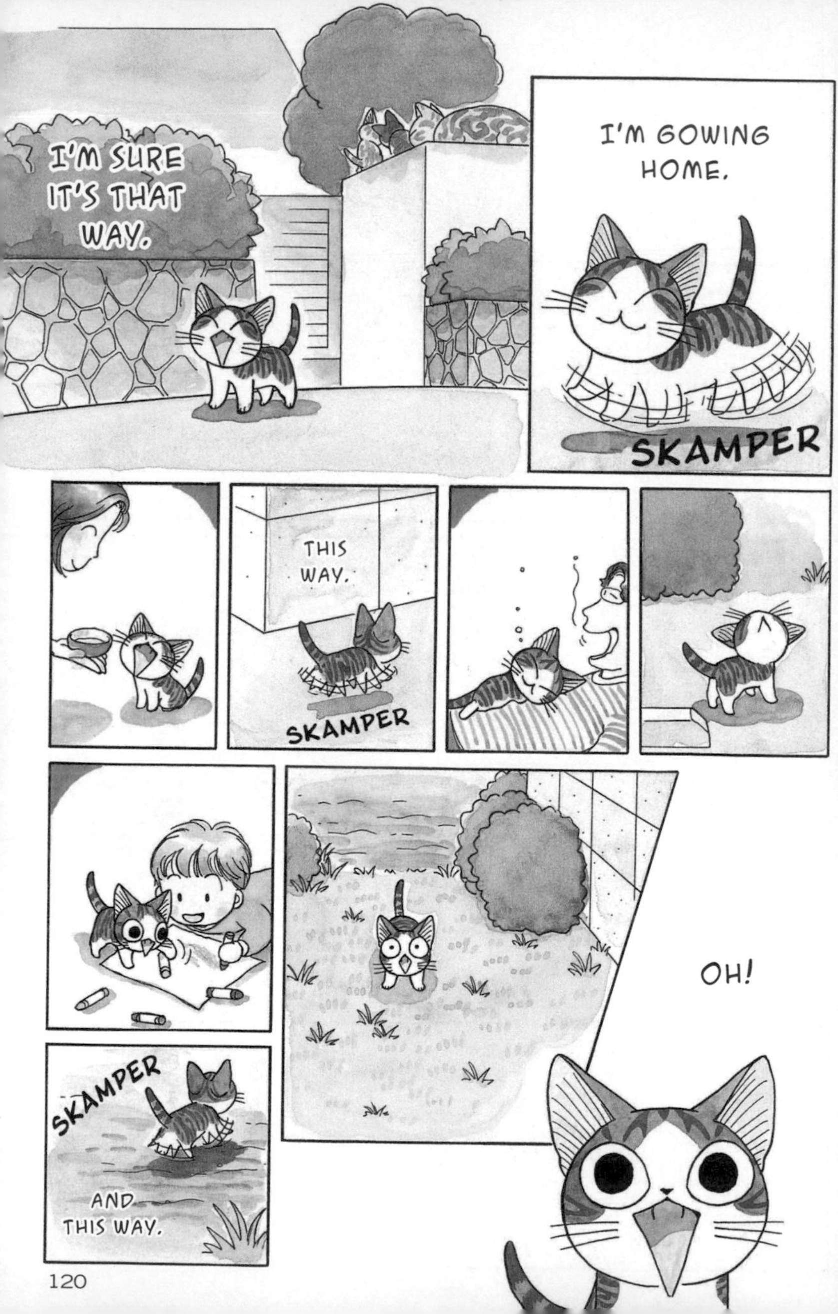
I'M SURE IT'S THAT WAY.
I'M GOWING HOME.
SKAMPER
THIS WAY.
SKAMPER
SKAMPER
AND THIS WAY.
OH!

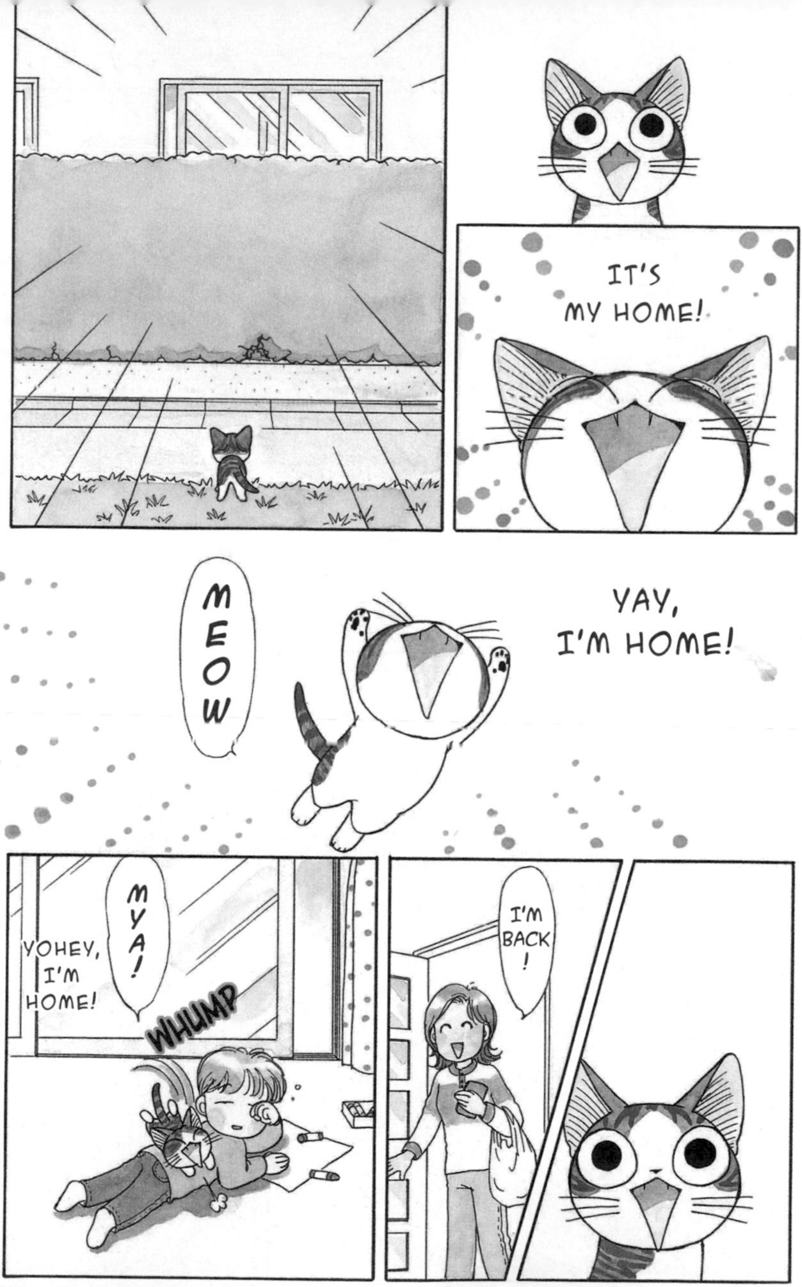
IT'S MY HOME!
MEOW
YAY, I'M HOME!
YOHEY, I'M HOME!
MYA!
WHUMP
I'M BACK!

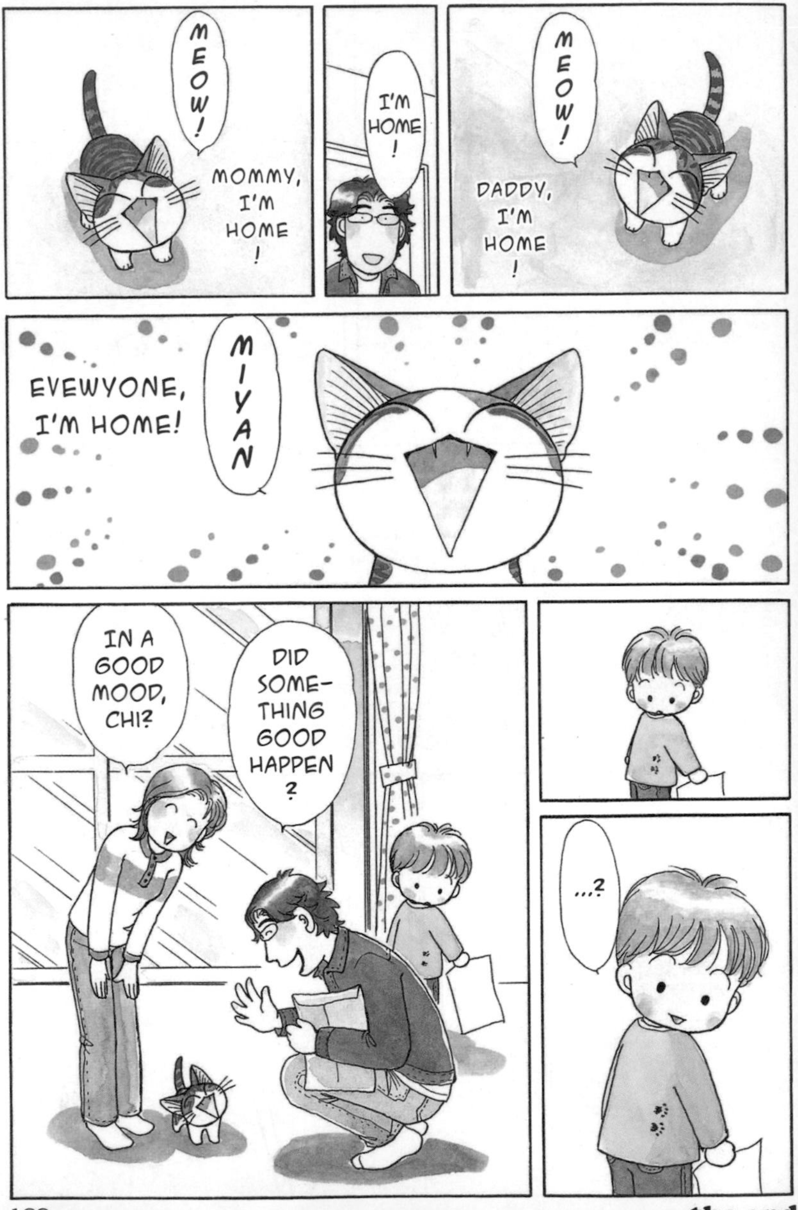
MEOW!
MOMMY, I'M HOME!
I'M HOME!
MEOW!
DADDY, I'M HOME!
EVEWYONE, I'M HOME!
MIYAN
IN A GOOD MOOD, CHI?
DID SOMETHING GOOD HAPPEN?
...?

the end

homemade 36: a cat resists

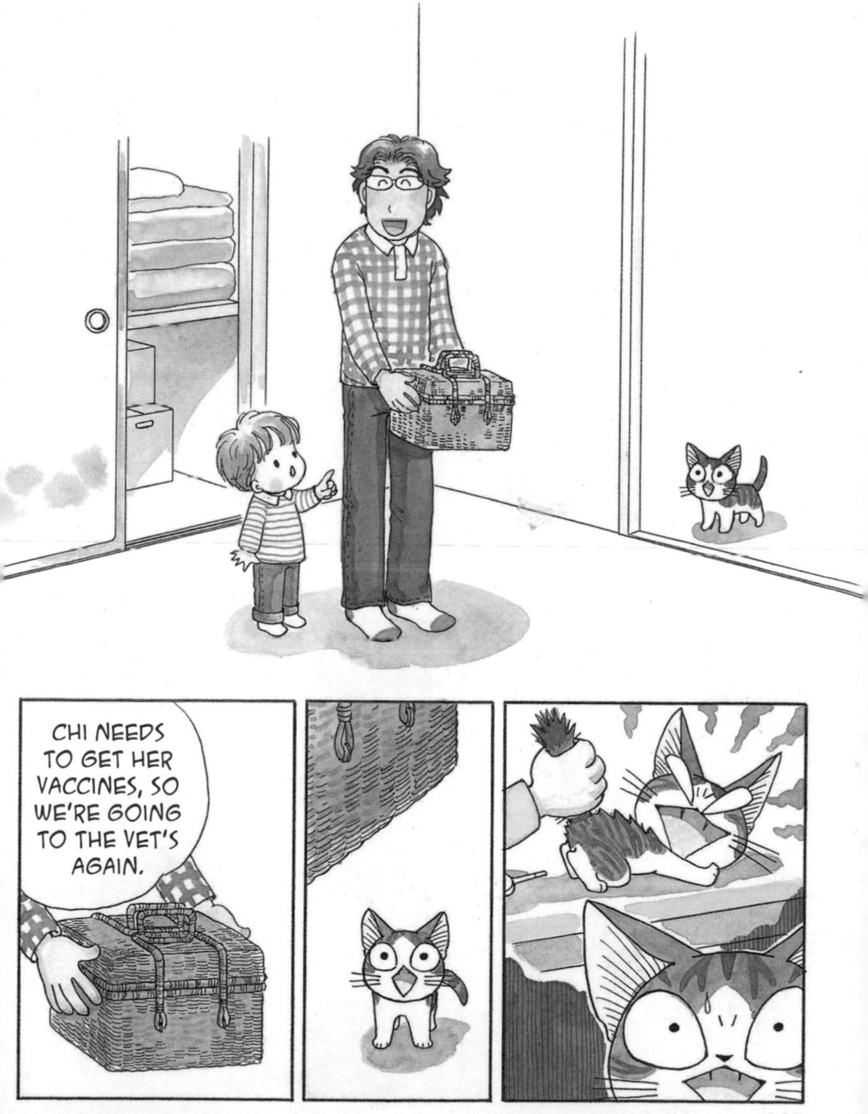
CHI NEEDS TO GET HER VACCINES, SO WE'RE GOING TO THE VET'S AGAIN.

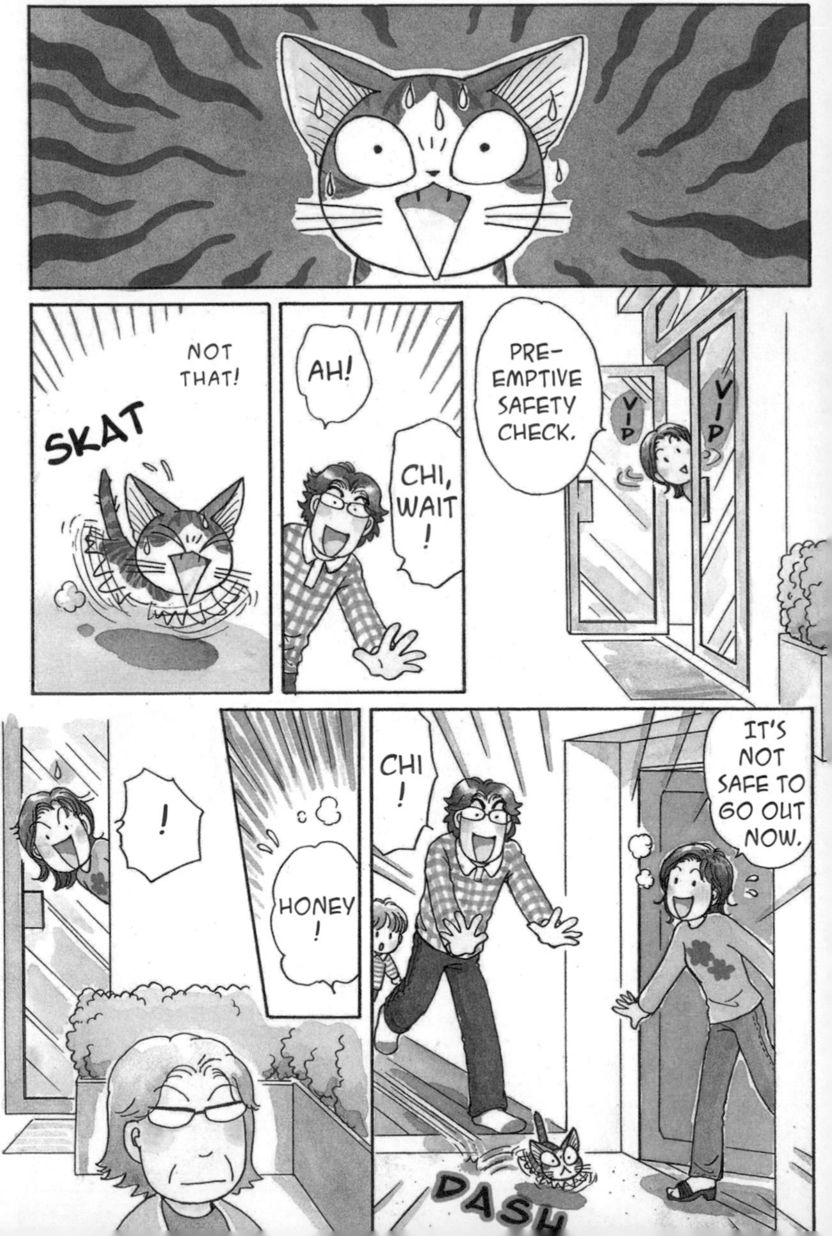
NOT THAT!
SKAT
AH!
CHI, WAIT!
PRE-EMPTIVE SAFETY CHECK.
VIP
VIP
!
HONEY!
CHI!
IT'S NOT SAFE TO GO OUT NOW.
DASH

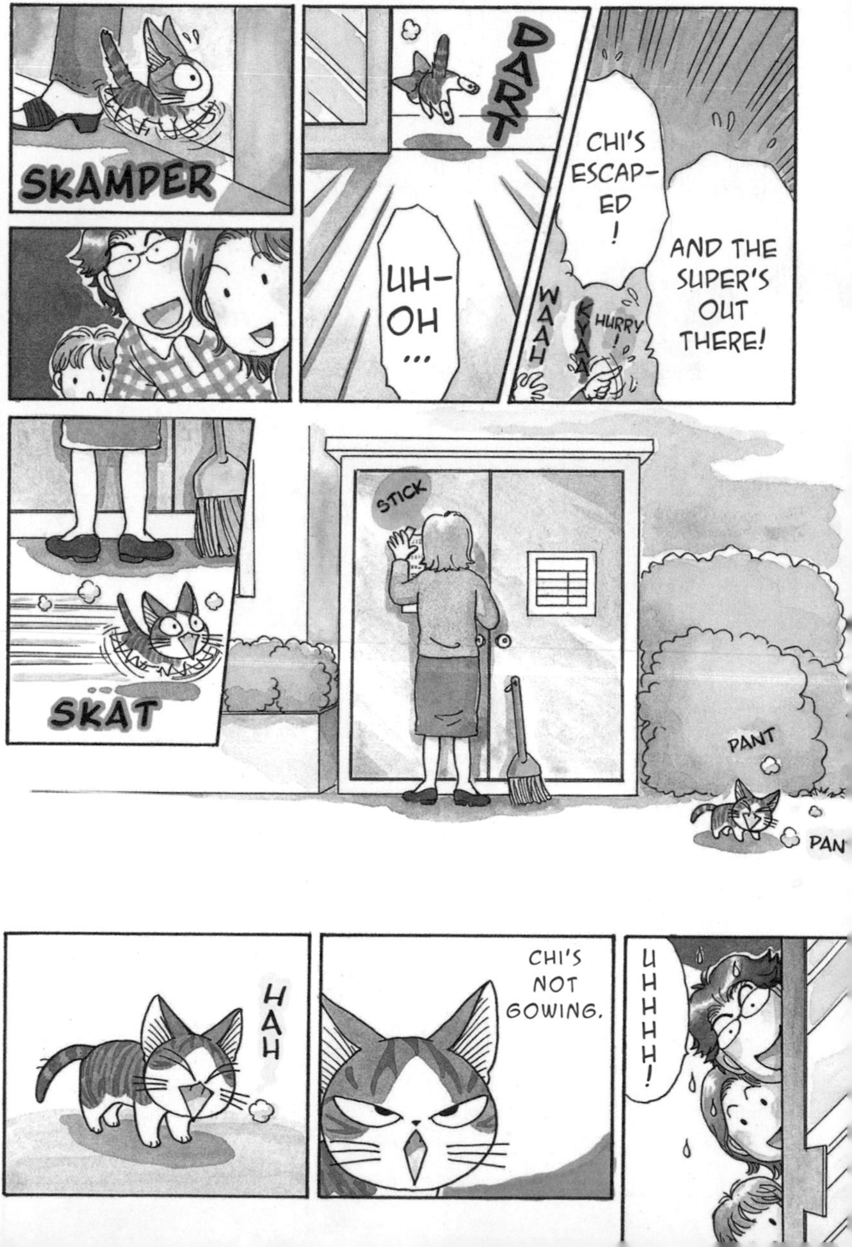
SKAMPER
DART
UH-OH ...
CHI'S ESCAPED!
WAAH
KYAA
HURRY!
AND THE SUPER'S OUT THERE!
SKAT
STICK
PANT
PAN
HAH
CHI'S NOT GOWING.
UHHHHH!

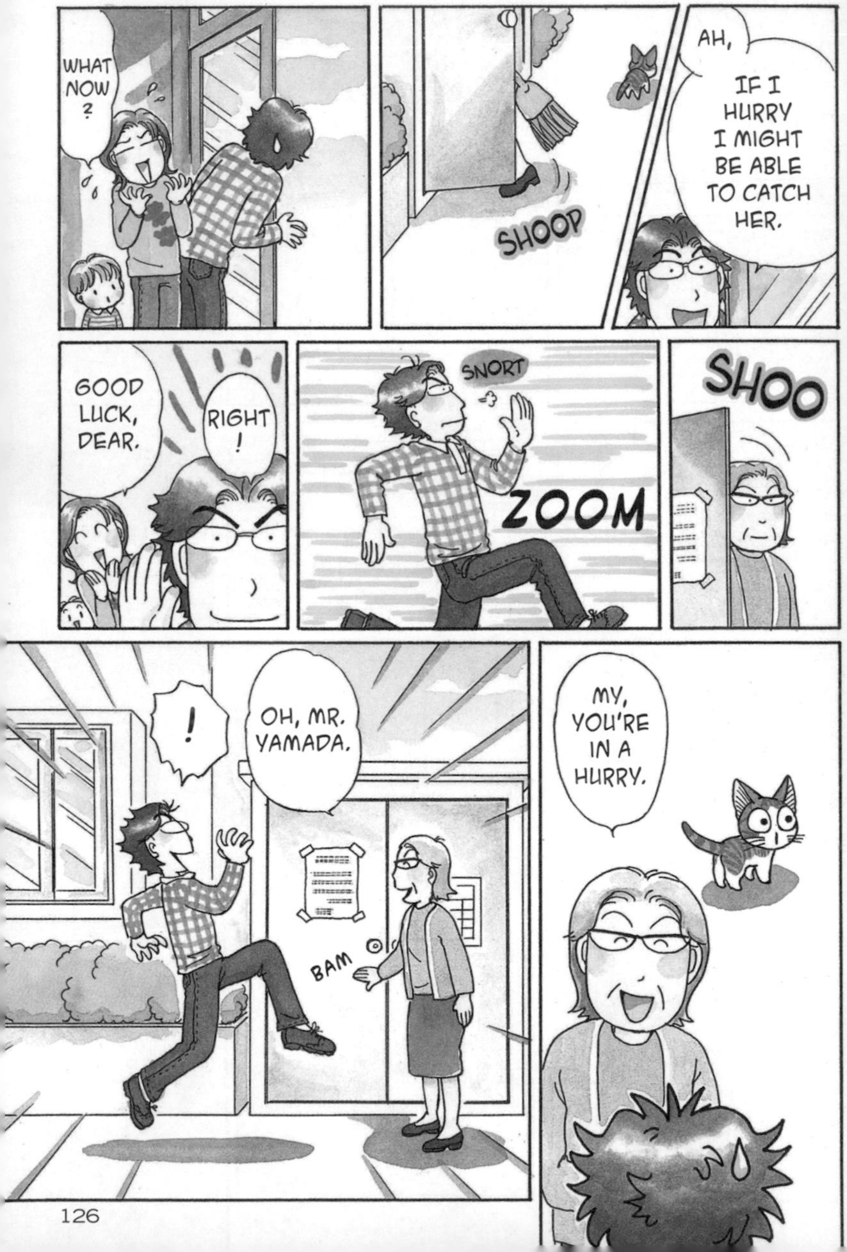
WHAT NOW ?
SHOOP
AH,
IF I HURRY I MIGHT BE ABLE TO CATCH HER.
GOOD LUCK, DEAR.
RIGHT !
SNORT
ZOOM
SHOO
!
OH, MR. YAMADA.
BAM
MY, YOU'RE IN A HURRY.

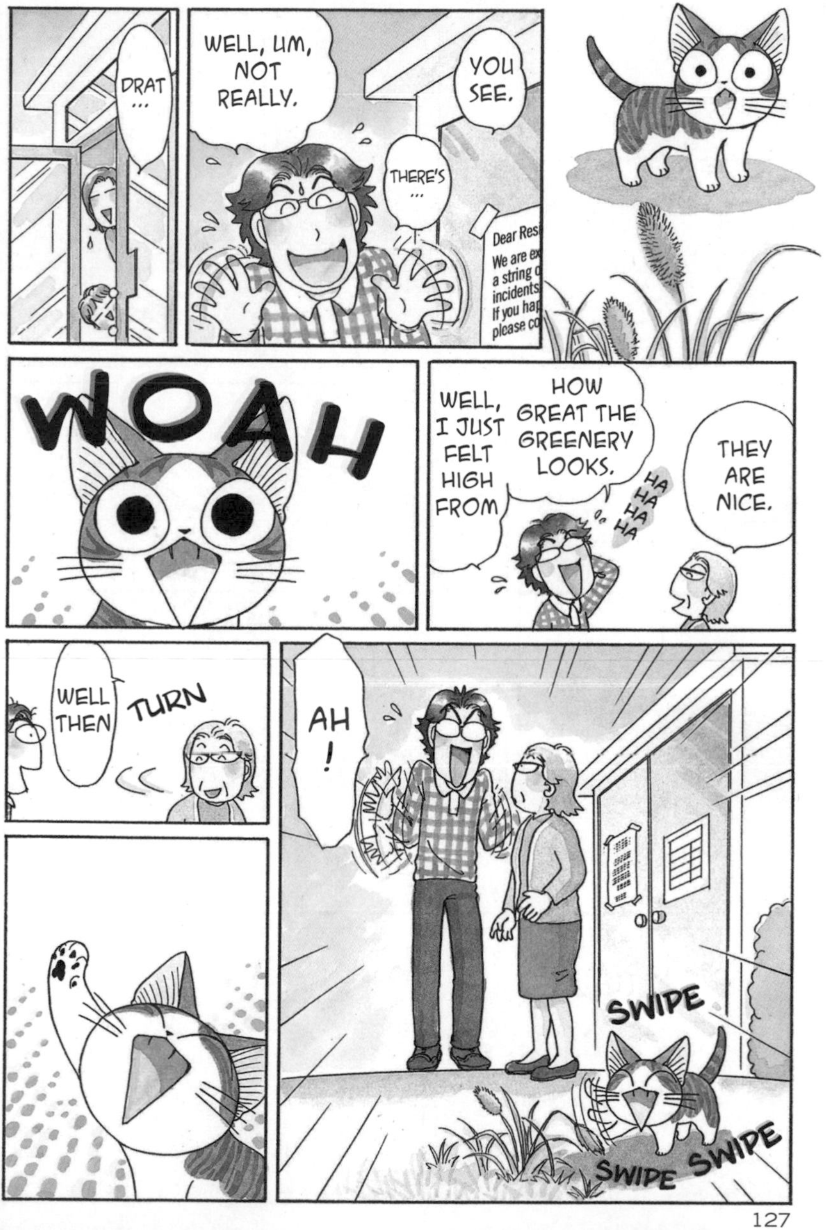
DRAT ...
WELL, UM, NOT REALLY.
YOU SEE.
THERE'S ...
Dear Resi
We are ex
a string o
incidents
If you hap
please co
WOAH
WELL, I JUST FELT HIGH FROM
HOW GREAT THE GREENERY LOOKS.
HA HA HA HA
THEY ARE NICE.
WELL THEN
TURN
AH!
SWIPE
SWIPE SWIPE

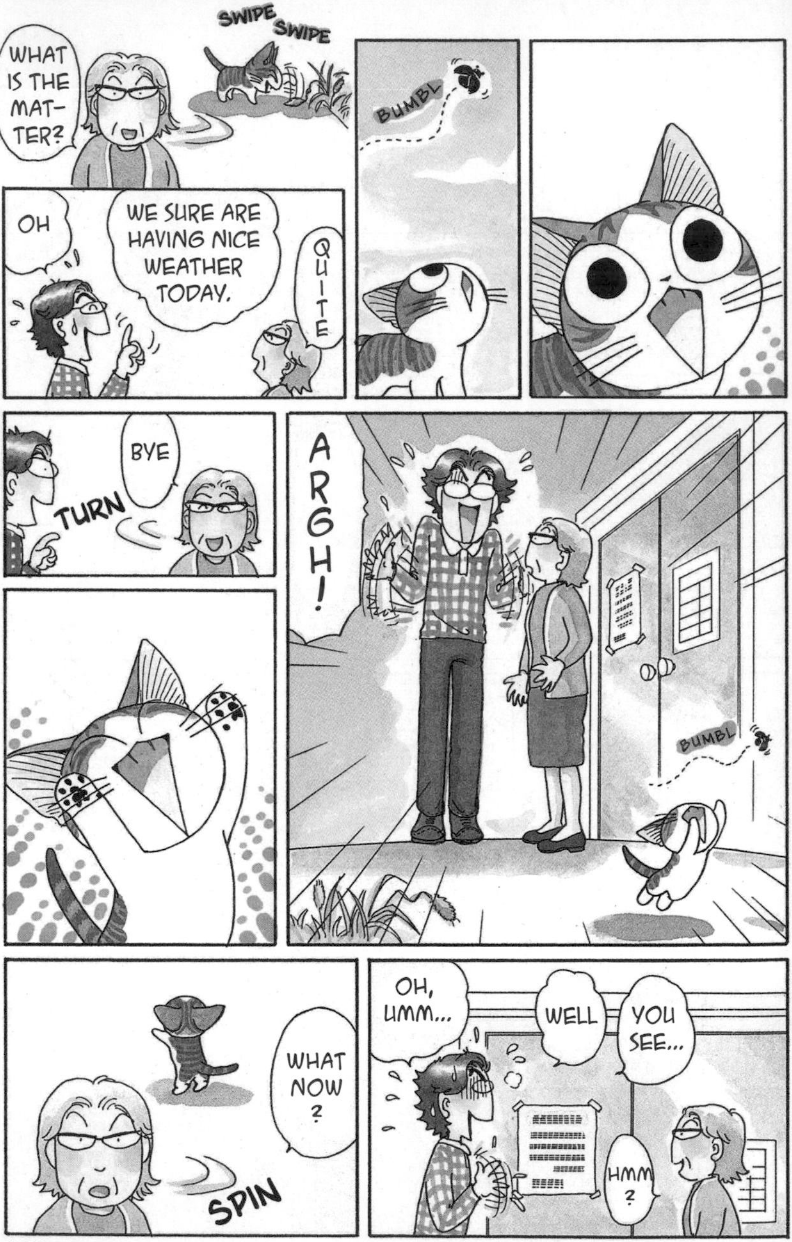
SWIPE SWIPE
WHAT IS THE MAT-TER?
OH
WE SURE ARE HAVING NICE WEATHER TODAY.
QUITE
BUMBL
BYE
TURN
ARGH!
BUMBL
WHAT NOW?
SPIN
OH, UMM...
WELL
YOU SEE...
HMM?

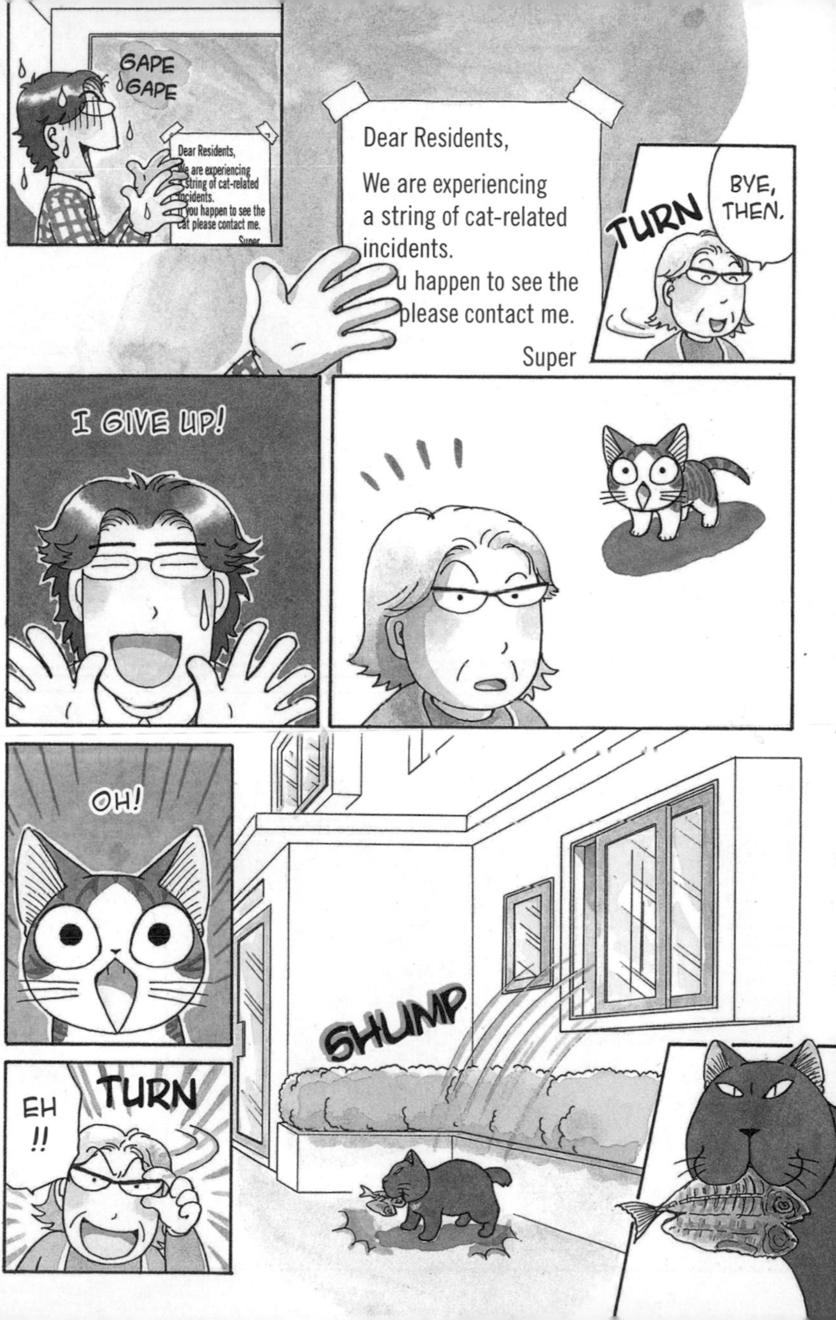

GAPE GAPE
Dear Residents,
e are experiencing
string of cat-related
cidents.
you happen to see the
at please contact me.
Dear Residents,
We are experiencing
a string of cat-related
incidents.
u happen to see the
please contact me.
Super
TURN
BYE, THEN.
I GIVE UP!
OH!
EH !!
TURN
SHUMP

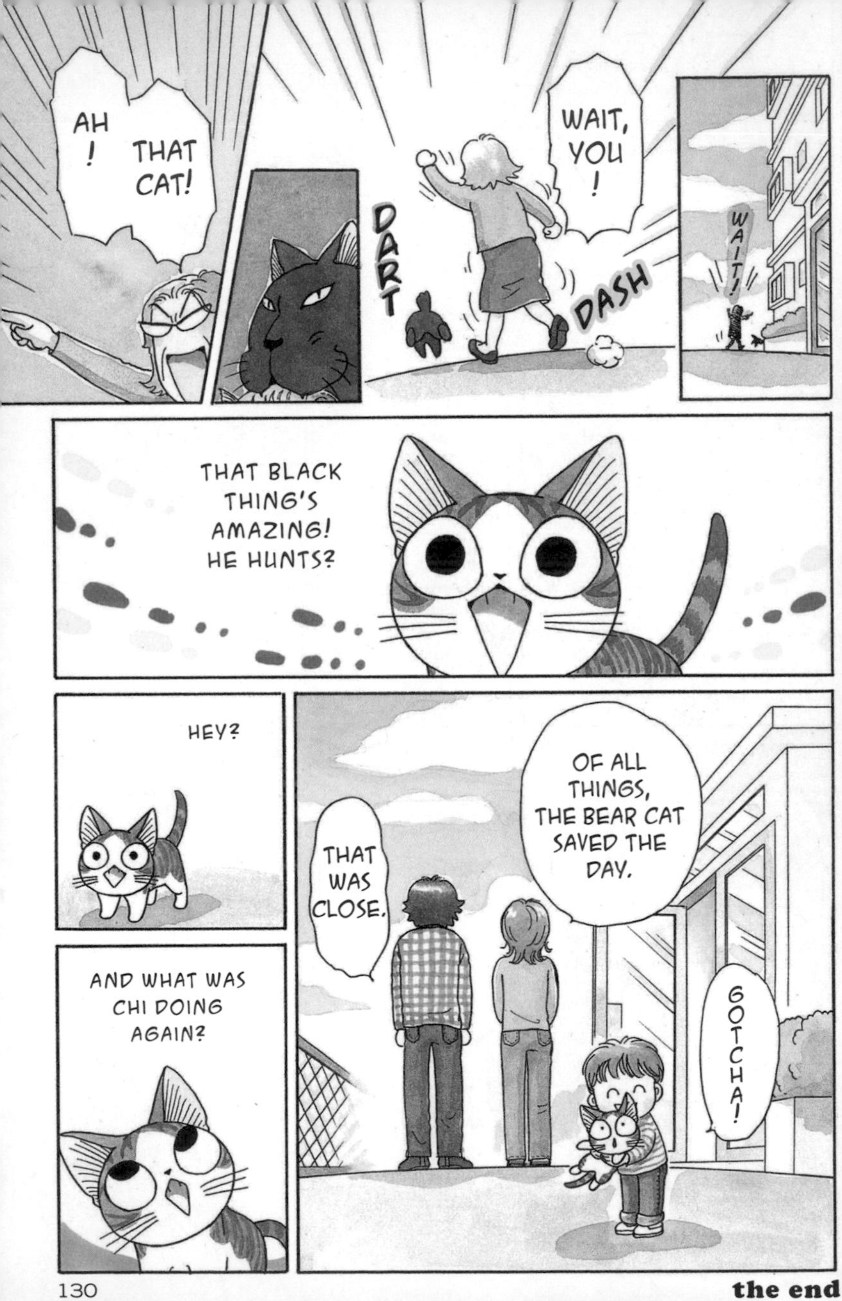
AH! THAT CAT!
WAIT, YOU!
DART
DASH
WAIT!
THAT BLACK THING'S AMAZING! HE HUNTS?
HEY?
AND WHAT WAS CHI DOING AGAIN?
THAT WAS CLOSE.
OF ALL THINGS, THE BEAR CAT SAVED THE DAY.
GOTCHA!

the end

homemade 37: a cat is defiant

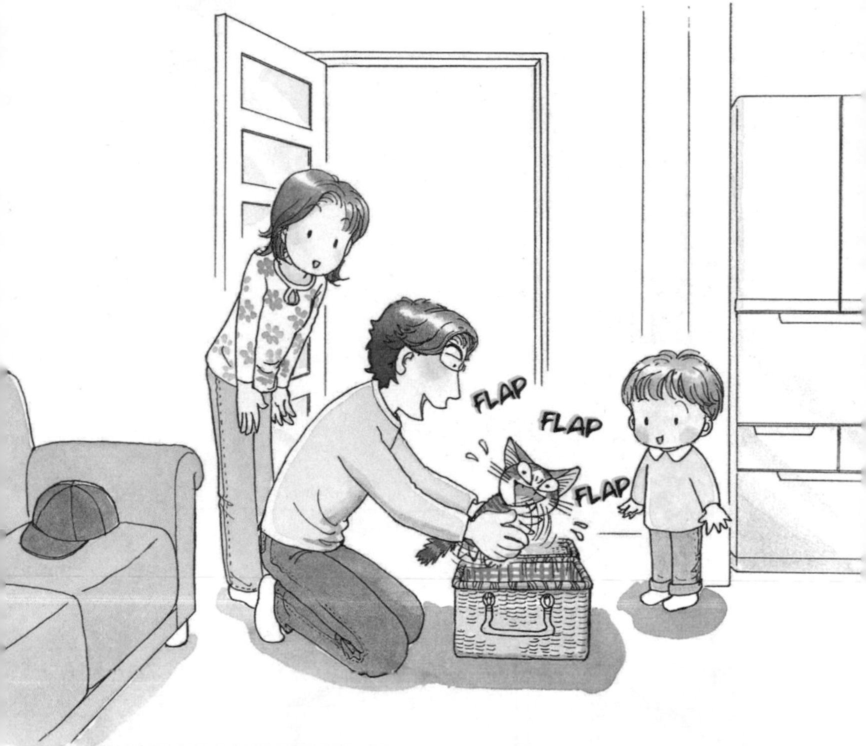
FLAP
FLAP
FLAP

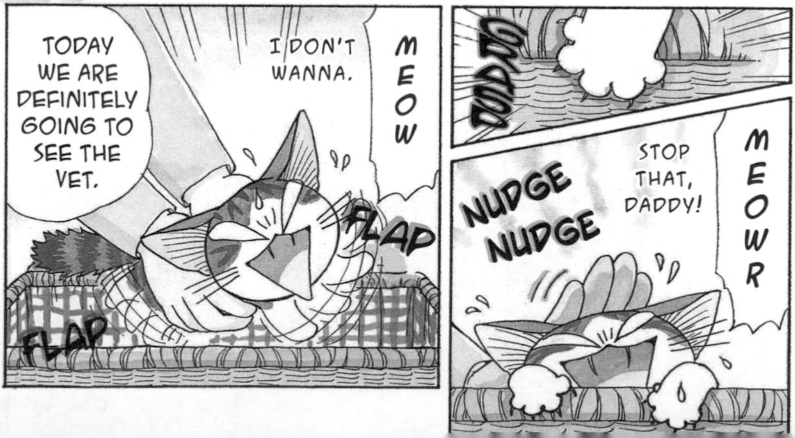
TODAY WE ARE DEFINITELY GOING TO SEE THE VET.
I DON'T WANNA.
MEOW
FLAP
FLAP
NUDGE NUDGE
STOP THAT, DADDY!
MEOWR

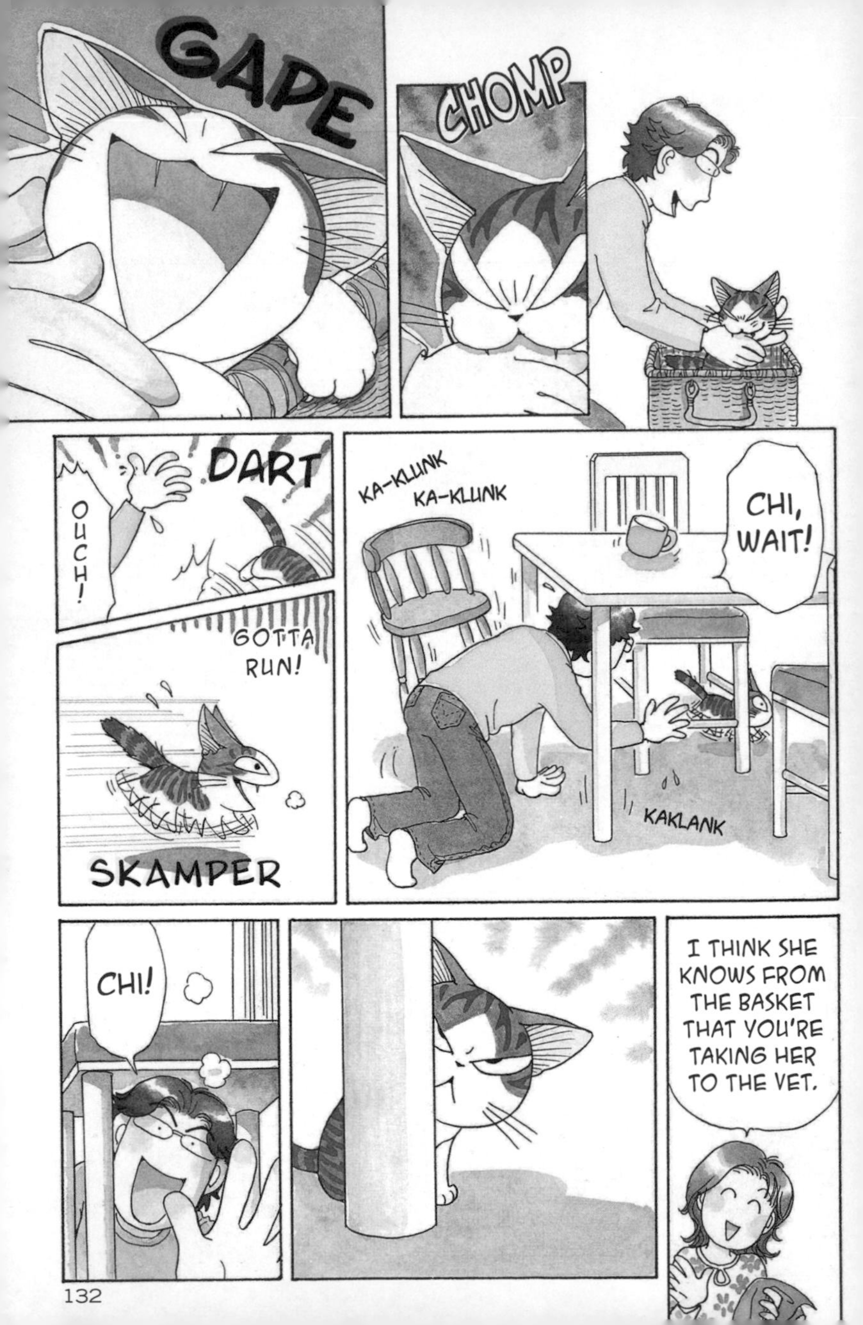

GAPE
CHOMP
OUCH!
DART
GOTTA RUN!
SKAMPER
KA-KLUNK
KA-KLUNK
CHI, WAIT!
KAKLANK
CHI!
I THINK SHE KNOWS FROM THE BASKET THAT YOU'RE TAKING HER TO THE VET.

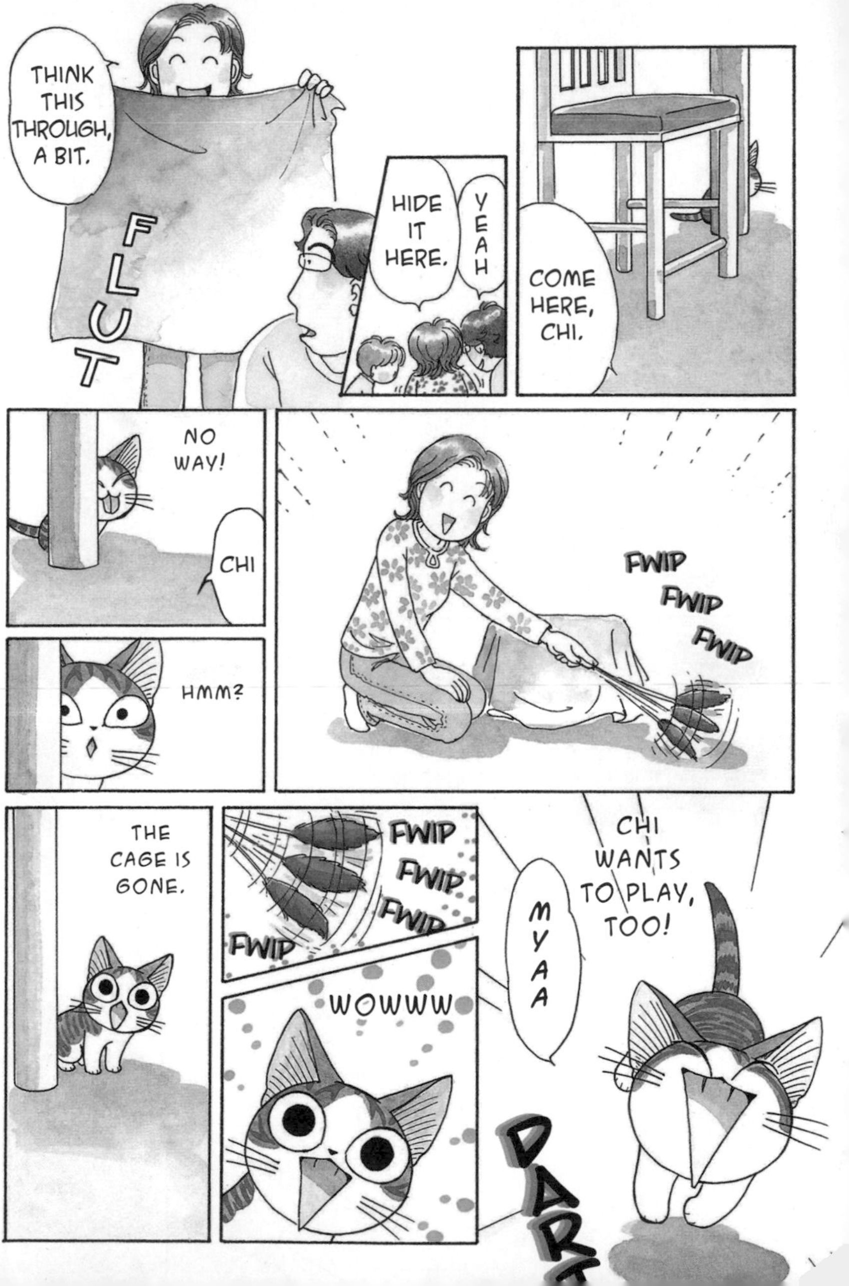
THINK THIS THROUGH, A BIT.
FLUT
HIDE IT HERE.
YEAH
COME HERE, CHI.
NO WAY!
CHI
HMM?
FWIP
FWIP
FWIP
THE CAGE IS GONE.
FWIP
FWIP
FWIP
FWIP
WOWWW
MYAA
CHI WANTS TO PLAY, TOO!
DART

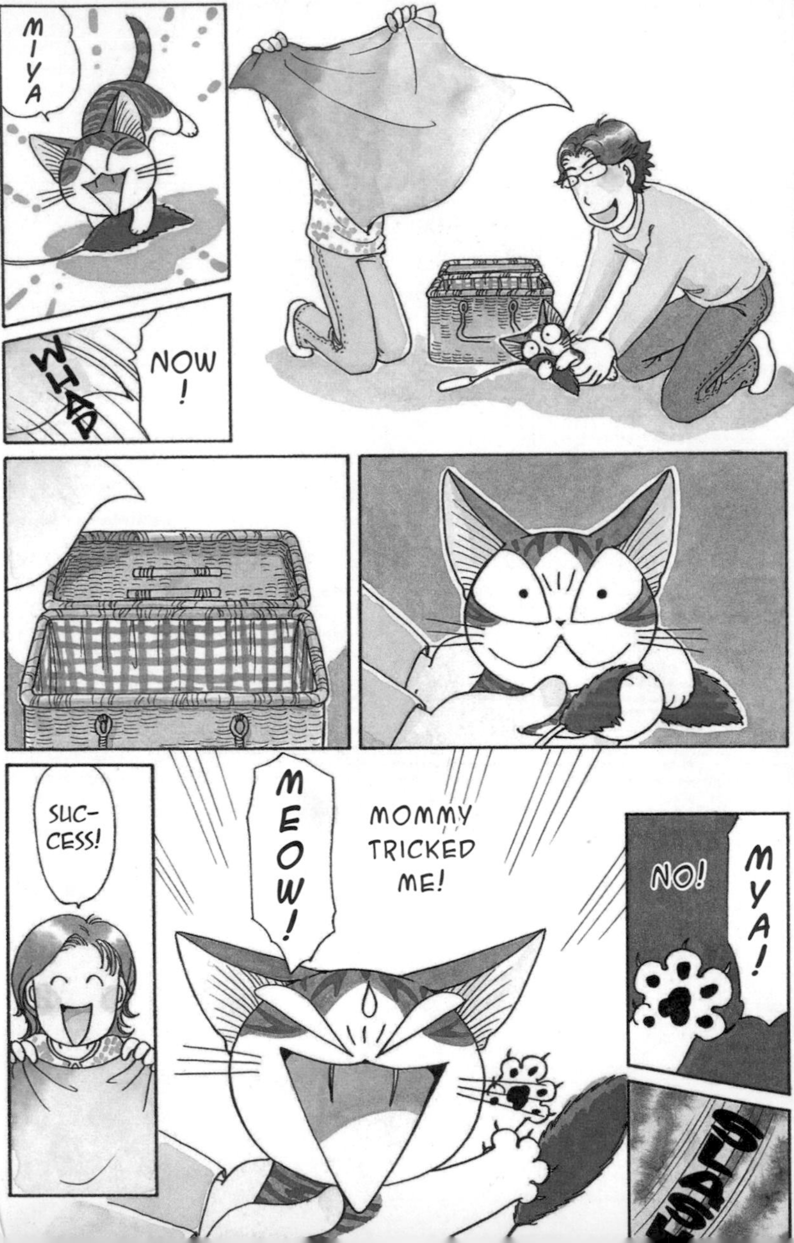
MIYA
NOW!
WHAP
SUC-CESS!
MEOW!
MOMMY TRICKED ME!
NO!
MYA!

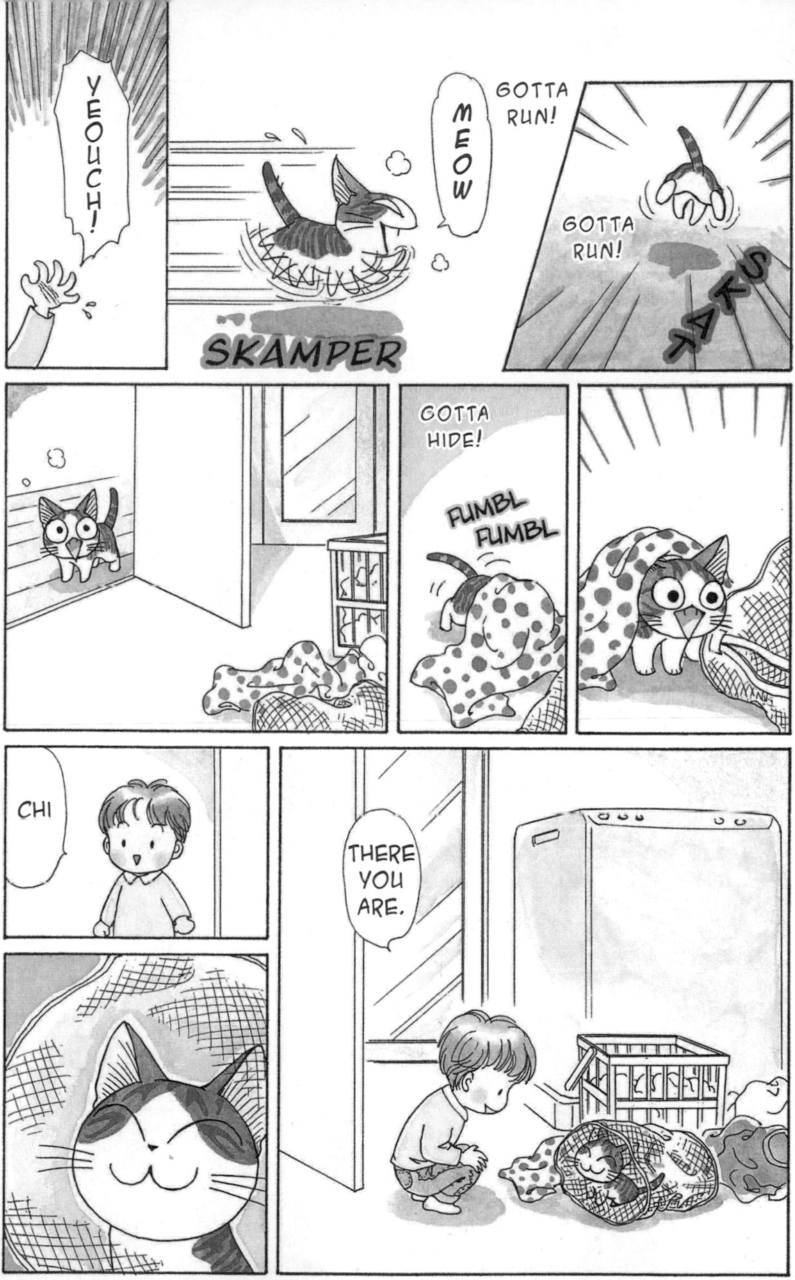
YEOUCH!
MEOW
SKAMPER
GOTTA RUN!
GOTTA RUN!
TAKUS
GOTTA HIDE!
FUMBL FUMBL
CHI
THERE YOU ARE.

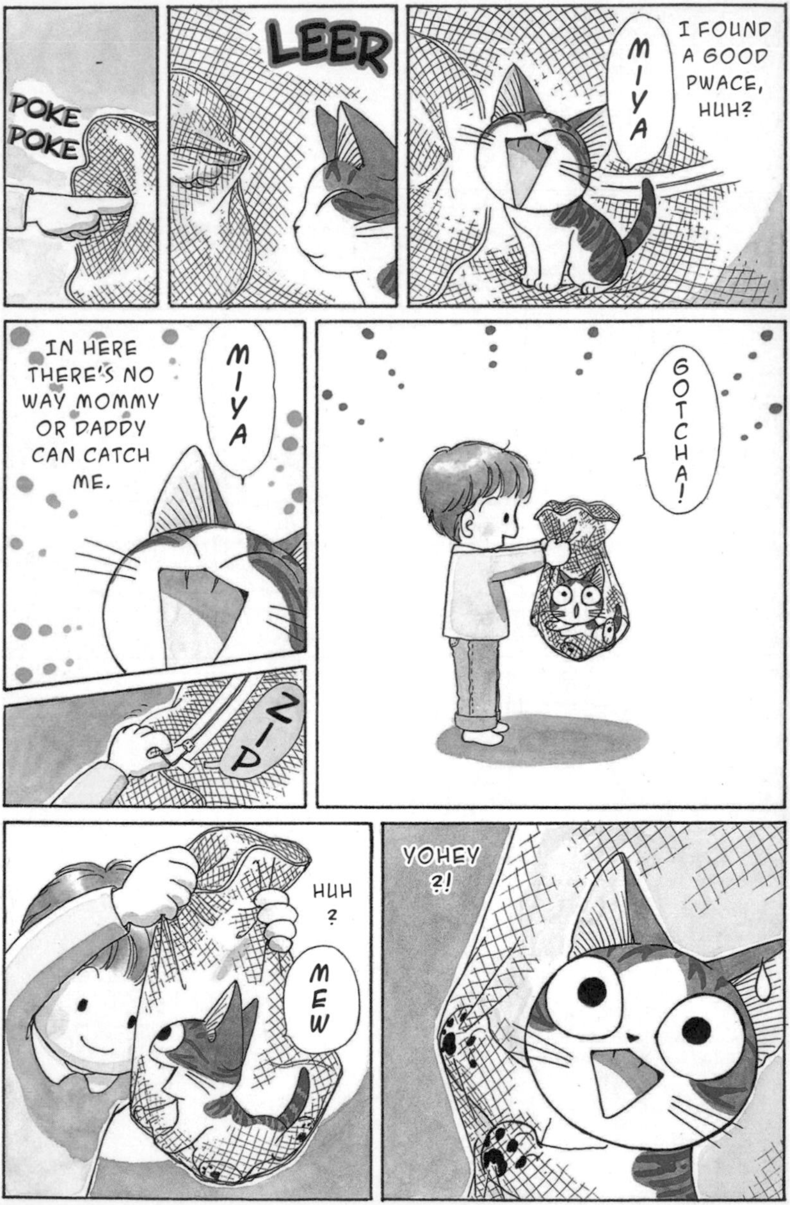
POKE POKE
LEER
MIYA
I FOUND A GOOD PWACE, HUH?
IN HERE THERE'S NO WAY MOMMY OR DADDY CAN CATCH ME.
MIYA
ZIP
GOTCHA!
HUH?
MEW
YOHEY?!

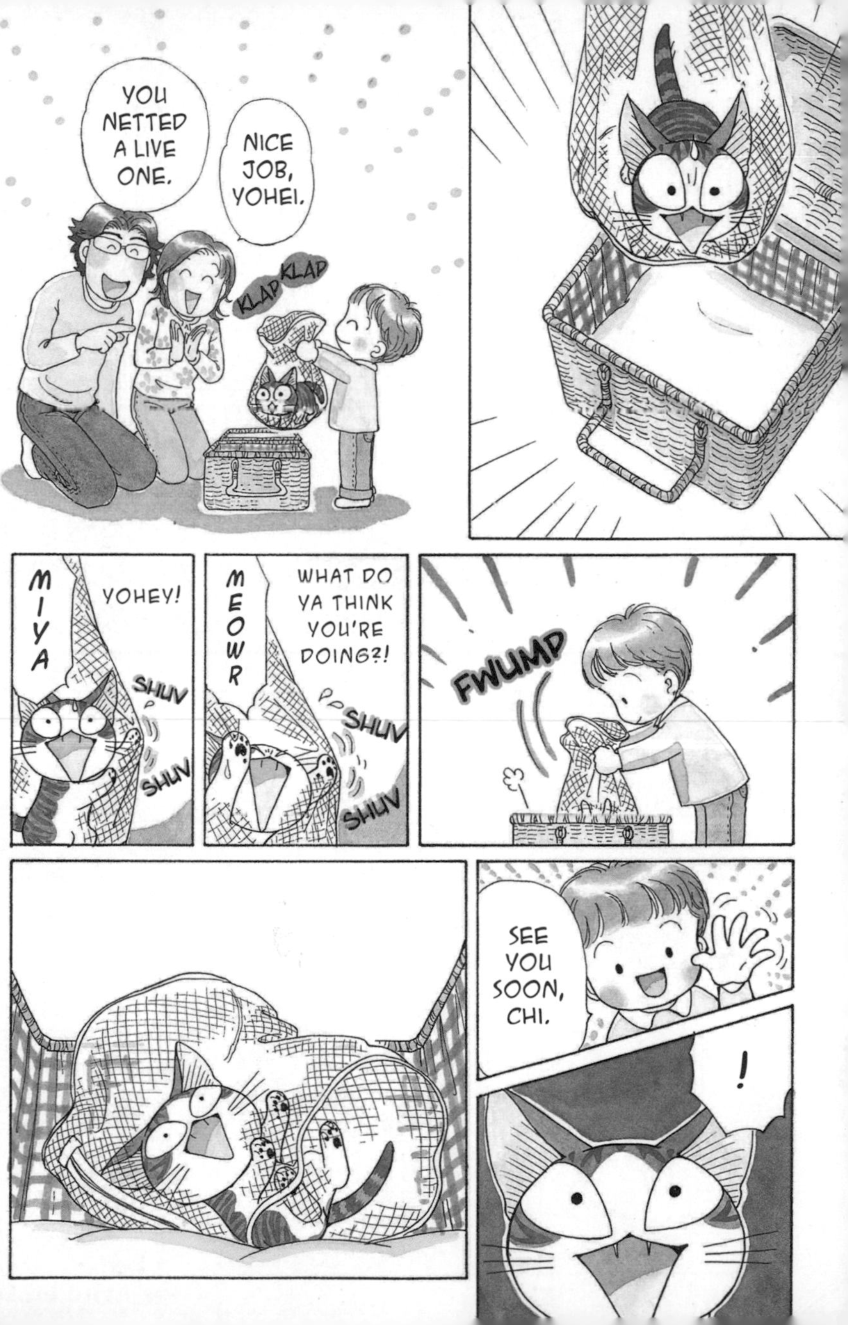
YOU NETTED A LIVE ONE.
NICE JOB, YOHEI.
KLAP KLAP
MIYA
YOHEY!
SHUV
SHUV
MEOWR
WHAT DO YA THINK YOU'RE DOING?!
SHUV
SHUV
FWUMP
SEE YOU SOON, CHI.
!

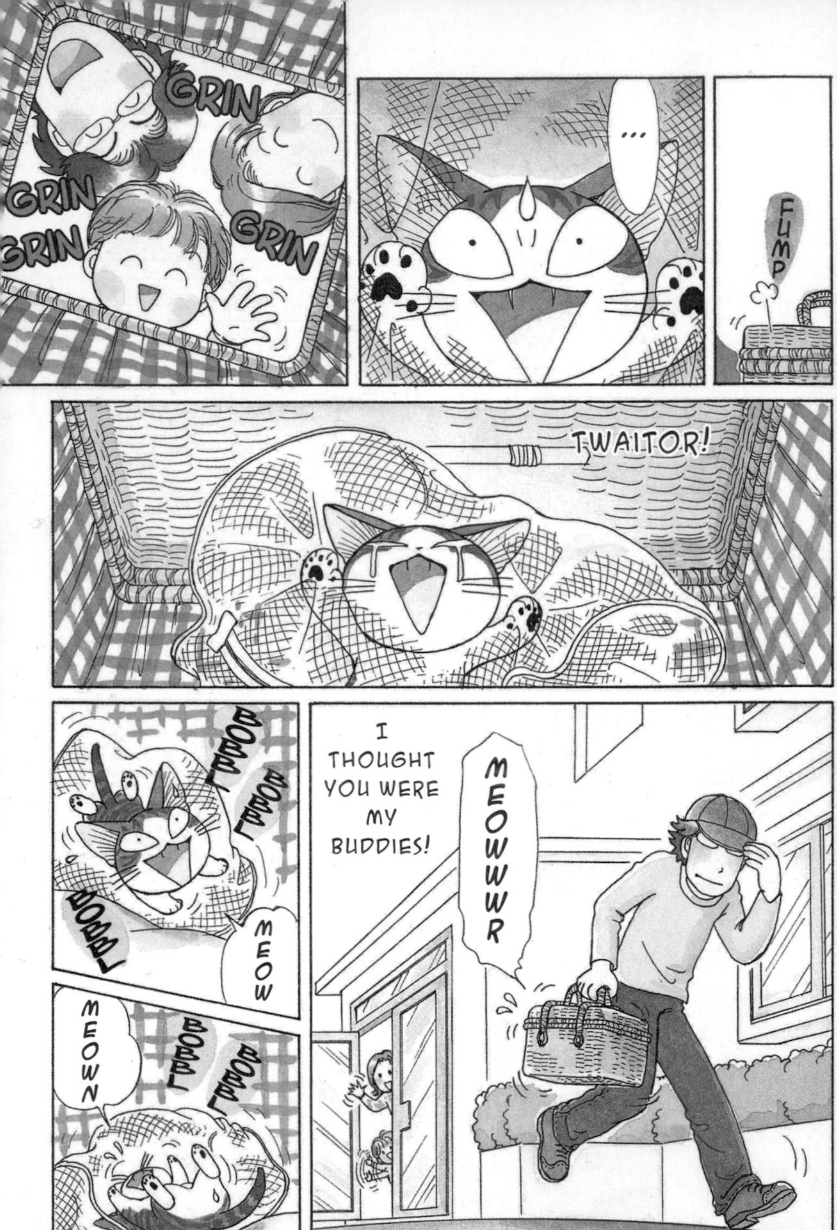
GRIN
GRIN
GRIN
GRIN
...
FUMP
TWAITOR!
BOBBL
BOBBL
BOBBL
MEOW
MEOWN
BOBBL
BOBBL
I THOUGHT YOU WERE MY BUDDIES!
MEOWWWR

the end

homemade 38: a cat sulks

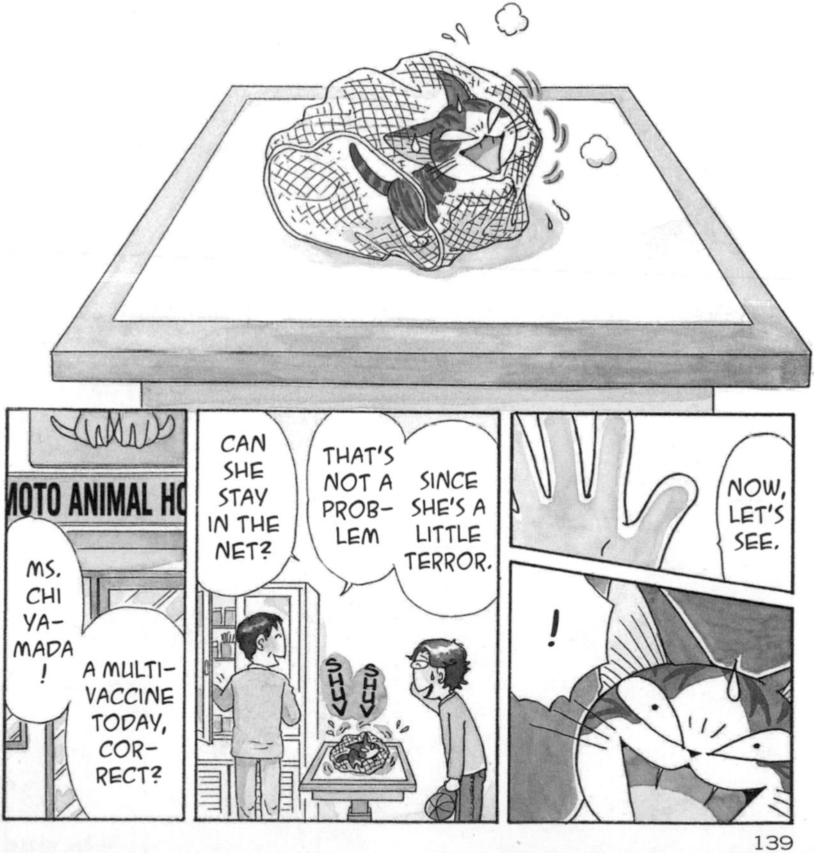

MOTO ANIMAL HO
MS. CHIYAMADA!
A MULTI-VACCINE TODAY, CORRECT?
CAN SHE STAY IN THE NET?
THAT'S NOT A PROBLEM
SINCE SHE'S A LITTLE TERROR.
SHUV
SHUV
NOW, LET'S SEE.
!

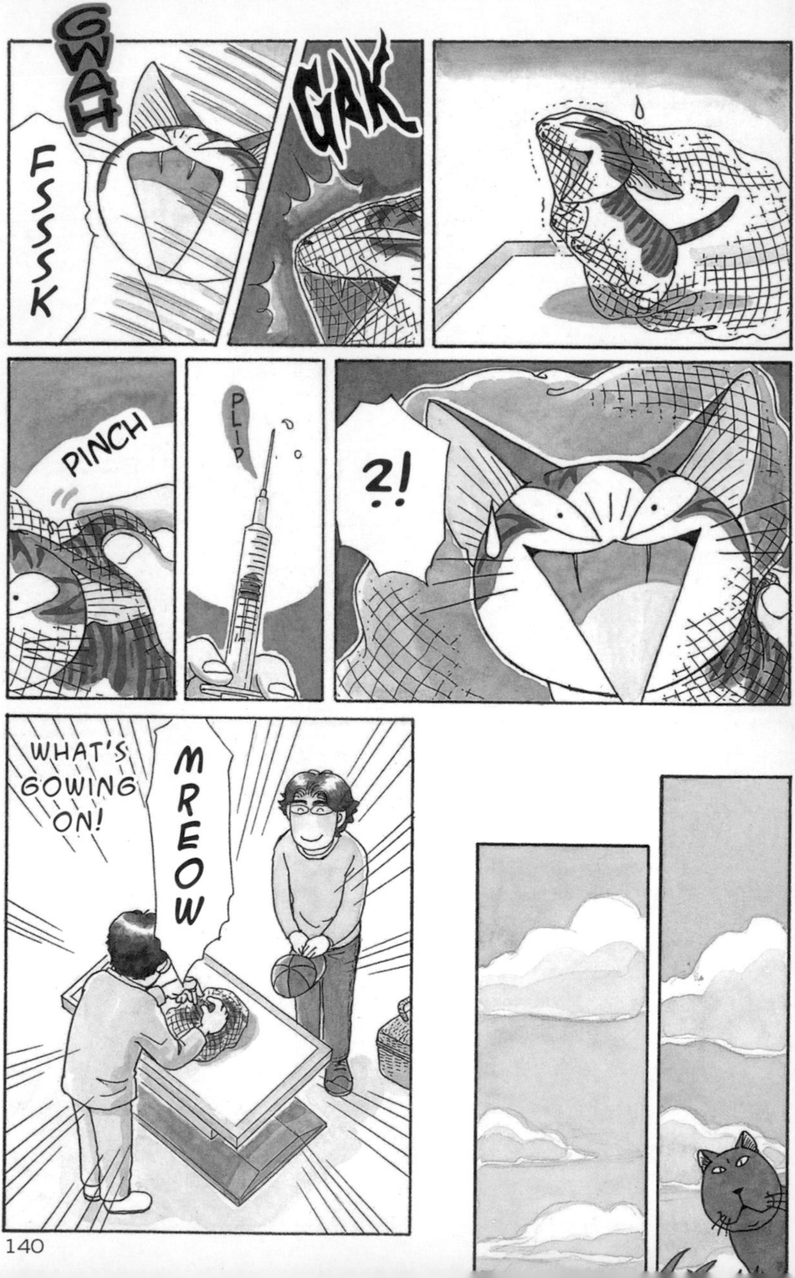
GWAH
FSSSK
GAK
PINCH
PLIP
?!
WHAT'S GOWING ON!
MREOW

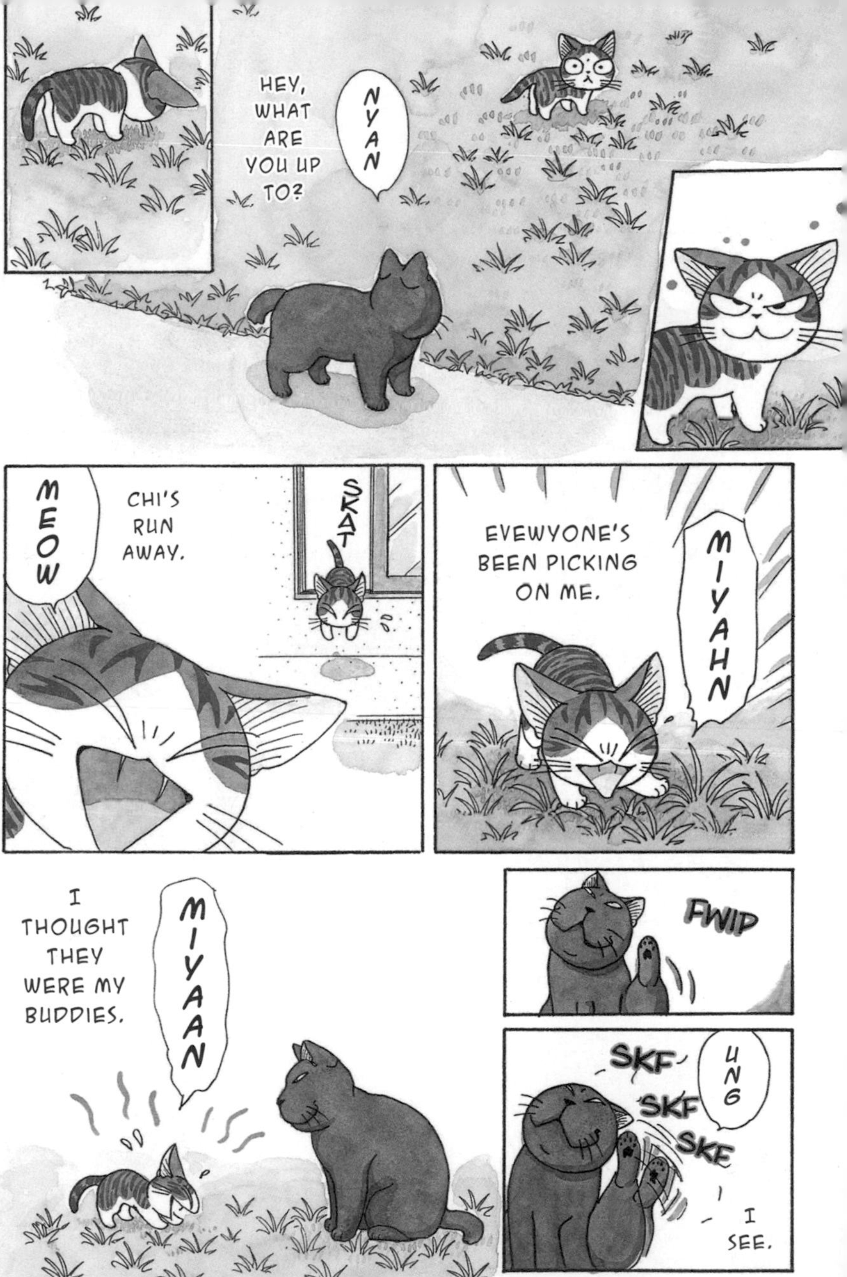
HEY, WHAT ARE YOU UP TO?
NYAN
MEOW
CHI'S RUN AWAY.
SKAT
EVEWYONE'S BEEN PICKING ON ME.
MIYAHN
I THOUGHT THEY WERE MY BUDDIES.
MIYAAN
FWIP
SKF
SKF
SKF
UNG
I SEE.

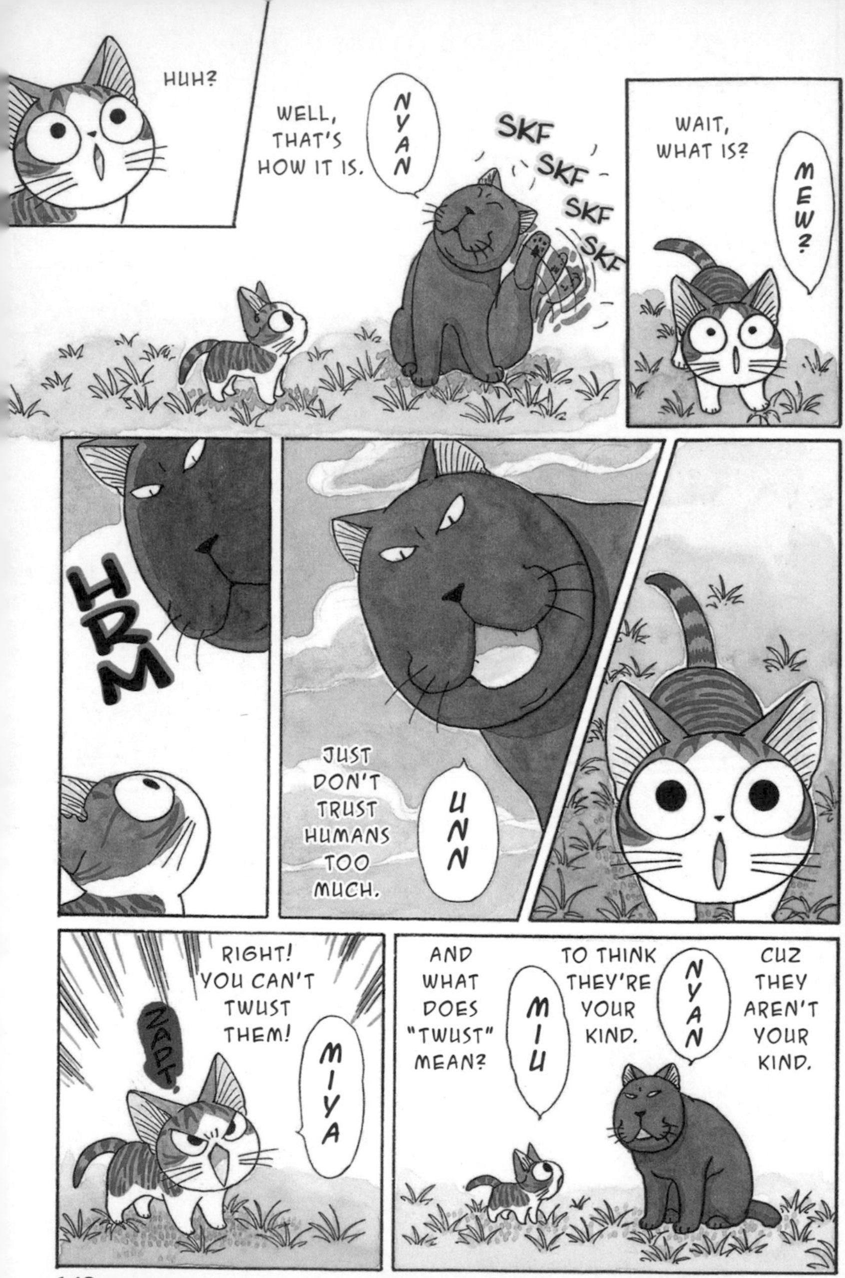
HUH?
WELL, THAT'S HOW IT IS.
NYAN
SKF
SKF
SKF
SKF
WAIT, WHAT IS?
MEW?
HRM
JUST DON'T TRUST HUMANS TOO MUCH.
UNN
RIGHT! YOU CAN'T TWUST THEM!
ZAPT
MIYA
AND WHAT DOES "TWUST" MEAN?
MIU
TO THINK THEY'RE YOUR KIND.
NYAN
CUZ THEY AREN'T YOUR KIND.

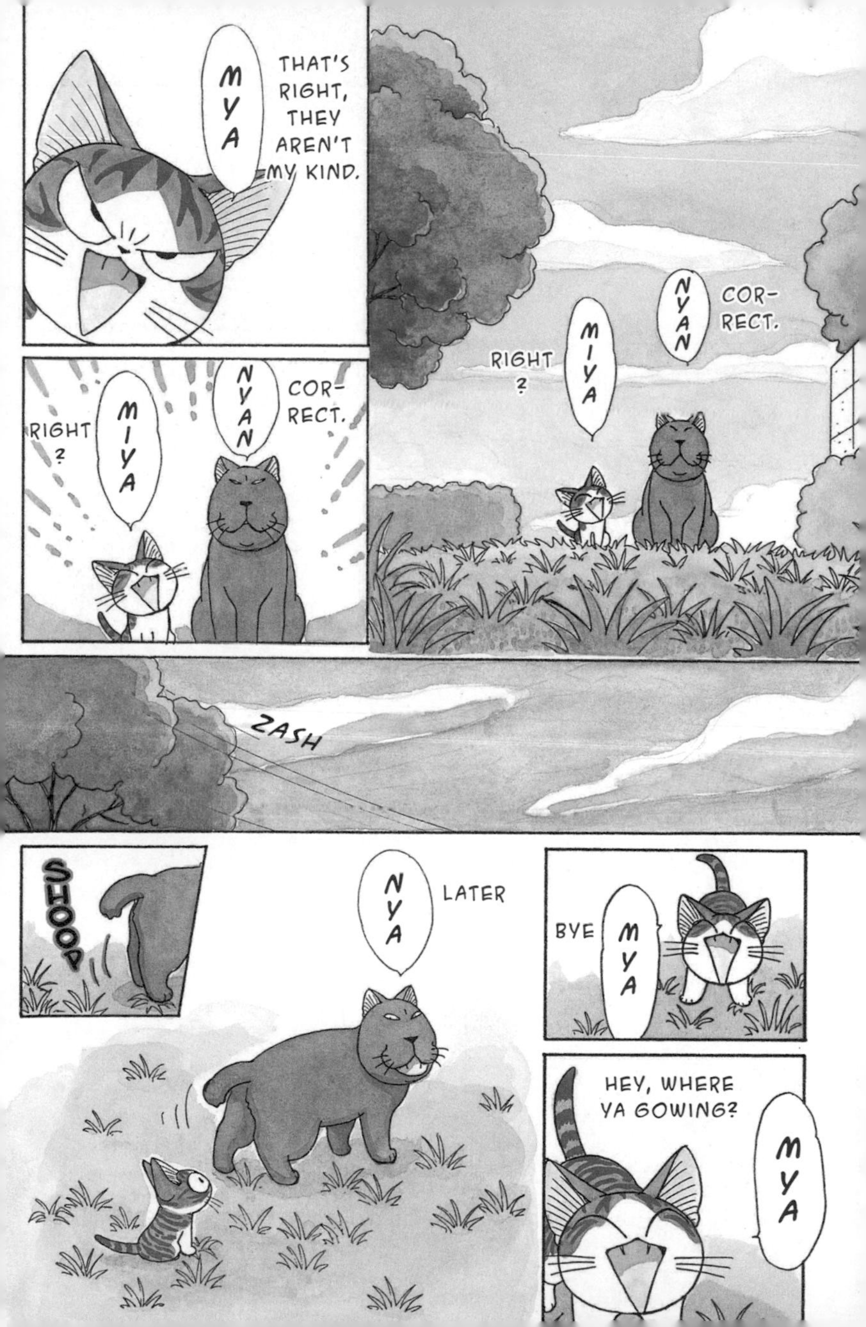
MYA
THAT'S RIGHT, THEY AREN'T MY KIND.
RIGHT?
MIYA
NYAN
COR-RECT.
RIGHT?
MIYA
NYAN
COR-RECT.
ZASH
SHOOP
NYA
LATER
BYE
MYA
HEY, WHERE YA GOWING?
MYA

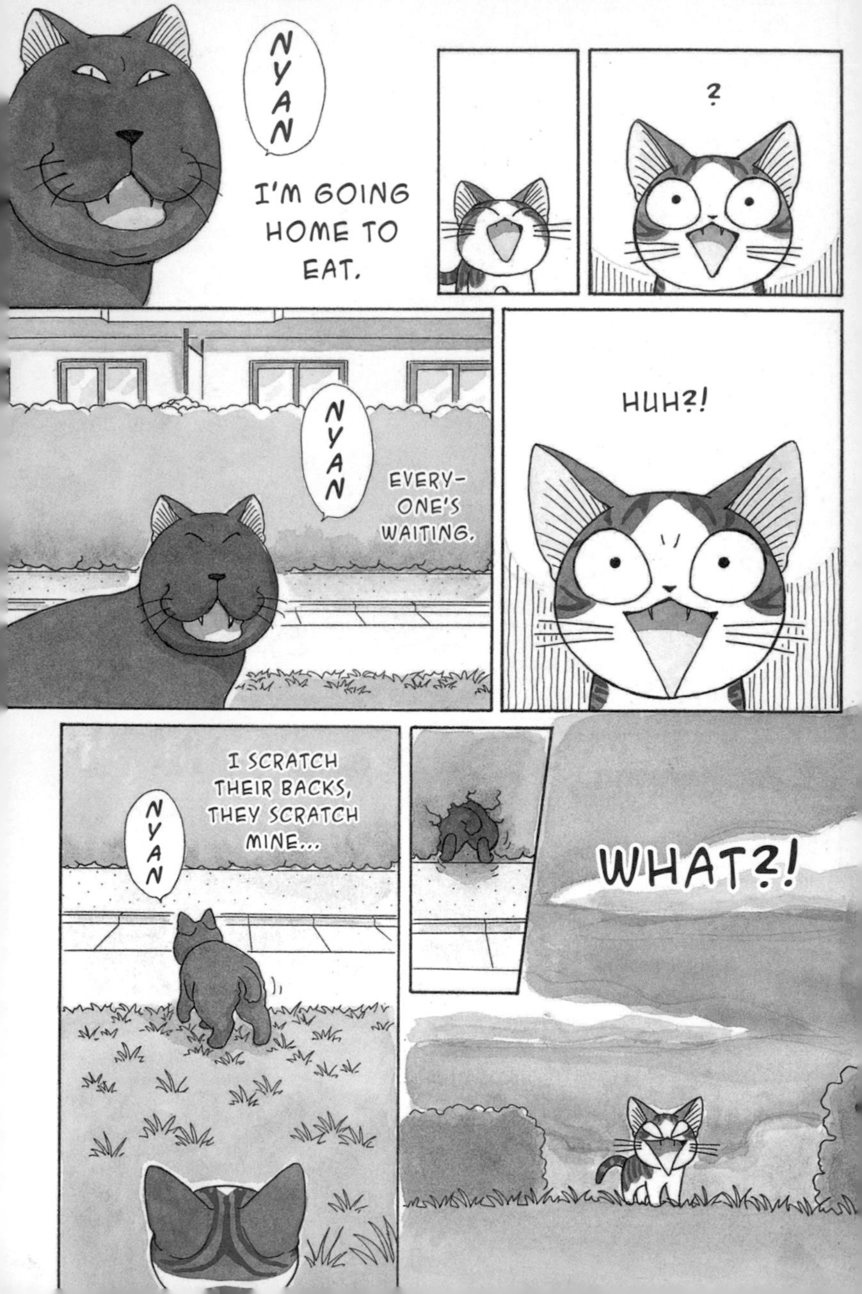
NYAN
I'M GOING HOME TO EAT.
?
NYAN
EVERY-ONE'S WAITING.
HUH?!
NYAN
I SCRATCH THEIR BACKS, THEY SCRATCH MINE...
WHAT?!

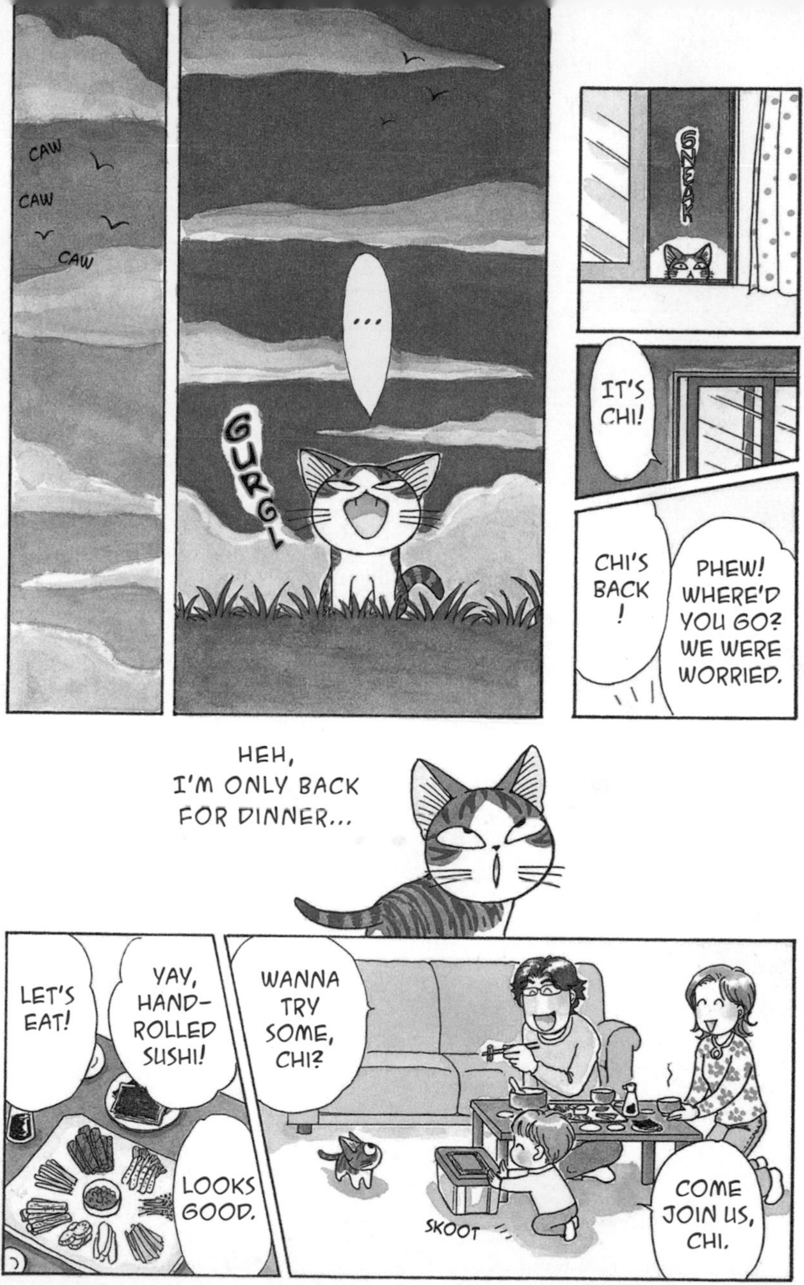
CAW
CAW
CAW
...
GURGL
SNEAK
IT'S CHI!
CHI'S BACK!
PHEW! WHERE'D YOU GO? WE WERE WORRIED.
HEH, I'M ONLY BACK FOR DINNER...
LET'S EAT!
YAY, HAND-ROLLED SUSHI!
LOOKS GOOD.
WANNA TRY SOME, CHI?
SKOOT
COME JOIN US, CHI.

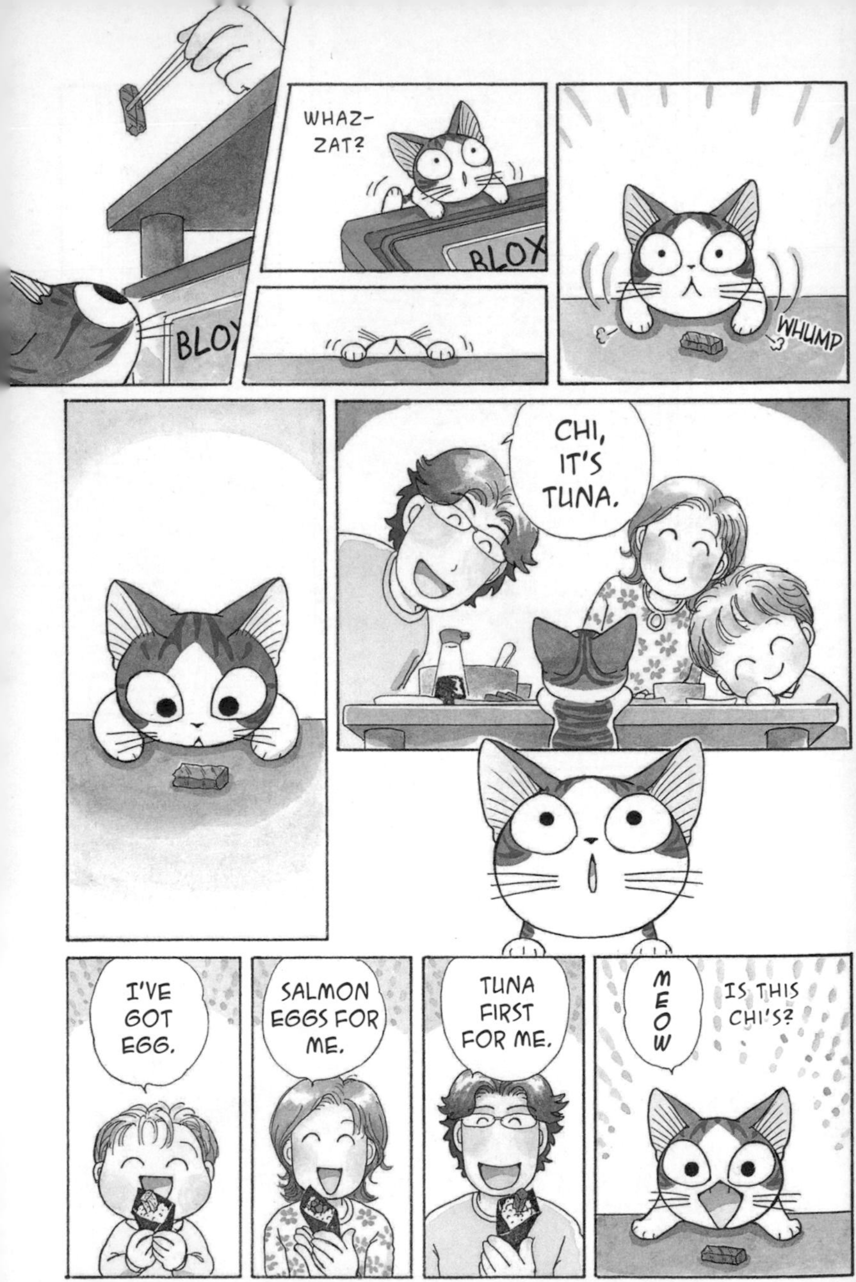

BLOX
WHAZ-ZAT?
BLOX
WHUMP
CHI, IT'S TUNA.
I'VE GOT EGG.
SALMON EGGS FOR ME.
TUNA FIRST FOR ME.
MEOW
IS THIS CHI'S?

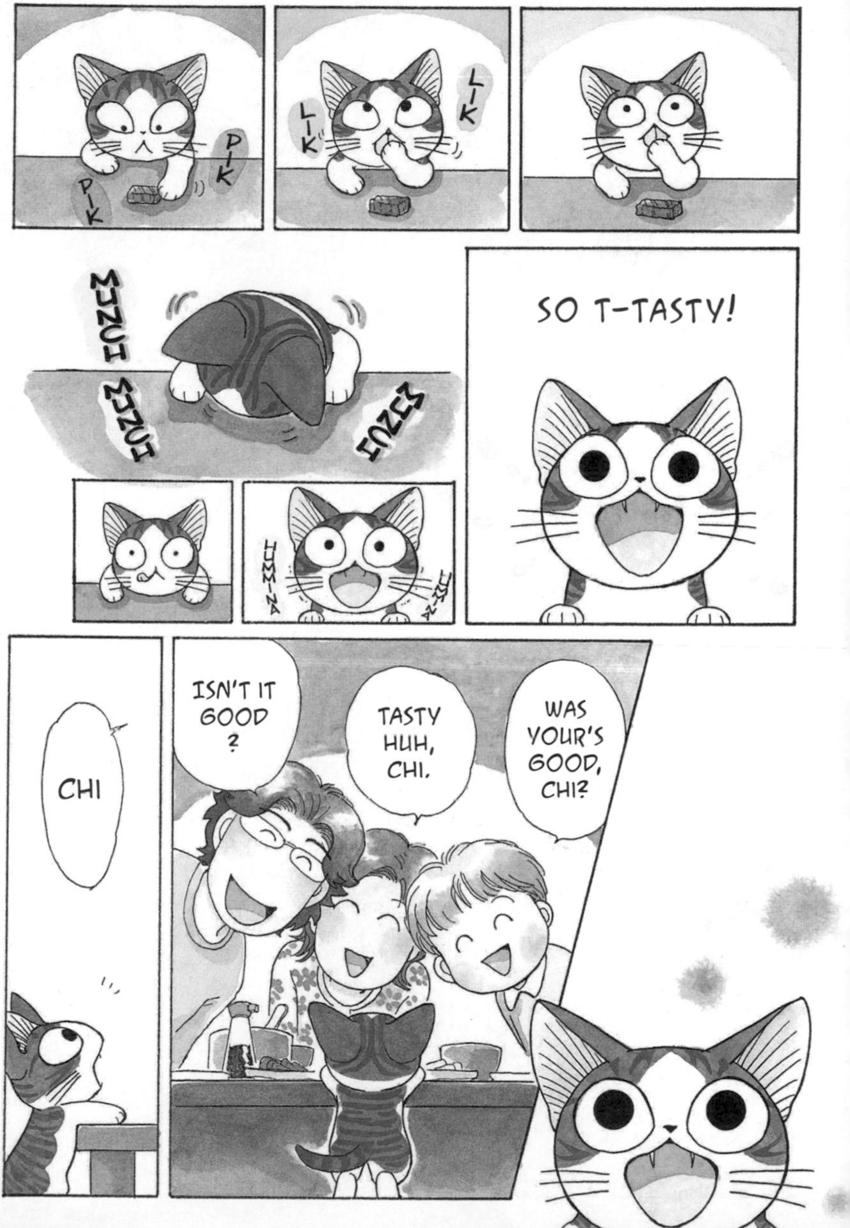
PIK
PIK
LIK
LIK
MUNCH
MUNCH
MUNCH
HUMMINA
SO T-TASTY!
CHI
ISN'T IT GOOD ?
TASTY HUH, CHI.
WAS YOUR'S GOOD, CHI?

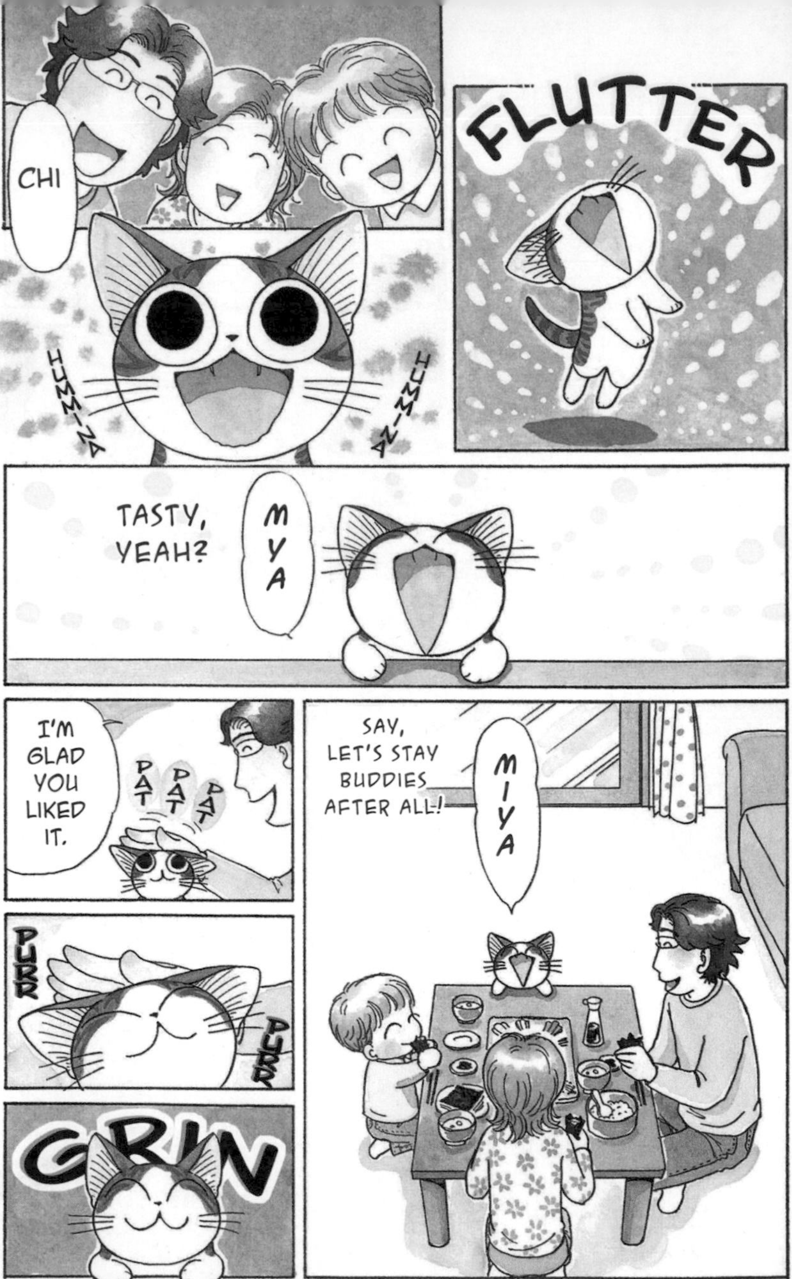
CHI
HUMMINA
HUMMINA
FLUTTER
TASTY, YEAH?
MYA
I'M GLAD YOU LIKED IT.
PAT PAT PAT
PURR
PURR
GRIN
SAY, LET'S STAY BUDDIES AFTER ALL!
MIYA

the end

special menu a cat meets FukuFuku

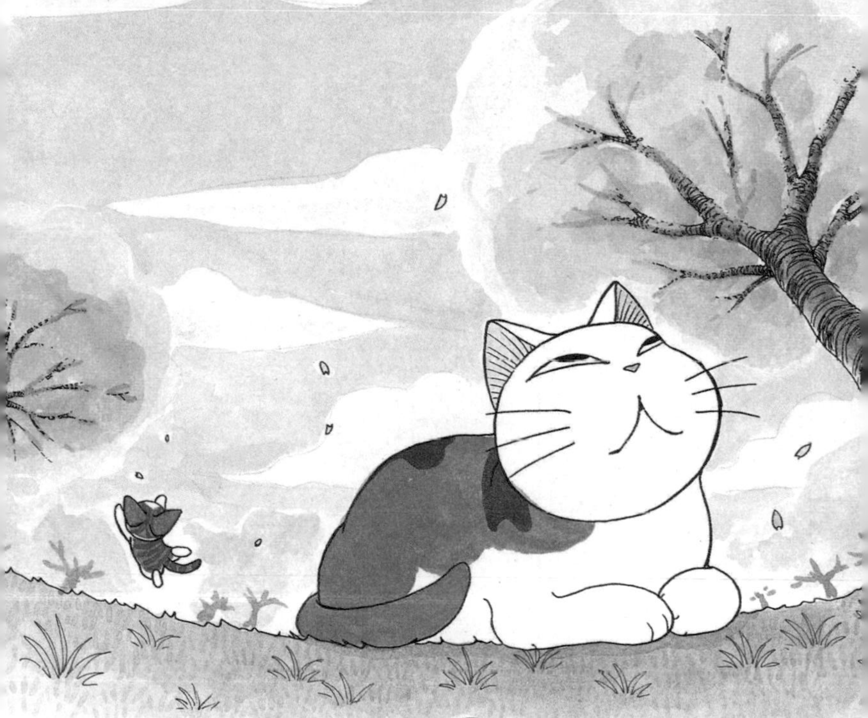

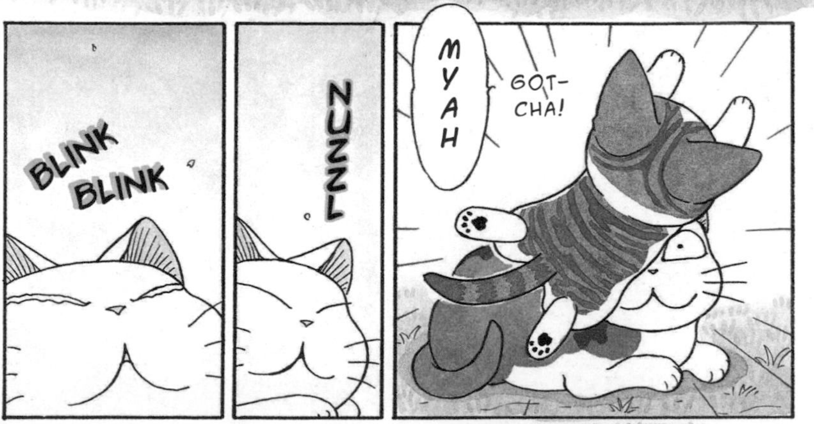
BLINK BLINK
NUZZL
MYAH
GOT-CHA!

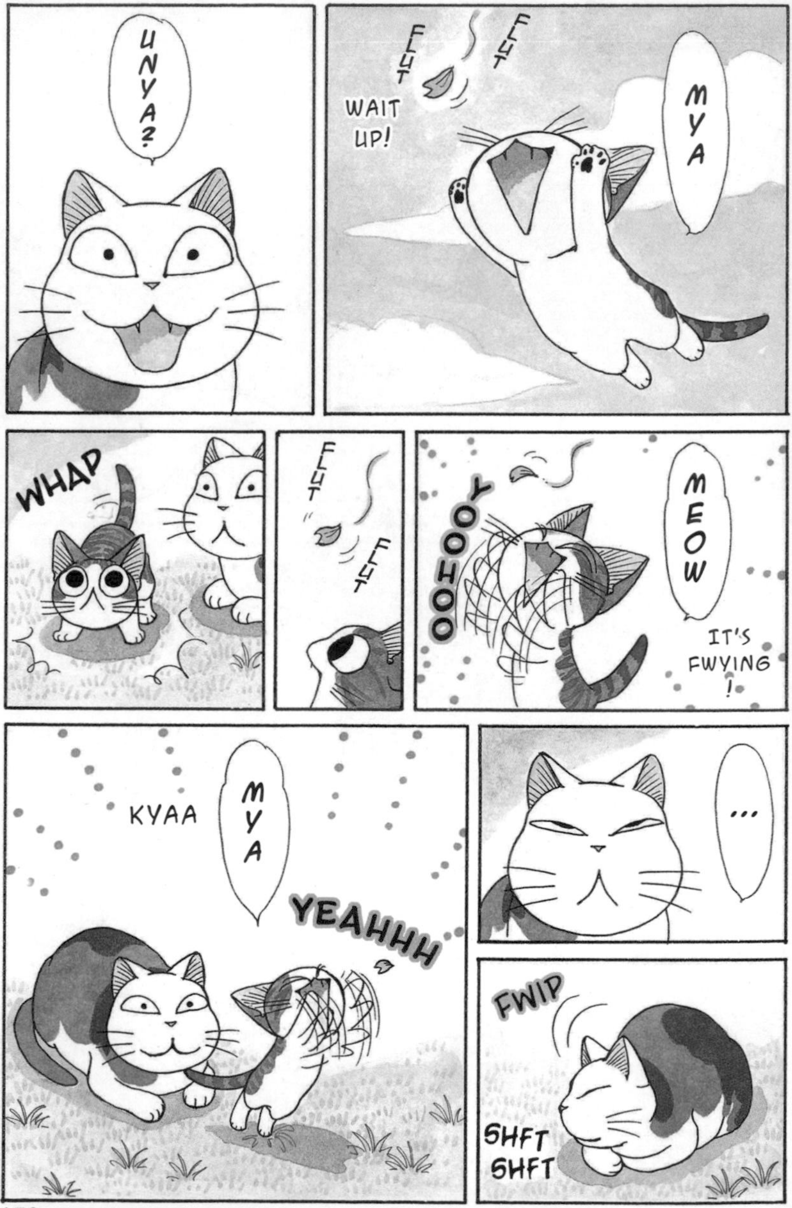
UNYA?
FLUT
FLUT
WAIT UP!
MYA
WHAP
FLUT
FLUT
YOOHOO
MEOW
IT'S FWYING!
KYAA
MYA
YEAHHH
...
FWIP
SHFT SHFT

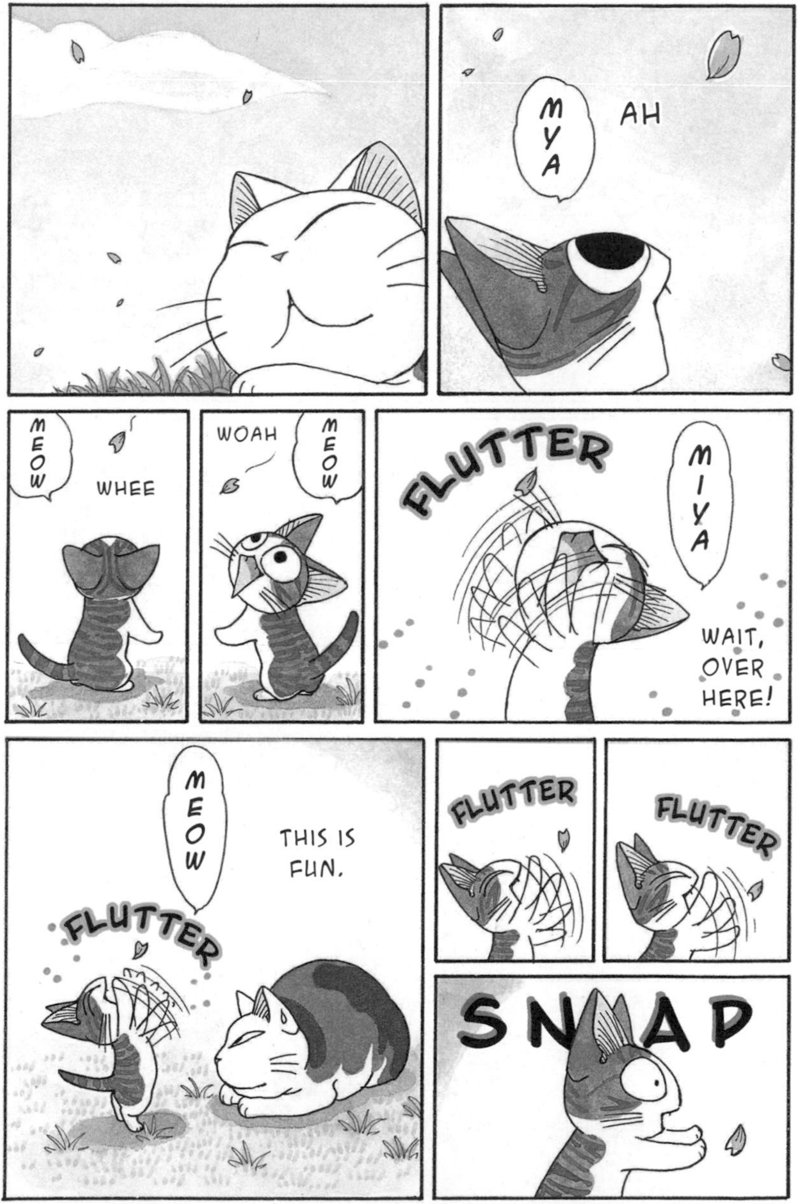
MYA
AH
MEOW
WHEE
WOAH
MEOW
FLUTTER
MIYA
WAIT, OVER HERE!
MEOW
THIS IS FUN.
FLUTTER
FLUTTER
FLUTTER
SNAP

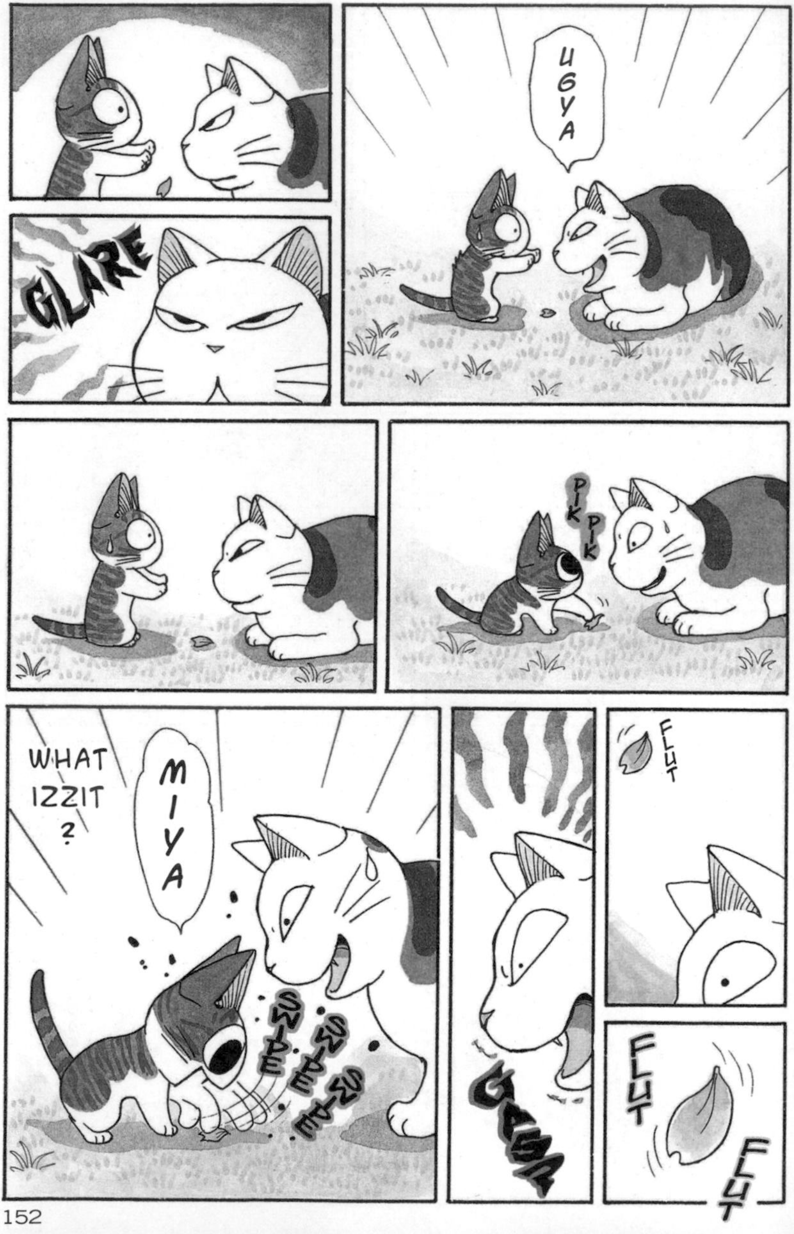
GLARE
UGYA
PIK PIK
WHAT IZZIT?
MIYA
SWIPE SWIPE
GASA
FLUT
FLUT FLUT

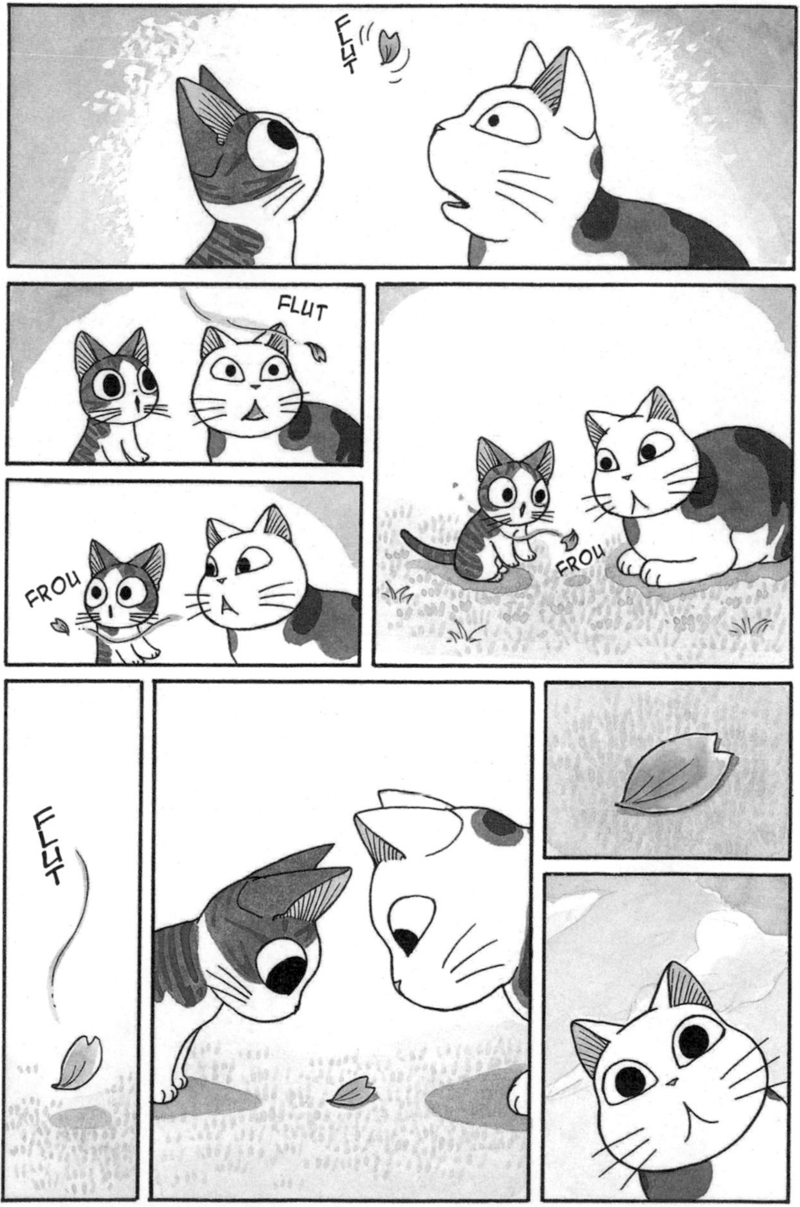
FLUT
FLUT
FROU
FROU
FLUT

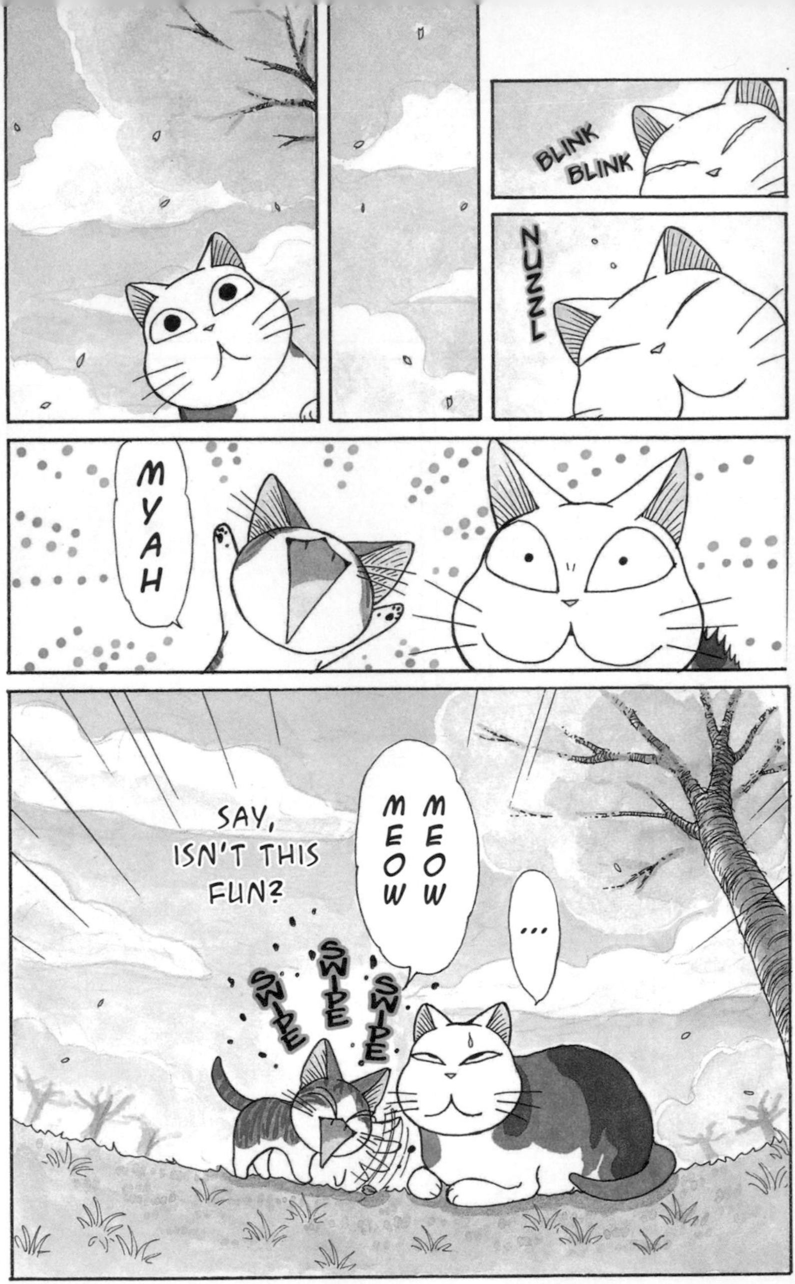
BLINK BLINK
NUZZL
MYAH
SAY, ISN'T THIS FUN?
MEOW MEOW
...
SWIPE SWIPE SWIPE

the end

A Note on the Special Chapter

Ms. Kanata's comic career spans over three decades, with the vast majority of her works focusing on the lives of household pets. Her debut work *Petit Cat Jam-Jam*, a *shojo* (girls') comic, distinguished her as one of the best graphic storytellers for young audiences, but it was her first hit *FukuFuku Funyan* with which Ms. Kanata's cats took Japan, and eventually the world, by storm.

Premiering in women's anthology *Me* in 1988, *FukuFuku Funyan* took pet comics to new levels of recognition. While the series ran, *Me*'s editorial staff was flooded with letters from readers of all ages detailing their personal feline experiences. Cat lovers saw just how well Ms. Kanata understood and rendered feline behavior.

In 2004, *Chi's Sweet Home* started running in Kodansha's comics anthology *Morning*. Though writing for a flagship *seinen* (men's) weekly marked a bit of a departure for Ms. Kanata, it was a highly successful one. Her first feline star FukuFuku makes an appearance in the special chapter exclusive to the graphic novel edition, giving new fans of Ms. Kanata a chance to become acquainted with this other kitty idol.

A relatively plump calico, FukuFuku is notorious for her poor eyesight, grumpiness, and tendency for napping too much. Though her interactions with Chi are characteristic of her behavior in her own series, they only reveal a small glimpse into her history and personality. While it's FukuFuku's only appearance in *Chi's Sweet Home* to date, in the coming volumes readers can look forward to a wide range of furry and feathery friends to follow and support.

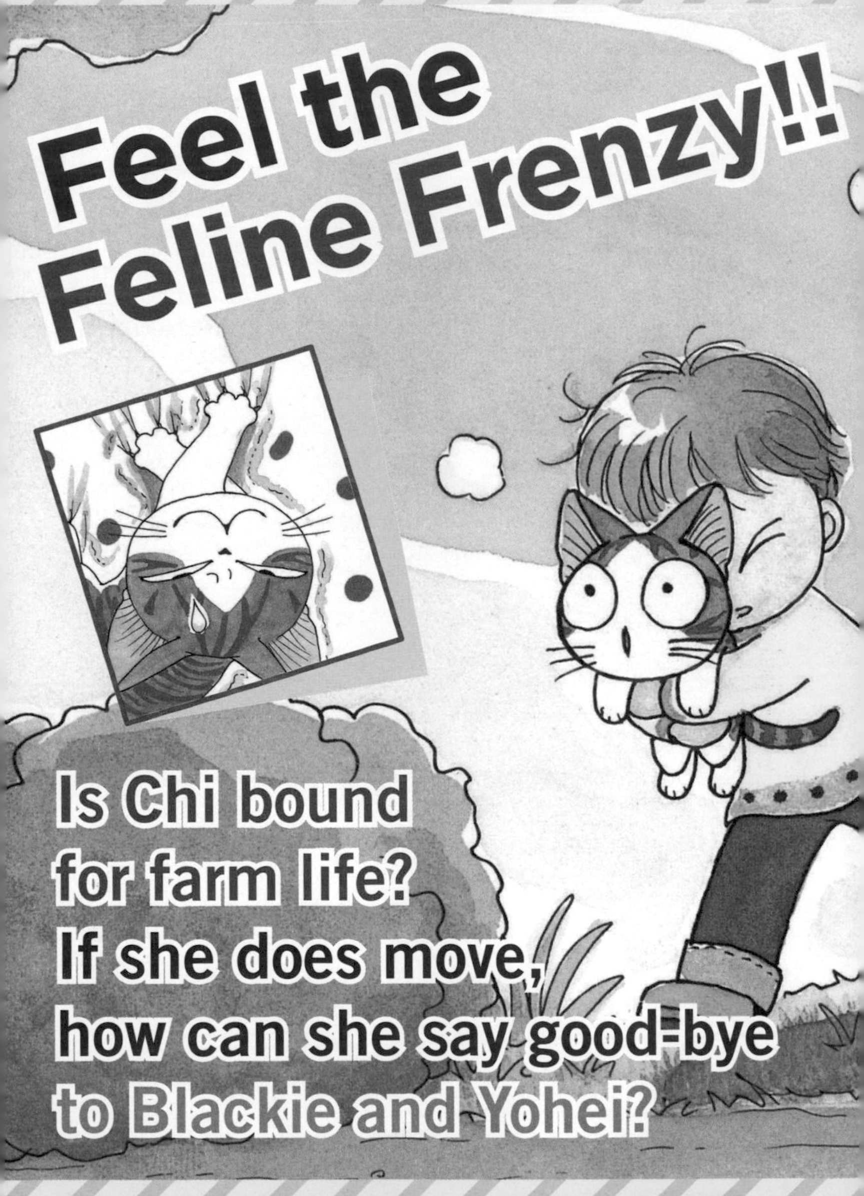
Feel the Feline Frenzy!!
Is Chi bound for farm life?
If she does move, how can she say good-bye to Blackie and Yohei?

Find out in Volume 3 of *Chi's Sweet Home*, on sale October 2010!

PREVIEW

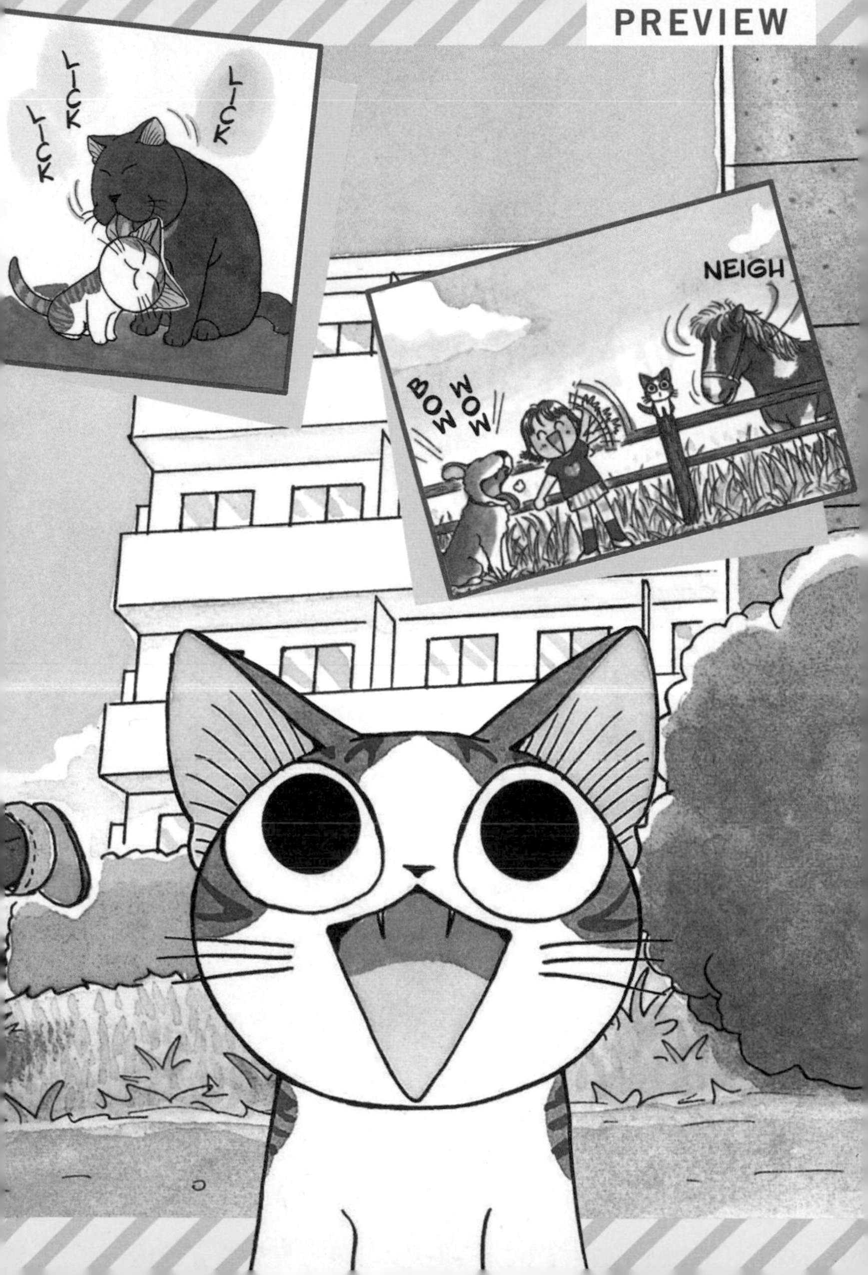
LICK
LICK
LICK
BOW WOW
NEIGH

TWIN SPI

Space has never seemed so close and yet so fa

"It's easy to see why the series was a smash hit in its native land...
Each page contains more genuine emotion than an entire space fleet's
worth of similarly themed stories."
—*Publishers Weekly*

Volume 1: 978-1-934287-84-2
Volume 2: 978-1-934287-86-6
$10.95/$12.99 each

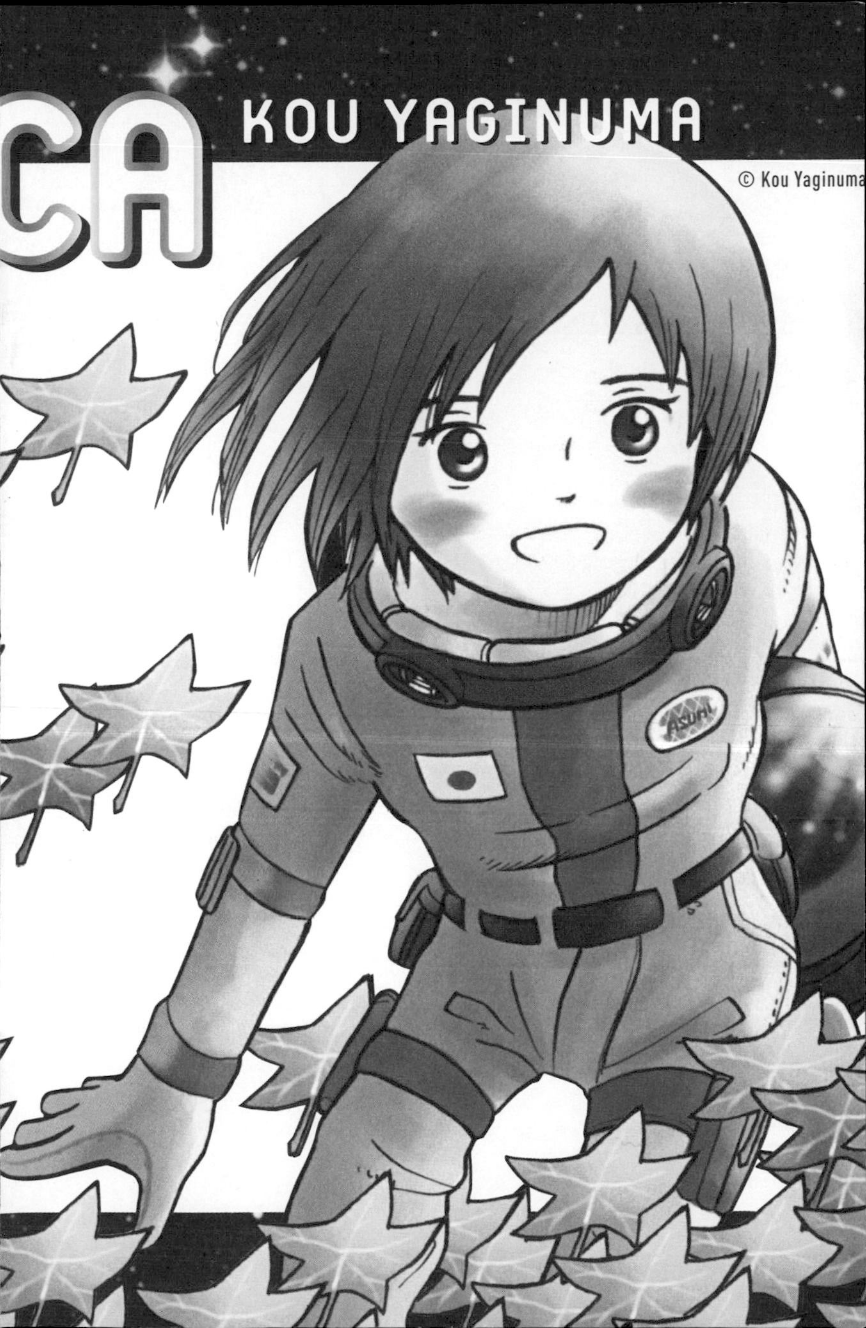
CA
KOU YAGINUMA
© Kou Yaginuma
ASUMI

Chi's Sweet Home, volume 2

Translation - Ed Chavez
Production - Hiroko Mizuno
Glen Isip

First published in Japan in 2005 by Kodansha, Ltd., Tokyo
Publication for this English edition arranged through Kodansha, Ltd., Tokyo
English language version produced by Vertical, Inc.

Translation provided by Vertical, Inc., 2010
Published by Vertical, Inc., New York

Originally published in Japanese as *Chiizu Suiito Houmu* by Kodansha, Ltd., 2005
Chiizu Suiito Houmu first serialized in *Morning*, Kodansha, Ltd., 2004-

This is a work of fiction.

ISBN: 978-1-934287-85-9

Manufactured in China

First Edition

Second Printing

Vertical, Inc.
451 Park Avenue South, 7th Floor
New York, NY 10016
www.vertical-inc.com

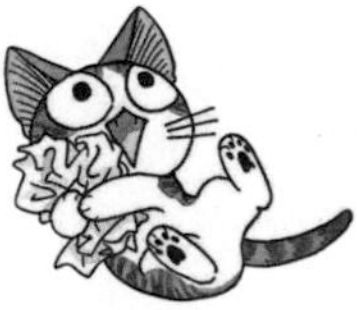

Special thanks to K. Kitamoto